A Nation
of
Guinea Pigs

A NATION
OF
GUINEA PIGS

Marshall S. Shapo

THE FREE PRESS
A Division of Macmillan Publishing Co., Inc.
NEW YORK

Collier Macmillan Publishers
LONDON

The Free Press
A Division of Macmillan Publishing Co., Inc.
866 Third Avenue, New York, N.Y. 10022

Collier Macmillan Canada, Ltd.

Library of Congress Catalog Card Number: 78-66977

Printed in the United States of America

printing number

1 2 3 4 5 6 7 8 9 10

Library of Congress Cataloging in Publication Data

Shapo, Marshall S.
    A nation of guinea pigs.

    Includes bibliographical references and index.
    1. Product safety--United States. 2. Hazardous
substances--Law and legislation--United States.
3. Drugs--Law and legislation--United States.
4. Chemicals--Law and legislation--United States.
5. Science and state--United States. I. Title.
KF3945.S53   344'.73'042   78-66977
ISBN 0-02-928550-X

FOR
HELENE
AND FOR
BENJAMIN AND **NATHANIEL**

Contents

ACKNOWLEDGMENTS   ix

INTRODUCTION   xi

1 THE SCIENTIFIC ENTERPRISE   1

2 VARIETIES OF EXPERIMENTATION   29

3 PERSONAL CHOICE   58

4 THE PILL   88

5 THE DELANEY AMENDMENT: ROUGH-HEWN REGULATION   142

6 DES: MAGIC WAND AND TERRIBLE SWORD   163

7 ASBESTOS DISCHARGES: A SHADOW IN THE LAKE   191

8 DNA REGULATION: LAW TO TAME THE GENIE   218

9 EXPERIMENTING WITH THE CONSUMER   248

NOTES   263

INDEX   291

Acknowledgments

I would like to thank many people for their help in connection with the writing of this book.

Richard Merrill sympathetically criticized the entire manuscript, and to him I am especially grateful not only for that help but also for the collegial experience of a seminar we taught using several draft chapters. I have also had the benefit of helpful criticism on various chapters by Glen Robinson, George Rutherglen, Steve Saltzburg, and Helene Shapo. Early encouragement to proceed with this project came from Julian Noble, and I appreciate his continuing colloquies with me on this and related subjects.

For editorial direction and stimulation, I thank Robert Wallace of The Free Press and his colleague Elly Dickason, my editorial supervisor.

Several students at the University of Virginia Law School aided me bibliographically, offered editorial criticism, and undertook the drudgery of checking and stylizing my citations. These excellent assistants include Bill Austin, Catherine Garcia, James Hammond, Mary Kearney, Louis Miller, and Kim Rosenfeld.

The Center for Advanced Studies of the University of Virginia, of which I was a member in 1976–1977, provided me with several months of precious time for scholarship that was indispensable for research and writing, and Dean Emerson Spies of the University of Virginia School of Law was a source of further encouragement and research help. For aid in the completion of the manuscript, I am indebted for support from the Northwestern University School of Law and its dean, David S. Ruder.

Many librarians have given me the constant support without which works of this kind could not be written. I express my thanks to Larry Wenger, law librarian at Virginia, and to Hazel Key for her extraordinary devotion in helping me get the needed books on time.

Several secretaries have cheerfully produced draft upon draft of the manuscript, and for this I thank the chieftain of the Publications Office at Virginia, Diane Moss, and her loyal co-workers, including Gail Branch, Madeline Branch, Kathy Burton, Gloria Keralakis, and Virginia Trenka.

Finally, I thank Helene S. Shapo for the help of a wifely comrade, now colleague, and Benjamin M. Shapo and Nathaniel S. Shapo for the moral support of sons who have grown up with the making of books and whose liveliness helps keep that endeavor fresh.

Marshall S. Shapo

Introduction

The march of science has proved a boon for most, but it also has brought tragedy to a few.

The media deluge us with stories about beneficial products of scientific progress that cause or threaten harm to those in no position to make meaningful choices. The case of oral contraceptives is a benchmark in the history of medical progress. Though the Pill has freed millions from sexual constraints, it has proved, over a decade of marketing, to have serious side effects for a relatively small number of users, and the returns on its long-term consequences are not in yet. The seemingly miraculous versatility of the sex hormones used to prevent conception has been utilized in other ways to preserve it, and in the fullness of the cycle of the life they control, to promote growth. Thus, the hormone diethylstilbestrol (DES) has been employed to prevent miscarriages, and also to improve the rate of weight gain in livestock. Yet in the former instance there is evidence that it has caused cancers in the very children whose conception it fostered. And in the latter case, controversy has arisen about the possible cancer-causing properties of the tiny residues of the chemical in marketed meat.

Controversy, indeed, is the hallmark of the problem this book addresses. An industrial plant on the shores of Lake Superior empties into its clear waters a slurry of asbestoslike particles, the jetsam of its mining activities, and at the same time also spews out microscopic bits of the stuff into the surrounding air. Faced with a choice between shutting down the plant or taking less drastic steps to reduce the emissions, how should the court view the potential risk to those who breathe in particles in the ambient air very similar to substances known to cause cancer in closed workplaces? What approach should it take to the problem of particles in water supplies which have not been shown to cause cancer but which also cannot be proved to be safe?

At the same time that these manufacturing and distribution

activities are progressing, interweaving the creation of hazards of the kinds described with the ongoing quest for scientific knowledge, research scientists are exploring unique frontiers. At the limits of our knowledge of the molecules of life, they have begun the recombination of those molecules, literally linking fragments of them together or introducing them into bacteria. The practical goals of this activity, some only dimly perceived, appear to promise enormous benefits for mankind. The risks are perhaps even more uncertain, but possibly could be immense.

These matters bring home to us that only recently has it been thought necessary to devise theories of legal control for the fruits of scientific enterprise as well as for the enterprise itself. The purpose of this book is to analyze the problems that law confronts with the fallout of scientific progress. I will focus this analysis particularly though not exclusively on issues involved with the long-term hazard of chemicals or processes whose danger slumbers through time, only to awaken in fatal or debilitating ways in individuals who have been playing a lottery whose rules they do not know. In adopting this approach, I hope not only to deal with legal issues engendered by the particular hazards under consideration, but to provide the beginnings of a more general theory of legal control of scientific endeavor and its consequences.

I should note that in contrast to the paradigmatic case on which I focus, there is a reverse image of the kind of research that presents short-term benefits and long-term uncertainties of risk. Sometimes practical applications of research may be viewed as immediately hazardous, whereas its eventual outcome could prove extremely beneficial. For example, at one point in recent scientific history it might have been argued that certain areas of microbiological research should be prohibited because the only perceived reason to transfer virulence between bacterial strains was to create new biological warfare agents; but such a ban would have blocked the studies that are credited with opening the age of molecular biology.[1]

I should note that many of the problems I have selected for analysis involve continuing controversies; I have chosen them because their intrinsic interest is a product of this urgent social concern. Yet although I have strived to present questions of topical interest, journalistic currency is not my primary intent. Rather, I wish to analyze these episodes as manifestations of a general social problem. In that sense, then, my approach is historical, entailing an effort to view these matters as lessons representative of possible trends in public policy.

I think it is important to establish the general framework in which scientific inquiry takes place and scientific judgments are made, and I shall describe this intellectual structure and continue to refer to it. I shall not, however, spend much time discussing the dangers of scientific progress as an abstract matter. As one commentator has said, writing from a social science perspective, technology itself is usually neutral, and its evils are products of the social system.[2] Thus it is my purpose to discuss a number of concrete problems that science and technology have produced, and to suggest methods of analysis which might be generalized with respect to analogous issues as they arise in the future.

The social drama in this subject comes from the clash of two great systems of thought. In connection with the great human endeavor called law, I must emphasize here some elementary distinctions among various kinds of legal responses to long-term hazards presented by new products and processes. These include the positive enactments adopted by legislatures and the case-by-case determinations—common law—made by judges. Also among them is the intermediate role, at times fashioning codes of conduct and at others making specific factual and legal determinations, which is played by administrative agencies. The chapters that follow deal with varying mixtures of these forms of legal process.

Broadly viewed, all problems that relate to the regulation of science are concerned with welfare defined in the economic sense. Some of them involve basic governmental decisions to push resources in one direction or another. Illustrative of broader issues are questions of whether to commit the country to a moon-landing project or to make all capital ships nuclear-powered. Others—problems in the penumbra of science—typically involve purchase by individual consumers, rather than the government as buyer of large-scale social projects. The lines between these categories are not sharply drawn. At the margin, for example, is the matter of the supersonic transport, concerning which it was argued that a government decision to buy an expensive program would create substantial harmful effects for the direct clients of that activity.

I shall develop a number of themes throughout this book. One of these will focus on the uncertain character of the hazards we face with new developments in science and technology. Associated with this will be a strand of argument based on a definition of experimentation that is broader than the usual connotations of that term. In particular, I shall speak of "market experimentation"—a term which describes the ongoing inquiry into hazardous effects, using members of the general public as subjects, that is a necessary part of the conduct of new activities and the marketing of new products. And I shall suggest a general approach toward decision-making about uncertain risks created by this broad form of experimentation. This approach is essentially cautionary and risk-averse in a time in which the burdens on our natures as well as on nature generally are accumulating at rates that even our best scientific minds do not understand.

Indeed a major thesis of this book is that over a period of about forty years a consensus has developed among the American people and their representatives about the risks that attend the benefits of scientific and technological progress. This consensus holds in effect that when concern and suspicion about these potential hazards find their way into the public eye, Americans adopt a generally risk-averse perspective on being exposed to dangers that are cumulative, unseen, and uncertain over the long term. A large part of this concern, articulated as well as implicit in several safety-focused statutes, is based in motives of self-protection against the uncertain danger. Part of it is founded in a sense that we should make strong efforts to limit the exposure of random groups of the population to the risks of serious physical injury or even death from dangers that are unpredictable and unknowable and may strike without warning. This view may be especially strong when the traumatic connotations of dangers that "strike" cannot adequately describe a process that may take months or even years in the human body. Further, when public anxiety about such hazards finds its way into legislation, judges tend to credit this risk-averse tendency, motivated interstitially by the factors described above as well as responding to the specific public concern embodied in safety statutes.

Americans have generally been a self-reliant, confident, and optimistic people. At the same time, a frontier heritage has given them a certain philosophical approach to the risks of living. Moreover, their principal choice of economic mechanisms, even well into a century that has seen increasing collectivization and regulation, has involved reliance on the market. It is therefore especially noteworthy when law, in the form of both legislation and judicial decision, manifests on their behalf a view of risk that is relatively defensive and regulatory.

The explanation for this, I think, lies in part in the relatively unknowable and insidious character of the risks discussed here. It also lies in the manmade origin of these dangers, as compared with the stark, natural character of the hazards that were the lot of our forebears. In addition, the hidden nature of these risks presents sharp contrasts with the glossy picture of the good life, achievable through new possessions and processes, painted by the mass media. When the heightened expectations thus created are disappointed by injury and disease, frustration and even anger set in. This has contributed to an increasing belief that regulation of technical progress must respond to the fact that progress often brings savage disappointment to some.

It is against this background that the view has developed that those who market new goods or create external consequences from processes that are novel or not thoroughly tested owe the community a scientific affirmation of safety at particular levels of use, or at least an abundance of warnings and opportunities to make a choice. It is for these reasons that legislatures, abetted by courts, have chosen to impose more caution on the development and marketing of new forms of products and processes.

This book both describes these developments of policy and law and suggests that they are sensible ones because of the uncertainties and sometimes unfair consequences of market experimentation. In the vernacular, it suggests that society has developed a short fuse about long-term risk, and for good reason. In developing this point of view, I shall analyze in some detail several outcroppings of danger signals and regulatory response, in particular episodes related to oral contraceptives and other prescription drugs, food additives, environmental asbestos emissions, and the regulation of gene recombination. Before analyzing these concrete examples of threatened hazard, however, I shall deal with the background of scientific activity and of the public and private choices with which it interacts. Thus, I shall first examine science as an enterprise with a view to understanding both its tendency to create risk and its ability to assess it. Then I shall develop the concept of experimentation as it works out in both clinical and market settings, emphasizing the role of law in protecting those who are made the subjects of experiments. And I shall counterpose a view of personal choice that emphasizes the ability of individuals to choose the risks they will confront, a perspective that sometimes contrasts with established governmental roles in what has come to be called "consumer protection."

1 The Scientific Enterprise

THE EFFORT TO DEVELOP PRINCIPLES for the regulation of scientific progress must turn first to the question of what science is. In this chapter I shall offer some definitions, cast in terms of the characteristics and attributes of the enterprise and the activities of its practitioners.

At first glance, it would seem that regulatory distinctions might be made between the purer science that seeks only to increase the store of knowledge and the technological inquiry that is much more goal-focused, and usually in one way or another more profit-directed. Yet this sort of distinction is facile, both in terms of the payoff for the investigator and the means he adopts. For even the scientist seeking knowledge for its own sake may require human experimental subjects; and in the extreme case, such as gene recombination, he may directly produce external hazards dangerous to the population as a whole. Moreover, the scientist's own measure of his utility, his own goal-striving, may represent a form of profit-directedness that rivals or exceeds that of the corporation-employed expert in terms of the need for public response.

Because of these functional overlaps, as a matter of definition I shall be commingling "science" and "technology" under both labels. This is appropriate because the problems that they present for regulation are quite similar. What is most important from the point of view of law is that both scientific and technological development have issues in common all along a continuous frontier, recurrently concerned with whether social trade-offs are acceptable either in terms of dollars or dignity.[1] However, in drawing definitionally on this similarity for regulatory purposes, I do not ignore, when relevant, the distinction between the two kinds of endeavor. I should add that in those cases in which I differentiate between science and technology, this does not imply a discrimination in valuation. As a report of the American Association for the Advancement of Science has said, the categories have equal rank, though different functions "as members of the scientific community."[2]

Jerome Ravetz, on whose excellent book I draw heavily in this chapter, has defined a "scientific problem" to include a "tentative statement" of what the researcher hopes to find in his investigation of the objects he will study, with a plan for the research that will allow him to establish his findings "as a conclusion to an adequate argument." A problem may be externally determined in a rather precise way and still be scientific; but it takes on a technical aspect when "the use to which the information will be put, its function, constitutes the major component of value of the . . . problem, and it determines the standards of adequacy by which its solution will be assessed."[3]

Many of the problems to which I address myself here concern new questions about the properties of objects which entail the hope of payoffs in specific modes of production. In that sense, they tend to be technological. One may compare Jacques Ellul's locution, in which technology, for purposes of definition and contrast with "science," is method; it is means and "the ensemble of means."[4] Ellul remarks the role of "consciousness and judgment" in technology, producing a "technical phenomenon" whose essence is to take "what was previously tentative, unconscious and spontaneous" and bring it "into the realm of clear, voluntary and reasoned concepts."[5] In this he finds the "clear technical intention"—a "precise view of technical possibilities, the will to attain certain ends, application in all areas, and adherence of the whole of society to a conspicuous technical objective"—which he calls the "distinctive characteristic of our time."[6] Yet the difficulty of drawing a line between the "scientific" search for these properties and their operational use does not concern me so much as the complexities and uncertainties that stretch across established lines of research and across the differing concerns with ends that characterize science and technology. In this book I am concerned primarily with legal and policy problems that grow out of the mix of these pursuits. These questions share elements of legal significance, whether they arise from the effort to develop new knowledge for its own sake or to solve practical problems of the world.[7] Indeed, the experimental use of a product or process may involve mixed motivations as to ends.

The definitions discussed above lead us to inquire as to the characteristics and attributes of scientific endeavor, for understanding these things will help us to formulate legislative and judicial approaches to its regulation. Given the complexity of science as it is, it seems particularly important to articulate these aspects of the activity because of the difficulties that present themselves for those who are trying to regulate processes that they do not quite understand. There is in this regard a significant contrast between law and science which grows from the goal of law in achieving results which are received as just, rather than describing an external reality.

Like many of the social sciences, academic law has developed branches in which the emphasis is on model-building and the use of mathematical tools.[8] But law's job as a social mediator retains a core that is relatively unyielding to this kind of analysis. The effectiveness of the most developed natural sciences lies in their use of computational and analytical techniques that yield a certain kind of precise information. The genius of the law lies in judgment. When judgment is required on conflicts that arise not only over the use of techniques but concerning prediction and choices under uncertainty, the law must proceed at a level of analogy and verbalization that differs from scientific judgment. This is both because of the character of the practical problems[9] and the need for perceptions among citizens that justice has been done. It is for these reasons that it is important that the process used to resolve socially significant conflicts over scientific fact be viewed as responsive to social needs and as a dispassionate mediator within the legal framework that defines those needs.

By significant contrast, if providing intriguing parallels, an important aspect of modern science is its concern with artifacts, representing a reality that the investigator will never glimpse directly. Einstein captured this feature of science in his statement that the scientist "will never be able to compare his picture with the real mechanism and he cannot even imagine the possibility or the meaning of such a comparison.[10] *Scientific discovery involves a substantial amount of judgment, even as to what as laymen we would like to call "facts."* This leads to the point that experimental science, involving as it does the production of information which represents "inaccessible classes of things and events," has an essentially craft character. It is not simply a matter of recording accurate measurements, but rather requires considerable skill in assessment and interpretation. This craft characterization applies not only to the production of data in experiments but to its transformation into statistical form and its testing; all of these operations are necessary to produce information that is considered genuine.[11] This aspect of science must give pause to those who rely on the information it produces and requires understanding by those who would regulate it. It emphasizes that one must view contested research results as the culmination of such a craft process, with all the intermediate judgments that this entails.

And these craft judgments are always subject to correction. For lawyers concerned with scientific "truths," it is important to remember that modern scientific hypothesis and discovery involve an endless process, including not only original assessment but continual investigation to refine the tentative knowledge that research has produced. It has been said that even published scientific conclusions have "rough-hewn" aspects.[12] If they are valuable, they will in turn give birth to a "lattice" of research descendants,[13] woven by investigations that take researchers into various side branches of the subject before producing the main lines of descent. This, although a very abstract description of the scientific enterprise, is important from the standpoint of regulation. Not only does it caution us to be wary of scientists' dicta about matters of social concern,[14] it also counsels that when the focus of social judgment turns to law, both legislators and judges should use a healthy dose of skepticism about seemingly definitive scientific conclusions. They must employ a social telescope that looks both backward to chains of conclusions that have been revised over time, and forward with a perspective that views new research discoveries as only the beginnings of complex processes and says, "wait and see."

Michael Halberstam, a physician who writes about medical matters, gives an eloquent statement of the depth of the mysteries confronting scientists in general, and medical scientists in particular. Describing the body as "a constantly changing mosaic of hundreds of interrelated systems," he notes that in only a few cases can doctors make simultaneous trackings of "two, or at most, three significant systems," although they must assume that dozens are involved in any particular pathology. In this view, medical science knows "comparatively little about how the body functions, and not much more about how it malfunctions." "The body has yielded only its surface secrets to investigators."[15] Statements like this keep us—citizens, lawyers, and scientists—cautious when we argue about regulating the production of substances suspected but not known to cause injury to the cellular stuff of our lives. They point up the complexity that restrains scientists from uttering the kind of definitive judgments we would like to hear, one way or the other. And they reiterate the uncertainty about causal linkages which makes our public law of product and process control such an exercise in the institutionalization of guesswork, and so dependent on wise determination of the appropriate level of risk aversion.

Another significant characteristic of modern scientific knowledge, one that reflects both the accomplishments of the last century of science and the depth of its remaining task, is its highly specialized character. Not only does its production require specialization in education, but it also needs a highly rationalized system of classification to make it practically available. Complex indexes and references, unknown to more genteel generations of investigators of nature's mysteries,[16] are part of the armament of all scientific and technical scholarship today. At the level of human organization, the labels of disciplines generally provide convenient territorial markers for the work of scientists, differentiating various tasks.

Harold Himsworth relates how an epidemic of beri-beri among sailors whose diet had been switched from unmilled to milled rice triggered a chain of events that produced an understanding of the biochemical role of vitamins. He notes that the different scientific disciplines involved had to wait for the ripe, or scientifically logical, time to make their contributions. Clinical medicine had to define beri-beri before epidemiology could articulate the existence of a widespread condition and associate it with a particular dietary deficiency. Only then could experimental pathology show that it was something in rice millings that prevented beri-beri. These findings in turn served as preconditions for roles played by biochemistry and cellular biology.[17] The episode demonstrates that logical progressions within conventional boundaries of scientific disciplines have "affinities" with other subjects.[18] There is in fact a double-directional thrust of research within scientific pigeonholes: in one way toward concentration on specific, often socially defined missions; in the other, toward the development of broad, unspecialized knowledge.[19] This dual feature helps to give modern scientific investigation its great solving power and suggests that the law should facilitate the development of these affinities. In particular, with reference to the problem of risks whose dangerous potential becomes gradually evident, it should encourage the cross-disciplinary sharing of both information and speculation about possible long-term consequences.

In terms of economics, modern science is capital-intensive. Large amounts of money are needed to start up research and to carry it out, and these sums typically come only from a relatively small number of agencies.[20] This fact is important not only with respect to scientific discovery but to a critical assessment of its products, an endeavor which itself may require substantial investment for research. Private enterprise must recoup in sales the high costs of research and development, often mentioned in the policy literature of science,[21] a factor likely to exert pressures for less deliberate experimentation and quicker marketing of goods. It is in the very areas where scientific and technical progress is the focus of concern that these pressures will weigh most heavily on entrepreneurs, and thus compel strict scrutiny of their evaluations of risk.

Another important aspect of scientific endeavor is the time frame in which it takes place. In the kind of investigative science now practiced, the fashioning alone of a proper grant application may require weeks or months, and bringing a major project to fruition often takes years. Thus the structuring of incentives by law will significantly affect the production of reliable scientific data. Legal rules that constrict the process of investigation will discourage discovery, and it is reasonable to believe that this holds true especially at the point where the scientist is investing his own venture capital—his time—in the development of projects. The kind of resource commitment that science requires also includes the background preparation constantly demanded of a dedicated researcher. Fleming's discovery of penicillin is one of the most famous examples of the maxim that chance favors the prepared mind. There is nothing that a scientist learns as he studies around his current project that may not be crucial as preparatory background for the chance discovery.[22] When we speak of how much of its resources society should commit to research, the implication is clear that public support of science should include interstitial accounts that promote this penumbral learning. This necessity for intellectual elbow room strongly argues that rules directly regulating the conduct of science should give scientists the benefit of the doubt. Although this proposition tends to slant against the main line of argument in this book, I must articulately recognize its importance as a balance wheel to risk avoidance.

These facts of life central to the discussion above—time and money—imply the next point: the depth of knowledge to which scientists can dig is, as with information generally, related in large part to the cost of acquiring it. One of the main preliminary obstacles to the completion of successful research lies in the fact that the definition of a problem to be solved requires a delicate balancing act in degrees of specification. The investigator must seek to make his decision on specificity in a way that precludes "aimless wandering" through many avenues of research, while still keeping the focus broad enough to avoid tunnel vision.[23] Moreover, scientists continually must make decisions about what level of adequacy is acceptable in their data.[24] These decisions have a counterpart in governmental choices about how much information must be accumulated about possible long-term risks. Among other particular problems arising at the stage of research design are the questions of how many persons should be subjected to experimental investigation and how long to permit experimentation to continue.

A related factor that is particularly characteristic of modern science is the enormous growth not only of the number of practitioners—it is estimated that about 85 per cent of all the scientists who ever lived are living now—but of its research product. The number of scientific journals now being published is approximately 30,000. More than 300 abstract journals—publications which print nothing but abstracts of articles—as well as a number of journals that publish only titles facilitate professional acquaintance with this flood of information.[25] These figures have grave implications for the regulation of scientific endeavor. Legislation designed to control potentially hazardous experimentation or the marketing of products that may pose a threat to human life should respond to the difficulties of unearthing as well as assessing information that may signal danger to the expert but is not within the ken of ordinary citizens. Consider the fact that in early 1960 there appeared in veterinary literature references to the birth of deformed lambs to sheep pastured on certain Idaho meadows. It is asserted that scientists with sufficient information could have analogized the chemical composition of plants in those meadows with the formula for the teratogenic drug thalidomide and blown an early warning whistle.[26] Although cost considerations inevitably exert limitations on background investigations of this kind, statutory and regulatory schemes should encourage the development of analytical screening techniques that bring such cautionary hypotheses to the surface.

The numbers of these battalions of workers and the indexes of this outpouring of data make plain the novelty that is the hallmark of discovery. And indeed the quality of newness colors our view of science and is an inextricable part of the role of modern scientists. As Paul Weiss has noted, whole areas of science now exist that half a century ago had "neither identity nor name, let alone university departments, societies, and journals for their specialties." In those days

> Virology did not exist, for viruses were just on the horizon. Endocrinology, pharmacology and biophysics had not yet split from their mother sciences; only twenty years ago the term "molecular biology," now in the daily vernacular, had not yet been coined.

Moreover, there have piled upon these problem-oriented or subject-centered specialties a wide range of subdisciplines focused on technique, ranging from electron microscopy and ultracentrifugation to tissue culture and radiology.[27]

Policy makers are constantly wrestling with the implications of this proliferation of the methods and the substance of investigation. They are forced to deal with them both in terms of the creation of risk and the measurement of effects. To take as specific examples the fields mentioned above, prescription-drug regulators may ask endocrinologists and pharmacologists what the chances are that chemicals used for contraception will produce malignancies; and persons drafting rules for containment of gene-recombinant experiments will have to consult virologists, among others, about the possible consequences of human contact with particular biological agents. Exemplifying the closing of the circle between measurement and assessment, officials dealing with substances added to the food supply must call on experts in the use of machines that can count residue particles down to the billionth of a part—as well as requesting other scientific workers to estimate the possibilities of danger presented by such minute quantities.

In this setting of high capital expenditure, long lead times, and continuing production of novelties an elite of superbly trained, and sometimes highly educated inviduals pursues its work. It is well to keep in view the qualities of mind and the habits that are part of the personalities of scientific workers. It has been remarked that one of the special attributes of science is the passionate dedication of its practitioners. In their search for knowledge they often become preoccupied in an extraordinary way.[28] Descriptions of this intense absorption, symbolized by the idealized portrait of the scientist grabbing catnaps in his laboratory while pursuing the newest lead, rival the images of great artists—Handel turning out the *Messiah* in a few days, painters pushing themselves to the utmost limits of creativity on starvation diets. And science does arc into the realm of art. From the incredible regularity of molecular biochemistry to the virtual poetry of the cosmological speculations of theoretical astronomers, there are powerful aesthetic attractions in scientific endeavor.

An inquiry into principles of public regulation of science also must consider the public's view of the activity and its practitioners. Critical perceptions and literary descriptions of scientists have varied from describing them as arrogant to emphasizing their "humanity."[29] Whatever the popular conception of scientific work, the delicate psychological structure needed to practice sophisticated science is manifest in the contrast, sketched by Ravetz, between the public communication of scientific knowledge and the "personal" experience of scientists at work, with their "private understanding[s]" of their "objects of inquiry." Another fragile link in the chain of discovery lies in the informal kinds of communication among scientists necessary to push the enterprise forward.[30] Against this background, the public image of the scientist is both stereotypical and ambivalent. At the same time, people may view him with awe as a worker of modern miracles and as a strange outsider with none of the bonhomie common to those directly engaged in commerce.[31] Yet it has been remarked that there is an optimism in scientists which rivals the boosterism of the traditional businessman. And the conviction that problems can be solved tends to the salutary result of generating human steam toward solving them.[32]

For purposes of devising systems of legal control, it is even more important to consider the internal social aspects of natural science—the personal relationships and combined ties of intellect and emotion that bind scientific workers. History counsels us not to underestimate the importance of collegial relationships in scientific research. Exemplary of early recognition of the advantages in scientific interchange is the formation of the Lunar Society of Birmingham, founded in England in the 1770s. This group included Joseph Priestley, the discoverer of oxygen, and the inventor of the condensing steam engine, Erasmus Darwin, the grandfather of Charles. It spawned not only technological developments contributing to Watt's steam engine, but also the finding that digitalis was effective for the treatment of heart disease and the discoveries of sulfuric acid as well as the bleaching properties of chlorine.[33]

Groups of scientists may be more or less loosely organized. The American Association for the Advancement of Science today provides a large umbrella for the exchange of scientific ideas and data. Within these catholic perimeters, it has been documented that there are grand "schools" of scientific thought dealing with broad fields of inquiry.[34] Presumably there are also smaller schools, with attendant orthodoxies, centered on particular problems. The existence of such scientific networks, however structured or informal, however broad or narrow, requires the regulator to know something about the sociology of the field he proposes to regulate. This knowledge may provide him with indicators about the reliability of predictions that a product or process is hazardous. For example, his analysis of disagreement about such forecasts among members of a given school or group may reveal unexpected, and thus telling, alignments within the group that either put him further on guard or signal that a hypothesis is trivial.

There is, of course, a danger that informal groupings of scientists may engender a clubbiness that stifles honest assessment as well as slowing the pace of discovery. One powerful force that does work against irresponsibility originates in the method of publishing scientific papers, which conventionally are subjected to scrutiny by anonymous referees and pass through a stringent process of selection and editing. This serves at least as first-line insurance that published results are duplicable and provides significant defense against exorbitant claims. The institutionalization of modern science thus brings significant benefits to the public, especially with its insistence on rigorous review of results. Additionally the stratification of science in a sociological sense, with a hierarchy of journals whose prestige serves as an index to the quality of their product,[35] has salutary features.

But when we speak of the relation of science to regulation of hazardous endeavors, we must be aware of the parallel rise of a priesthood of scientists and of a concomitant personal interest in certain modes of investigation or review of evidence. Despite the formal controls imposed by the now established traditions of refereeing and publication in journals, the dangers of intradisciplinary political control by established high priests have grown. Ravetz has asserted that they are at the point where a "Big Scientist" may perpetuate himself by stringing together hastily produced papers in journals under the control of himself and his friends. Moreover, he says, such leaders may effectively control "the government of a field," which for practical purposes means its pursestrings.[36] In this structural framework, the fresh discovery or the new hypothesis about hazard—or sometimes its absence—may find it difficult to penetrate the hierarchy and acquire the professional certification which assures regulatory recognition.

A related point is that the more sophisticated science becomes, the greater will be the tendency that methods of formulating problems, adopting strategies, and interpreting criteria of adequacy and value will involve "informal and largely tacit precepts of method." This kind of lesson among scientists, Ravetz says, is learned "entirely by imitation and experience." It is quite different in character from the knowledge that is found in published results, because there are not the same possibilities for controlling the diffusion of this informally transmitted information, nor the same kind of quality control. Thus, it is argued that it is "subject to particular weaknesses from which public scientific knowledge is protected."[37] This slippery form of intrascientific communication poses special difficulties for regulation. It involves premises buried within arguments, informal assumptions about methods of inquiry and, one assumes, inarticulate value choices. It is an important and difficult job of law, and lawyers, to probe the informal intellectual history of these teachings and understandings in the effort to arrive at social judgment.

Important among the characteristics of modern science that have implications for legal control is a particular kind of neutrality that characterizes scientists' views of their work, which is associated with a belief that their reports should be limited to the presentation of data. A recent example of the social implications of this position arises from gene-recombinant experiments: a first preprint of a paper which described a means of transmitting a DNA molecule into a bacteria contained a cautionary note concerning the "implications and potential biohazards of experiments employing this approach." In the process of review, this note was deleted, apparently in part because of the feeling that this warning should not be printed without elaboration, but also because of what one commentator calls the "assumed ethic" that limits scientific publication to reporting the data.[38]

Of course, science as a method of inquiry is neutral. But science as a producer of data and as a creator of new physical and chemical entities may start chains of events with destructive consequences, and these results may be mysterious to the general public. Speculation about sabotage as a cause of the baffling arrival and departure of "Legionnaire's disease" in Pennsylvania in 1976[39] illustrated public apprehension about the possible secret uses of science. Shortly after the explosion of the first atomic bombs, Frédérick Joliot-Curie published a short story in which he imagined the use of biological weapons which mimicked natural human illnesses but were more virulent.[40] Running divergently from the creation of risk known only to the creator is a problem that arises from secrets which nature continues to hold, rather than those which scientists and their governmental or corporate employers keep to themselves. This is the problem of external consequences of scientific progress which may not be known until after the introduction of a new product or process, sometimes months or years later. It is a task of law to limit such occurrences, and it must provide incentives to scientific professionals to identify possibilities as well as probabilities that they will happen. When experience and scientific intuition indicate that there is a significant experimental component involved with safety of a product or process, this will call for regulation, at least as a matter of disclosure and sometimes in the form of constraints on production. In this regard, law is a natural foe of secrecy.

We should make further reference here to the often subtle and inarticulate way in which established scientists communicate the process of analysis that is at the core of successful science, and to the general problem this creates for regulation. Ravetz has spoken of the "partly informal and even tacit" character of the methodology of various scientific fields, noting that the transmission of these methods employs "informal, interpersonal channel[s]," rather than the avenues of published scientific communication.[41] Thus a ground for social regulation lies in the elusiveness of the process; apparently what breeds success in this most successful and mysterious twentieth-century endeavor is something that people cannot quite pin down. The indefinable character of this method of communication implies the argument "Don't make laws that bruise the delicate membranes of this.always developing enterprise, for this will have subtle and unpredictable deleterious effects on the process of discovery." Thus science presents us with a special irony. Regulation too stringent in the name of protecting the public from uncertainty will produce unknowable damage to the process itself, which has given society so much. An abstract condemnation of cabals does not advance solution of this problem. Our recognition of this aspect of science, however, does inform our general approach to legal control.

One source of problems attached to scientific endeavor is, and historically has been, its mystique. An interesting parallel may be drawn between the arcane nature of science for laymen today and the mysticism that became associated with Pythagorean science in the fifth century B.C. It has been speculated that although that ancient effort at scientific endeavor achieved a promising beginning with its advancement of ideas, however rude, that might be subjected to verification, the secretiveness of its practitioners may well have contributed to this air of mysticism.[42] Today even slightly educated people know that science is not mystical, but the mystique remains, a product of the enterprise's ability to solve extraordinary problems as it unlocks what are popularly but properly referred to as the secrets of the universe.[43] The point of science as craft, well developed by Ravetz, is worth emphasizing here. As science becomes more sophisticated, it deals less with "things" which laymen can readily observe and more with "intellectually constructed things and events."[44] Thus there is an artificiality about the objects of scientific inquiry, and it follows that the arguments that scientists make toward their conclusions include many kinds of inferences: inductive, probabilistic, and analogical.[45] The most interesting point from our perspective is the consequent "lack of demonstrative certainty," which must itself fuel both public awe and distrust of science.

In more specific relation to our subject, the mystique of science constitutes an important background factor in its relation to law. Public obeisance to science, manifested in the practice of the rituals of a vulgarized "scientism," is a product of this mystique.

The promoters of products which owe their being to scientific development take advantage of it; one author has cited illustrations in mundane contexts, ranging from decay-fighting claims for toothpastes to advertisers' injunctions concerning diet. Unswerving obedience to dosage directions on pill bottles exemplifies the same respectful attitude.[46] Sometimes the wide-eyed citizen runs headlong into contradictory evidence, as with conflicting opinions on the claim that one product will reduce cholesterol in the blood, complicated by arguments that another which raises it is on balance a positive contribution to diet. But the very authoritativeness with which such pronouncements are offered illustrates the high regard in which "science" is still generally held. Playing on this public favor in efforts to increase budgetary shares and boost sales, scientists and promoters tend to project a sense of infallibility, an impression which requires consideration when laws are drafted and interpreted.

Associated with the scientific mystique is the difficulty that lay persons have in understanding these scientific problems. The general point that "some sciences' rate of development even outruns some scientists' efforts at comprehension"[47] has been specifically made in the case of work on gene recombination.[48] Indeed, the main problem to which this book addresses itself is the case in which scientists and technological innovators are themselves quite uncertain about the long-term consequences of their activities. Yet even in their uncertainty, they are prone to make technical statements that are impenetrable to the layman. In situations of this kind, the legal system requires translation of scientific dialect, though it must also check the inclination to oversimplify. In situations where translation fails, the best working principle would appear to be that if those charged with legal decisions on scientific questions cannot understand their potential consequences, they should draw back, or at least proceed very slowly. The most recent paradigm for this approach again involves the development of gene recombination research, in response to which NIH guidelines imposed several levels of regulation on a technology whose momentum seemingly threatened to spin it out of control. This case illustrates a point where scientific activity which many practitioners think is well justified must yield to a government whose being is dependent on knowledgeable consent of its clients. It is worth noting the application of the principle in two settings of DNA regulation. At the federal level the resolution achieved in the guidelines was fashioned in a situation in which the decision makers found themselves in the same state of ignorance and uncertainty as the investigators. What is especially interesting is the much-praised decisional process of the Cambridge City Council, which involved lay persons whose lack of knowledge was similar to that of scientists who wanted to proceed with the research, the only difference being in the degree of sophistication about uncertainty. The message may be that while experts are required for explanation, expertise is not so important in decision as intellectual openness and a process that encourages rational persuasion.

I should stress here a point made earlier about the judgmental content of scientific research results. Shocking reports of statistical error in laboratory reports as well as scientific studies[49] become more explainable when one considers Ravetz's comment about the tendency to "accept statistical information as facts, rather than evidence." As he says, using a word with legal overtones, "This can lead to negligence even in testing the reliability of such information in relation to the populations whose properties it describes."[50] It is this tendency, as well as documented episodes of error, that must put regulators on their guard against the intuitive belief that science always deals with "facts" and "certainties."

The system of having anonymous referees review scientific papers does serve as partial insurance that they will have a certain technical integrity; but it will not insure that they will contain "facts." Indeed, as Ravetz has pointed out, "It is hardly ever possible to reproduce the data on which the evidence is based." The referee, rather than duplicating the research under review, must call upon his own knowledge of the science as a craft in order to make a judgment of the work's adequacy.[51] Moreover, as techniques improve, adequacy is a matter of the moment. Scientific discoveries are always subject to the possibility that new developments will show them to be based on crude data.

The tentative nature of scientific conclusions is only another indication that what takes place in the assessment of scientific "discovery" is a judgment of judgment. A striking parallel appears between law and science in this regard because, as Ravetz has said, this is a social judgment, subject to various influences and errors.[52] We have underlined here the differences between law and science as agencies of justice and truth-seeking, but Ravetz's statement that "the objectivity and certainty of science seem to

dissolve before our eyes" reminds us remarkably of the psychology of the first-year law student who discovers the malleability
and vulnerability to change of the common law, as well as of any
legislative scheme.

Another problem in scientific inquiry, which is cumulative to
the ubiquity of possibilities of mistake, is the difficulty of guarding
against errors and even of discovering them. There are many
ways in which research may go awry. For example, data may be
produced on equipment with a concealed systematic error, or the
theory of the equipment "may have a hidden error which vitiates
the inferences from the readings."[53] These "pitfalls," Ravetz
notes, involve "false assessments of the quality of evidence or insufficiently strong inferences," rather than logical errors. And he
notes that they cannot easily be identified even retrospectively,
because of the difficulties in unraveling the "patterns of argument" in scientific problems.[54]

This terminology leads to a further point, which is that science
does in fact proceed as a series of dialectical arguments, with its
tradition that hypotheses are proposed and tested, to be discarded, broadened, or amended as the evidence requires. The job
of law, in those areas where scientific knowledge is at issue, is to
facilitate this process of argument among scientists, and especially
to encourage it in situations in which the inner politics of science
or the larger politics of the nation would tend to hide it.

The problem of secrecy and nondisclosure is one that infects
all areas of scientific advance where safety questions are involved.
It is true that there are strong forces that impel basic scientists to
publicize their work. Besides the desire for recognition, the entire
ethic of contributing knowledge to an ongoing process of investigation pushes in that direction. Yet as the products of science
approach commerce, in cases in which a need to stave off government intervention or to secure official approval presses upon
investigators or exploiters, there may be reasons of self-interest to
suppress information. Sometimes these reasons may be found directly in the profits being made by a product currently on the
market, which retains its usefulness for the purposes for which it
is advertised, but whose risks appear greater than when it was
originally offered to the public. At other times the drive to proceed with premarketing research and development without government surveillance will be foremost. In each of these cases the
investigator or promoter (sometimes these functions are joined)

may be perfectly sincere in believing that he is producing a boon to mankind. But what counts is not this subjective inner state; it is the right of public representatives to review the evidence with an eye to safety.

The conduct of scientific endeavor sometimes makes it difficult to fix responsibility. This can be so, it has been pointed out, because of the team nature of much scientific work.[55] Moreover, the production of bad science, which might be assumed to affect employment adversely, may not necessarily cost a scientist job opportunities. Some firms may prefer the scientist-advocate who can throw up a strong defense while they reap short-term profits. It has even been contended that scientists who misadvise the government need not fear for their livelihood because of university alternatives, although this argument implicitly derogates the standards of academic employers. Yet there also remains the option of moving from government to industry, even assuming the highest standards of competence in the private sector, if the complaint about a scientist's work concerns his bias rather than his technical competence. Additionally, it should be noted that the most difficult behavior to trace is that of the scientist—whether employed in government, academia, or industry—who recognizes a problem and walks away from it without saying anything, or even fails to recognize it at all.

In our consideration of the facts of scientific life, it is well to note that levels of morale may differ considerably among various branches of the enterprise. In this connection, one must recall the craft nature of science, and the inexactitude of its seemingly exact product. One must also refer constantly to the need for internal, informal checks on the conclusions drawn by scientists whose desires for publication or publicity may, if they are left to their own devices, outweigh their motivation to do good work. Ravetz has abstractly described the evolution of a Gresham's law syndrome within a field of science in which those who assess research products are driven by a general demoralization to approve marginal work, a process which feeds on itself to the detriment of quality in the field as a whole.[56] It would seem that this problem might be especially acute in those fields in which the public controversy is greatest about the potential direct benefits of scientific work. Regulators surely must concern themselves with general conditions of deterioration in the acquisition of knowledge and the formulation of research conclusions. But it is also incumbent on them to respond to pressures on the one hand to conform to existing orthodoxies—which may have vested interests in presenting images of relatively riskless consequences of research and development—and to incentives on the other hand to produce well-publicized predictions of grave danger. Both the etiquette and the ethics of individual scientific communities may be strained by the task of keeping these pressures under control,[57] and the law should operate as a backup line of defense against the kind of demoralization that contributes to misestimation of risk.

It has been well said that many problems that are attributed to technology have arisen because "an activity previously carried out badly can now be carried out well."[58] The case of motor transportation provides a broad example of this sort of phenomenon. The rise of the automobile produced severe economic dislocations, practically destroying the industry that had grown up around horse transport. At the same time, of course, it produced large numbers of manufacturing and service jobs related to cars and trucks. This story of new job categories springing up as old ones are rendered obsolete by technology is a familiar one,[59] but the motor vehicle especially exemplifies the double edge of progress in the area of personal injury. The automobile that repeals old meanings of miles carries a striking force that produces more death than our wars.

More precisely related to our present inquiry, controversy in the area of public regulation about requirements of "technology forcing,"[60] and in private law about the "state of the art" as a defense for defective product design,[61] demonstrates that progress itself often opens up grounds for complaint that were not there before. Sometimes problems become problems only because of the existence of new technological tools. This has occurred with progress in instrumentation which has enabled us to discover the presence of substances which previous measuring techniques were not able to detect. Exemplary is the development of ever more sensitive devices for the measurement of additives in animal tissues.[62]

Thus far the discussion has dealt generally with the way science poses problems that may create fallout on the public, entailing some remarks about the tasks thus posed for the legal system. I now continue with more of a focus on the role of law as controller and mediator of science.

Lee Loevinger has pointed out a conflict in roles between scientists and lawgivers. He characterizes science as "completely nonauthoritarian and dedicated to the proposition that every rule and datum is open to challenge and testing," as contrasted with government, which he views as "necessarily authoritative and even somewhat authoritarian."[63] Yet, as Loevinger himself recognizes, there is a tendency in votaries of science to claim a special authority for their expertise that will win them political power.[64] This has exposed scientists to conflicting pressures between their role as seekers after knowledge and as suppliers of public policy judgments.[65] This book proceeds on the premise that scientists possess a method of approaching problems which offers social benefits, but that when there is social controversy over either the information or counsel they provide, the ultimate judgment is one for law. This arbitration function is performed both by the technical kind of law manufactured by attorneys in courts and agencies and the policy-oriented preferences expressed by the general citizenry, principally nonscientists, through their legislators.

In this analysis of the "law-science confrontation," it is appropriate to stress a fundamental social tension created by scientific work. The conflict is one between encouraging innovation, a goal which requires incentives for being first to announce a discovery, and serving the competing social interest in rigorous critical review, designed to weed out shoddy, trivial, or erroneous material.[66] The emphasis on priority of discovery may lead to the taking of dangerous risks—either by imposing them on subjects in controlled experimental settings or by exposing segments of the population to the external effects of industrial activity or product marketing that remains experimental. It also will produce pressures to steal the ideas of other scientific workers.[67] We must remember, in this regard, that there is a great distance between the creative hypothesis with which a scientist may begin his work and the understated dispassionate report in which he announces his conclusions. Between these events, as Ravetz says, is "demanding and subtle craftsman's work on the very special objects of scientific knowledge."[68] The law must aim to preserve the incentives for this kind of labor while recognizing the craft nature of the work, and its inevitable openness to interpretation, argument, and error.

These tensions intrude themselves into the arena in which law must judge conflicting opinions of scientists. One should keep in mind the varying roles that scientists and technically trained persons play in the formulation and articulation of conclusions about scientific matters with public policy implications. It has been pointed out that "experts" employed by organizations will try to argue—"perhaps with sincerity"—as if they were scientists, "establishing [their] conclusions on supposedly known and irrefutable facts."[69] And attorneys operating in many branches of the law would recognize the force of the statement that even when a scientific project has been subject to "ghastly pitfalls," "the firm can usually find an expert to assure the public that the matter is really in competent hands."[70] It should further be noted that often the impressiveness of experts' technical or scientific qualifications will be taken into consideration by legislatures resolving political conflicts or courts when they judge evidence from disagreeing experts.

The authoritative cast of statements by experts, somewhat at variance with the model of science articulated by Loevinger, makes it necessary to provide ways for the law to cut through impressions of expertise to gain dispassionate analysis. It is a turnabout from what we ordinarily think of as the opposed roles of science and law. Special recognition of the need for critical assessment has appeared in the executive branch, where instances of bias and tunnel vision among various scientific chieftains have made it clear to top-level policy makers that they must have independent advice on matters involving substantial resource allocations. Thus, for example, President Eisenhower created a post of Special Assistant to the President for Science and Technology in 1957.[71] There followed the development through the 1960s of what has been called a "pluralism" of scientific advice on policy matters, evolving under the Johnson Administration to a situation where the "institutions of science policy" became "indispensable" in aiding the President to balance conflicting technical advice from various parts of the government and "scientist publics."[72] The lesson here is that in public controversies over dangerous products and processes, persons with the most genuine scientific credentials may for a variety of motives place their reputations at the service of particular political positions. It is important for both legislators and judges to ask where professional judgment and personal stakes simply coincide and where scientific conclusions may be swayed by self-interest.

Thus the task of law is to mediate among persons who have powerful prima facie claims to integrity, and who, according to their own lights, generally are acting in good faith. Judgments favorable or derogatory to a particular line of technological inquiry or development would be corrupt if they were made with the knowledge that the evidence on which they were purportedly based did not justify these conclusions. But corruption—in the sense of a betrayal of public trust in the divergence of actual goals from professional social functions[73]—is not usually an overt component of these problems. If it exists, it is in a very attenuated form. However, law must concern itself with outcomes for citizens who may be affected by scientists' evaluations; and it must be structured to guard against subtler tendencies to tailor scientific judgment to private goals.

One description of the work of the scientist is that it involves an effort to achieve a consensus of public knowledge. In this view, although the scientist may privately be interested primarily in solving a puzzle of great interest to him, he is also trying to convince his colleagues about the value of his findings.[74] From this perspective science has been contrasted, perhaps somewhat simplistically, with law, which is characterized as not involving consensus. An author who pursues this line of argument says that law can "never be a scientific discipline." Using trials as an example, he declares that the only reason for them is that there is no consensus: "A trial judgment, almost by definition, is a matter of judging the data and then giving an opinion on the basis of the limited data available."[75] But as we have also pointed out, science has craft aspects, with much room for judgment and disagreement, and sometimes the disagreement becomes a matter of public controversy. When this happens, it often becomes a matter for the law to resolve, either through legislation or more interstitially through the judicial process. At that point, the divergent lines of the disciplines intersect.

Indeed, we must note the similar ways in which the boundaries of human knowledge restrict law as well as science. Legal demands for proof face limits in what science can produce. Exemplary of these limits is the constraint inherent in the Heisenberg Uncertainty Principle, which declares that it is impossible to measure all the variables in an experiment with unlimited accuracy.[76] To state this principle only underlines the fact that the seeming exactitude of science always represents a way station along the road to a perfection whose achievement is restricted by these limitations on measurement.

A question of legal process that will recur in our consideration of science-created dangers is that of who will assess their hazardous potential. In principle, critical judgment on risk factors might come from competitors, from government agencies and from academic or free-lance specialists. However, when one is dealing with frontier technologies, there may be no competition that generates criticism; and potential competitors may be reluctant to speculate that certain dangers are possibly associated with a product when expertise is closed and confined within a few firms, if they perceive more utility to themselves in a policy of silence. With respect to governmental review, the picture is a mixed one. Dedicated government professionals have performed important jobs in keeping harmful products from the general public. The publicized case of Dr. Frances Kelsey's work for the Food and Drug Administration on the thalidomide problem is exemplary.[77] Many other such episodes probably are buried in intraagency memoranda. Yet there is conflicting evidence even about the work of the FDA, and indeed its statutory mandate. At one pole are complaints by staff personnel that the agency has been ignoring their recommendations and thereby endangering consumers;[78] at the other, there is the argument that the best risk assessor is, after all, the market. This contention receives powerful analogical support from studies suggesting that statutory regulation of drug efficacy creates a negative welfare balance because of the useful drugs it keeps from the public.[79]

In the background of problems with governmental assessment of possible product hazards is the prospect of future private largesse, a carrot for agency workers who eventually plan employment in industry. And the lack of sufficient personnel, as well as lower salary scales compared with private enterprise, also conspire against the most rigorous review.[80] Academic specialists are themselves subject to possible pressure from private sources of funds whose projects and products are proper targets of critical inquiry. In general, analogous to the realities in the industrial sector that damp down criticisms of prospective risks, there are similar forces at work among scientists. Often it may be more advantageous to "get along by going along," in the sense of keeping one's peace about apprehensions of possible danger from a particular line of inquiry or development.[81]

Although these problems may have been exaggerated by journalism, and even if the magnitude of each of these potential threats to dispassionate analysis is open to question, taken together they constitute a matter of serious concern. But although there are disincentives to critical evaluation of possibly dangerous technological developments in every quarter which might produce responsible criticism, the serried ranks of potential critics will still produce plenty of inquiry on specific subjects. Competition will generate reports of hazards in other firms' products. Pride in doing the public's business will lead government scientists to raise warning signals. And independent investigators will frequently be independent enough to publish research conclusions that force political review of complex risks. Personal experience with academic scientists persuades me that many maintain a prickly independence against pressures to compromise their scientific integrity. With respect to all of these possibilities, a primary goal of the law in this area is to keep the channels of communication open, and to make the incentives to communicate adequate.

Here I wish to make a preliminary statement of certain premises that guide this study. I shall add to them and elaborate on them as I progress through a consideration of specific processes and products.

A cardinal maxim for controlling scientific progress is that discovery should be publicized. There occasionally may be reasons of national security to withhold from the public useful findings already made, although in many cases even this is disputable.[82] But generally, on occasions when some experts believe there is a possibility of physical risk to members of the community, my working principle is that this should be public information. In the case of publicly supported enterprise, the citizenry at risk pays the bills, and it does so under a political form in which appropriations must be justified after a statement of the merits and demerits of proposed ways of spending. Moreover, when the principal investment in dangerous products and processes comes from private industry, the existence of governmental regulatory bodies usually entails requirements that information about risks and injuries be communicated, at least to those agencies. It is true that overemphasis on public communication about hazards could foster hysteria about events that are in fact rather trivial but which the media may transform into monsters coming over the next hill. But the advantages to be gained from publicity have generally been thought to outweigh the costs of uninformed public choice. Both as an abstract matter of democratic theory and as a calculation of practical politics, our faith has been that in the long run people will react soberly in their best interest.

A reverse aspect of this concern with publicity relates to regulatory attitudes toward claims made by those who develop or produce potentially dangerous things. In considering the profile of activities that are candidates for regulation, we must always ask who benefits from a product or process and how product claims affect perceptions of benefits. Certainly if the subject of proposed regulation is something on the market, one group of beneficiaries consists of the purchaser and those who use it with or for him. But because of lack of information about the hazards of a well-advertised product, ordinary consumers may not be in a position to assess its risks. A product which appears from current sales figures to provide a net benefit may eventually turn out to be a social liability. Thus one important question is whether goods perceived as beneficial really are advantageous, on balance, to the consumer group which views them that way.

There will always be certain groups whose advantage is much more direct and unalloyed; these are the developers and producers. It is true that in theory, given an assumption of active markets and widespread publicity about product failures, these persons have a substantial interest in seeing to it that their goods do not produce dangerous side effects. But given the fallibility of memory even when failures are well publicized, and sometimes the confinement of injurious results to particular classes of consumers, there is a powerful incentive to market products that will reap gains in the short run. This exists especially when there is just a prospective possibility of harm, which if it does materialize will affect people only after a period of years. Because of this, it is especially important to scrutinize claims made for products, and to apply at least an initial discount to defenses raised by developers and sellers to charges concerning safety, whether made by public gadflies or private litigants.

Continuing my articulation of premises, I wish to mention some assumptions I make about governmental obligation, and to ventilate some related concerns about the role of scientists and their relation to the commonwealth. Important among my social premises is the notion that twentieth-century government owes protection to its citizens in situations where they are incapable of acquiring or assessing information about potential risks which have a scientifically complex and uncertain character. This obligation arises in part from an economic aspect of general welfare: The notion is that the total national product will be diminished, causing most of us to be marginally worse off in varying degrees, when people are harmed by hazards whose character they could not judge and which they would have avoided had they been more knowledgeable. But the duty also stems from a sense that even when economically measurable gains and losses are in balance— sometimes even when a harmful product promises a net monetary gain—government has a compassionate obligation to prevent the imposition of disproportionate, fortuitous harm on random victims.[83] This is not only because of the morale-destroying potential of such occurrences, but because of a belief that individual citizens should not be violated by invasions to which they have not consented.

An important rationale for public intervention arises from the fact that government provides so much direct funding as well as indirect financial encouragement for scientific and technological endeavor. This largesse provides a basis for regulation of advanced processes and products when they present threats to the people who pay for their development through taxes as well as purchase them in the marketplace. It is an important background factor in judicial as well as legislative decision-making which affects safety allocations, contextually related to the desire to allay public apprehension, as well as to the motivation to provide safeguards for the long-term citizen interest in protection from insidious dangers.

The question of who benefits from research, and in what way, is entwined with this effort to define premises. When one considers the bedrock issue of whether to allow risky forms of experimentation to proceed, a large factor in the decision will concern their perceived social value. Such judgments of the worth of scientific investigation may be removed from traditional market considerations.[84] Close to the surface of a recent controversy has been the contention that there are nonmarket scientific values to be served by pursuing experiments in gene recombination, although the proponents of the research have principally appealed for support on the basis of predicted tangible contributions to social welfare. When such cases arise, regulators must be in a position to know the personal investment of those—the high priests of the scientific temple as well as politicians—who offer assessments of value.[85]

In this connection I should also state my assumption that scientists and their corporate or governmental employers should be given neither more nor less credit for moral sensitivity than anyone else with similar incentives. I must stress that my conversations with scientists and the record of scientists' capacity for self-regulation impress me that there is an admirable sense of social responsibility abroad in that community of workers. The convening of the Asilomar conference on gene recombination in 1975, in which scientists with considerable professional stake in continuing a line of research made a persuasive case for restricting it, provides a prime example. Yet my general view is that in a democratic state, the conduct of risky activity must be open to public inspection and if necessary subject to public control, no matter who the principals may be. Thus, when the law's oversight of analogous nonscientific activities tends to give free rein to human creativity and invention, this perspective should be applied to science. On the other hand, when scientific work produces conditions of latent danger for others, the case for regulation should parallel that concerning hazardous activities generally.

In taking this position, I do not deal with questions such as whether the scientists of the Manhattan Project were "morally responsible" for the destruction of Hiroshima and Nagasaki.[86] Although I do not denigrate the philosophical importance of such issues, I restrict myself here to the less flammable but still complex question of what approach government should take to the creation of risks whose potential for damage is uncertain. I should add that I generally do not occupy myself here with such metaphysical speculations on technology as those of Ellul, who refers to "technique" as involving "but one method for its use, one possibility," and distinguishes the "bad use" of technique from the careless use of automobiles.[87] My concern is with outcomes and consequences, with specific technologies being viewed simply as processes, functionally equatable for purposes of this analysis with conventional products. The problem that I principally address here is one of defining attitudes toward risk in concrete situations, not one of making abstract value judgments.

A further premise that guides me here, one aspect of which I have introduced above, involves the worth of the physical and psychological integrity of persons. A valuation of those components of personality, which is at least implicit in all forms of government regulation of hazardous products and processes, is made after the fact of harm by courts that award damages for personal injury. Thus both private litigation and public regulation place dollar values on human life or at least assume that these values exist. These valuations tend to focus on conveniently measurable items of economic loss, particularly earnings and medical bills. But it also would appear that the law, inarticulately but properly, expresses a value on human life that cannot easily be broken down into such discrete categories. This is a subject that demands much fuller treatment, but it is enough for my present purpose to point out that this seems to be the case. And I wish to emphasize that both easily calculable and relatively unquantifiable valuations of life rank high as goods on the scale of established legal policy. They are important pillars of that policy that sometimes provide counterweights to values of free scientific inquiry as well as to projections of measurable social benefits from new discoveries and designs.

In connection with this valuation point, we cannot blink at the difficulty of quantifying risks of uncertain dangers when human intangibles are part of the damage equation. Not only are the risks uncertain; there also is theoretical controversy about the compensable elements of the harms that do occur. This is a problem that appears across the spectrum of law involving relief from physical and psychic dangers. The common law has developed a system of damages which in dreadful cases of personal injury may require payments of upwards of a million dollars to one victim, and this is exclusive of the substantial punitive damages that may be awarded in cases of intentional or reckless conduct on the part of the injurer. Compensatory damages often include substantial dollar amounts for an item loosely called "pain and suffering." This item is both symbol and reality of the difficulty of valuing intangibles. What are the elements of "suffering," and how do we determine what they are worth? There is respectable scholarly opinion opposing this kind of award altogether; but in a rather rough way, it has tended to represent community judgments of both value and vengeance.

Several currents of law and policy run together on the valuation of life and limb for the purposes of public regulation. We have noted the importance of an original lack of information about hazards from a standpoint of traditional welfare economics, with its premises of citizens choosing combinations of utility and risk that are most congenial to them at particular price levels. In addition to this technical focus on what people know about risk are concerns about their defenselessness against unknown hazards. There is an especially powerful equitable argument in favor of regulating dangers that will affect people who are ignorant of them. But considerations of fairness also motivate government to intervene against hazards about whose existence citizens may be nominally aware, because of the ethical problem of unequal exposure to harms that fall disproportionately on particular segments of the population. This mixture of concerns, and particularly the tendency to place special societal valuations on the worth of individual lives, colors much of our recent legislation.[88] I shall contend also that it has provided a basis for courts to act as backup guarantors of public safety, pushing as they do this to the limits of the relatively narrow spectrum of their historically defined competence.

2 Varieties of Experimentation

THE STORY OF MEDICAL SUCCESS in combating disease in the 1940s and 1950s was primarily that of attacks on infectious illnesses—pneumonia, scarlet fever, whooping cough, and diphtheria. Tuberculosis therapy has emptied large, specialized hospitals; tertiary syphilis is virtually a thing of the past. Truly, immense frontiers remain with respect to causes and cures of heart disease, vascular illness, and cancer. But a physician reciting this unfinished agenda, although admitting its dismal sound, also emphasizes its finite character and the fact that all of these illnesses are "recognized as respectable, approachable, and potentially soluble biological problems."[1]

For our present purposes, the important point is that the information necessary for an attack on these problems will be obtained in significant part through human experimentation. More broadly, it can be said that all improvements in human welfare require some form of experimentation. Notably in the purview of this book, these include advances in drug therapy, the development of other useful new consumer products, and the discovery of techniques for boosting agricultural yields by manipulating the basic chemicals of life.

In this chapter I shall try to define the concept of experimentation and to describe some of the characteristics that make it an important subject of legal concern. I shall then examine some of the premises which support the conduct of the more controversial kinds of experimentation, and the policy problems that attend these activities. And I shall suggest tentative solutions for some of these problems which are designed to advance the analysis of our particular subject, with its focus on long-term, uncertain risks.

Ravetz has summed up the principal problem of experimentation in this powerful sentence: "At every stage of our exploration of the unknown, we are at risk of being mistaken, and of remaining in ignorance of our mistakes until irretrievable damage has been done."[2] The experimentation that is necessarily involved in the development of new scientific processes and technologies often carries risks to physical integrity, sometimes immediate but often over the long term. Of special concern is the fact that in a mass-production society it carries them to the market at large.

Against this somber background, it is useful to say what we mean by experimentation. Walsh McDermott defines experiment to mean "either . . . the first occasion of new observational techniques within the human body or the choosing of some intervention in the course of human disease or human condition and subjecting that intervention to experiment." He emphasizes that the question of whether a procedure involves an experiment is one that involves judgment on quantitative questions, particularly with reference to the element of experience: "the more experience, the less a particular intervention could be considered an experiment; the less experience, the more."[3] This definition can encompass a broad range of innovations in research designs and observational techniques. However, in this book I am concerned particularly with the use of techniques which are not only new but potentially invasive. One might therefore distinguish between the measurement by social scientists of what an employee already is doing, for example by a time-and-motion study of existing work practices, and an effort to introduce new variables into a job that might cause physical or mental stress.[4]

More broadly, experimentation is a label which connotes an attempt to solve problems in a fresh and novel way, using the subjects of the attempt as means to gather information. The image that the term conveys in the context of hazards involving products and processes tends to be a laboratory image. But much experimentation goes beyond the laboratory. In the process of testing and marketing new drugs, after procedures first limited to testing for toxicity and pharmacological effects, it takes place with increasingly large groups of patients in clinical trials. And although we do not conventionally attach the label "experimental" to the general marketing of products, it is clear that widespread distribution in fact involves a continuous process of experimentation. Especially with goods that are scientifically complex, the information-collecting goal of the experimenter is never perfectly attained in the formally investigational stages of the process. Some hazards may become apparent only after the products are used by millions of people, and over extended periods of time.

During this period of what we properly may call "market experimentation," a product carries with it, at least implicitly, a multitude of negative hypotheses about its safety—for example that it will not prove unstable on the road, or that it will not cause cancer. Sometimes these hypotheses are entirely implicit, in the sense that the marketers themselves would not have given any thought even to the possibility of such eventualities. This experimental feature of general public distribution provides a central concern of this book. However, in order to gain perspective on that problem, we should first consider the developing controversies about experimentation in the sense that it is more generally understood— as a laboratory process or a field project involving relatively small numbers of preselected individuals.

I shall summarize here a few features of the subject which are relevant both to our initial concentration on medical experimentation and to our later, broader focus on market experimentation.

It has been suggested that there are two principal conceptual models of medical experimentation. One of these is a sociological model that uses the paradigm of a teaching hospital as a kind of cooperative enterprise between investigators and patients. In this view, the emphasis is on participation—the patient's participation in experiments as well as the physician's in the enterprise of diagnosis and cure.[5] In this discussion I will generally follow a more legal model, using as a point of departure the conventional tort notion of battery as an unconsented contact and viewing the physician as having a duty to inform patients about the risks of particular procedures. I posit also a fiduciary obligation the force of which not only prohibits exposing persons to unconsented risk, but also proscribes approaching patients in a way that is formally correct but which virtually paints them into a corner requiring submission to experiments.

An important aspect of experimentation which will affect the applicable legal rules has to do with the question of whether the proposed procedure may bring benefits to the "subject." The HEW regulations on protection of special classes of human subjects—among others pregnant women and fetuses—are slightly euphemistic in this regard, being cast in terms of "therapy" and "research" and not specifically referring to experimentation. The regulations define "therapeutic research" to mean activities designed to improve the subject's health "by prophylactic, diagnostic or treatment methods that depart from standard medical practice but hold out a reasonable expectation of success." By contrast, "nontherapeutic research" is that which is not designed to improve the subject's health.[6]

A distinguishing aspect of medical experimentation is the ability to deliberate that characterizes the experimenter's choice, and which also is possible for a subject who is truly informed about the nature of the project. This provides a significant comparison with the ordinary "accident" that forms much of the corpus of tort law, which generally evolves from a situation in which one or both parties are inadvertent and cannot readily avoid the initial harmful contact. However, it must also be emphasized that the very nature of experimentation implies uncertainty as to the *result* of the transaction; an experiment is in fact a deliberate effort to acquire information that reduces uncertainty for future occasions.

Exemplary of the frustrating complexity of research risks, in a form somewhat less obvious than trauma directly caused by experimental products, are problems of hazard that arise from testing processes. Medical dogma may also rear its head in this connection. McDermott shows how these problems combine by referring to the aspiration of sternal marrow, a dangerous procedure which he characterizes as having acquired a "sanctity" for use in the diagnosis of blood disease. Because it has taken on this aura, the use of the sternal marrow procedure is often extended to patients who have a risk of only "theoretical damage" to blood-forming organs; this provides an example of "an observational method aimed at protecting [the patient] but actually increasing the risk."[7]

A related, significant feature of experimentation, one often associated with the problems addressed in this book, is the difficulty in tracing results and assigning causation. In biochemical terms, human beings are polysystemic creatures, and the cause of their injury or death is not always clear. This makes it difficult to found a system of regulation purely on compensatory principles.[8] If one cannot trace causation after the fact, one cannot establish the legal linkages necessary to make out a case that one person or another should pay for the consequences of an event. At once, this difficulty renders impossible the effort to control experimentation entirely through detailed regulations which mandate investigatory procedures or to specify conditions appropriate for the use of such methods, for example, in the administration of certain kinds of chemicals. For if causation presents a lottery aspect before one embarks on a particularly hazardous course of action, no manual of procedure will prevent harm. Indeed, in some cases the need is for proscription rather than prescription.

Not only does experimentation involve the use of a multitude of techniques, but its different forms entail a wide variety of impacts on subjects. We may refer illustratively to the unfinished research agenda of medical science, specifically to some distinctions which may be made between investigations involving heart patients and experiments dealing with the many forms of illness collectively known as cancer. Both kinds of illness may require major surgery, but cancer surgery is more likely to be mutilating than coronary operations. Too, experimental chemical and radiation therapies for persons with advanced carcinomas are likely to put a greater burden of pain and discomfort on them than treatments for heart ailments. Such differences bring home the point that the kinds of experimentation to which the law must respond are many and varied, and that its responses must reflect that variety.

We now consider some of the fundamental justifications and criticisms of experimentation in a rather narrowly defined scientific and medical sense, a review which should help us to analyze more clearly the issues involved in market experimentation. The social benefit of unfettered experimentation is undeniable, and it is a value for which lives and careers have been sacrificed since before Galileo's time. The history of medicine with the approach of the age of Pasteur confirms the need for observation and scientific experimentation. Well into the nineteenth century physicians referred to "laudable pus," which was thought to play a part in the healing of wounds, and surgical progress was stalled by the high incidence of infection.[9] Symbolic of medical opposition to new ways of doing things was the condemnation poured on Semmelweiss for his successful attempt to reduce childbed fever by having his medical students wash their hands in a chlorine solution.[10]

Against this historical backdrop, whether one makes the case within the confines of religious tradition, embracing the notion that "since God gave us our senses, we certainly must be allowed to use them to study what we can,"[11] or argues from a more agnostic viewpoint, experimentation has generally tended to increase human welfare. But modern rationalizations of maximum social protection for scientific investigation invoke a notion that knowledge—objective facts about the universe—is worth seeking for itself, as well as for the promise of socially useful gains. A related area of legal liberty involves commitments both to increase the total social product and to permit people to exercise personal preferences for material goods. These values made it an article of faith that not only should inquiry in the marketplace of ideas be untrammeled, but that there should be free traffic in goods, the only exceptions being where clear cases are made for regulation.

We do not, of course, justify experimentation as a modern version of ritual for the good of the community. It is true that the notion of enforced sacrifice is not unknown; it is imbedded, for example, in the "selective abrogation of personal inviolability" that one finds in the military draft,[12] and indeed in some programs of compulsory vaccination. But this kind of selectivity is justifiable only in emergency situations, in which the entire fabric of society is threatened, wars and epidemics being the most compelling cases. If there is a social property in parts of the body, it is one that becomes concrete only under unusual pressures.[13]

It follows from this discussion that the philosophical basis for the usual kind of experimentation is basically "melioristic"— aimed at improving society—rather than one emphasizing the need to save it. As Hans Jonas has said, this rationale pivots on science as a necessary instrument of the progress which is regarded as the normal course of things, with experimentation being viewed as a means to carry out the research necessary to that progress. But in nonemergency situations—cases in which the goal is typically one of trying to enhance the conditions of a life that has generally involved given percentages of death from certain diseases—this justification does not support the conscripting of experimental subjects. The "oughts" of positive commands to help others here are theological rather than social; they describe relationships between man and God rather than man and society.[14]

Proceeding from these rationales for experimentation, we may readily subscribe to the assertion of Jonas that nontherapeutic experimentation should aim for free willingness to serve as subjects on the part of understanding members of the community. He posits that the appeal should be to the highest level of both intellect and emotion of the society's leaders. This effectively insures the moral purity of the enterprise, as contrasted with an approach that seeks as research subjects the most dependent and least understanding citizens.[15] The central concern here, applicable across the board from conventional experiments to market experimentation, is understanding—not merely the "information" of which economic theory speaks. The effort to achieve that goal should infuse legal standards related to all impositions on citizens of uncertain risks, whether over the long term through the market or in the carefully controlled conditions of the laboratory.

With this focus on understanding fixed, we may move to consider one case of experimentation that found its way to court, and then to summarize some principles and codes that have been fashioned as guides and standards for experimenters.

Perhaps the most chilling episode to appear in a published law report is one in which the judicial decision did not reach the merits of the case. This is *Hyman* v. *Jewish Chronic Disease Hospital*,[16] in which a prestigious cancer investigator undertook to elaborate important research which already had revealed that healthy persons without cancer would reject foreign cancer cells injected into them much more quickly than cancer patients—although ultimately even cancer patients' bodies would reject foreign cancer cells. The researcher, Dr. Chester Southam, now wondered whether persons who were debilitated but did not have cancer would react with the same speed of rejection as healthy individuals rather than that of persons with existing cancers.

To conduct this test, Dr. Southam and his associates selected twenty-two aged persons who were patients at the defendant hospital. They did not tell these patients that the injections they proposed to give contained cancer cells, but only that they were conducting a skin test for immunity or response. In withholding the information that the cells were cancerous, the researchers argued that the precise nature of the tissues was "irrelevant" to the reaction that could be expected—the appearance of a lump that would gradually disappear. They reasoned that the injections would not cause increased risk, since predictably the lump would go away. Thus they opted not to create what they believed would be unnecessary anxiety in the patients. Southam had declared that there was essentially "no risk" in the procedure. It should be noted, however, that he was quoted as explaining his own reluctance to volunteer for cancer cell injections on another occasion by saying that although he "did not regard the experiment as dangerous ... [l]et's face it, there are relatively few skilled cancer researchers, and it seemed stupid to take even the little risk."[17] Moreover, there was at least some medical opinion that in some cases cancerous tumors would occur from such injections and would spread.[18]

But despite the fear of some that such injections might cause cancer, there was no evidence that they did in any of these elderly patients, whose bodies did in fact throw off the injected cells as promptly as did healthy patients. This result was a telling one from a biological point of view. It suggested the possibility that the body might possess defense mechanisms against cancer that could be stimulated before or even during the onset of the disease. It is for this reason that the Hyman case, although litigated to reported decision only on a question of right of access to the patients' medical charts, is a classic in the field. For the experiment was not a trivial one: the possible payoff was very high. And on the other side, even assuming the accuracy of the hypothesis that none of the patients was at risk from cancer, the case focuses the dignitary interest of persons to be fully informed about any procedure that violates their bodily integrity.

Thus the case serves as a baseline for analysis of questions involving experimentation on various scales, ranging from procedures closely controlled by scientists to marketplace experiments, when subjects are ignorant of the possible long-term consequences of what they are ingesting or otherwise encountering. If there is a social judgment that people have a right to know about the "precise nature" of things that are being introduced into their bodies, even if it is assumed that these things cannot harm them, then it would seem to follow that they have broad rights to be told about possible dangers and long-term hazards. And whatever the medical facts of specific procedures, another important point lies in what the Hyman experiment reflects about the attitudes of some researchers. Although there is little judicial precedent on experimentation, we now know that there have been many cases of highly questionable experiments performed on human beings in this country. Providing another striking example of the need for some public control of experimentation is a research proposal, seriously advanced, that would have involved withholding food from a random group of children while supplying their siblings with protein-rich dietary supplements. The fact that a trained professional could even bring such a proposal to a review committee illustrates that when some investigators find the ends of a proposed line of research worthwhile they may sometimes be inclined to treat people as means. What is also troubling is the statement of a critic of the proposal that there was "considerable evidence on hand already" to show that protein deprivation had serious consequences in child development.[19] It is not clear from the available brief summary of the study whether this critic would have thought the research should be approved on the basis of balancing risks against projected benefits if there were no such body of evidence. A slightly different attitude, manifesting some tension in moral perspective if a rather wooden view of the law, appears in a statement of an anonymous respondent to a survey of psychologists, who opined with respect to an informed consent form which used only the technical name of the drug LSD, "Legally the research was covered, but ethically, I am not so sure."[20]

Implicit in statements that exhibit some soul-searching, as well as in research procedures entirely insensitive to considerations of personal dignity, is the nature of the motivation that pushes researchers toward unconsented to, invasive procedures. An index to this motivation appears in the self-serving nature of the justification advanced to require research participation by students in psychology courses. An American Psychological Association document characterizes as "the heart of [this] argument" the view that if this source of participants did not exist, it would be much more difficult and often prohibitively expensive to recruit research subjects. Thus, "some potentially valuable research would not get done." Moreover, the remaining pool of participants, being self-selected, would introduce biases into the data. The impulse behind these arguments is the same drive that generates industrial production generally. It stems initially from the self-interest of the producer—in this instance the investigator. The APA's statement of research principles places this motivation on a high moral plane, speaking of "the first and most important ethical obligation of the researcher—to conduct meaningful research."[21] This transformation of ambition into an ethic captures the strength of the researcher's desire for success, and implies the discount which must be attached to his own ability to regulate unwarranted interferences with the persons of his subjects.

Perhaps the fundamental historical document on the rights of experimental subjects is the Nuremberg Code, which was applied in the German war-crimes trials. It says that persons being subjected to experiments "should be so situated as to be able to exercise free power of choice, without the intervention of any element of force, fraud, deceit, duress, over-reaching, or other ulterior form of constraint or coercion." The Code requires that subjects should have "sufficient knowledge and comprehension of the elements of the subject matter involved as to enable [them] to make an understanding and enlightened decision."[22]

Building upon this framework of free choice, we may now examine a rather highly developed American code of regulations dealing with human experimentation, that involved with the investigational new drug (IND) process.[23] The IND rules require sponsors to take drugs through three separate phases of human testing. In Phase 1 studies the subjects are healthy volunteers, and they are used, in the common parlance, purely as guinea pigs. There is no effort in Phase 1 to employ the product to influence the course of a disease. With these healthy subjects the drug is given only to test its pharmacological effects, including toxicity, effects on metabolism and safe dosage range, and at least in theory its administration is monitored very closely. Phase 2 experiments represent the first time that the drug is used to combat the disease at which it is aimed. The subjects here are few, highly selected, and carefully supervised to determine the safety and effectiveness of the product.

In Phase 3, clinical investigation becomes large-scale. The FDA emphasizes that Phase 3 studies should be carefully monitored, but they may lack the on-the-spot supervision of trained drug investigators. These investigations proceed unless someone discovers a problem with the product. The law requires the sponsor to report serious or potentially serious adverse reactions, but there is room for judgment as to what is serious, and the early warning signs of eventual tragedy may be very faint or even nonexistent when the risk is a long-term one. A collateral problem is manifest in one commentator's notation that in large-scale clinical testing a few patients are likely to be victimized by the withholding of established treatments. He suggests that there is a tendency to view large groups of patients in a rather sanguine way as to gross results, while ignoring the fact that "one or two individuals within the group could have a very sad outcome" which would be prevented by the use of a particular technique.[24]

After a manufacturer has accumulated evidence from the IND process that it thinks qualifies a product for general marketing, it proceeds to the New Drug Application (NDA) stage, where the manufacturer must convince the FDA of both safety and efficacy. If the manufacturer makes this showing, it may sell the drug on the general market under the specified conditions of advertised use for which the NDA is approved. But in recognition of the continuing experimental features of new drugs that have passed through this process, the law requires information about side effects and adverse reactions to be reported to the FDA.[25]

The requirements of consent for administration of new drugs vary from detailed standards associated with the IND stage to the application of conventional "informed consent" law to physicians who administer new drugs cleared for marketing under an NDA. The IND regulations, with which we are principally concerned here, require consent from *all* persons whose bodies are being used essentially only as experimental vehicles.[26] They allow for exceptions to the consent requirement only when the drug is being used therapeutically, and then only in "relatively rare" cases in which it would not be "feasible" to get consent, or when the investigator's professional judgment is that it would be "contrary to the patient's welfare" to do so. The need for considerable self-restraint in the administration of the latter exception is apparent. It seems principally designed for the patient for whom a proposed treatment is objectively mandatory but who, because of a peculiar psychic attitude, will be irrationally scared off by a recitation of the dangers in experimental therapy. Yet it does have a potential for paternalistic administration.

The heart of the matter lies in the definition of "consent," for that is the standard for all nontherapeutic experiments and almost all cases of therapeutic ones. Tracking the Nuremberg language, the IND regulations say that the subject must be "so situated as to be able to exercise free power of choice."[27] Presumably they imply the same injunctions against the use of fraud, deceit, and duress which that Code contains, and which would clearly have invalidated the procedure in the Hyman case.

Further spelling out the concept, the IND regulations require a "fair explanation of pertinent information" which will enable the subject to "make a decision on his willingness" to take the drug. This means, the regulations say, that the investigator should carefully consider and make known the "nature, expected duration, and purpose" of the experiment, and the "method and means" of the administration of the drug. As best he can, considering the subject's well-being and ability to understand, the investigator must also inform the subject of the hazards known to be associated with the drug and the existence of alternative forms of therapy, as well as the benefits that the product under testing may confer. These elements essentially duplicate the language of the Nuremberg Code.

There may be variations among institutions and investigators with respect to the dedication with which these regulations are followed. But they are publicized, and the existence of committees on human experimentation at all institutions where drug investigations are conducted creates a built-in surveillance mechanism for them. Under typical procedures a scientist who wants to use the bodies of human beings for any purpose that is not therapeutically accepted must submit a document that summarizes what he plans to do and why, explaining the potential harm that the procedure may cause to subjects, and attaching a copy of the consent form which he will ask them to sign.

I must note that the advent of this scheme of regulation is relatively recent, a fact which emphasizes to us that the question of what limitations government should impose on experimentation presents issues of continuing controversy. With consent remaining in the vortex of these issues, it is interesting to refer to a distinction that Guido Calabresi makes at an abstract level of analysis. He stresses the importance of requiring articulate consent in situations in which the choice of risk-taking is relatively direct or official.[28] By contrast, he asserts that when the lidded mechanism of the market works—when the choice is "indirect, unclear or uncertain"—we may rely on relatively imprecise consents. The very way that the market facilitates impersonal choice makes clear that when governments select risks or experimenters make direct choices to expose persons to hazards, "only consent keeps us from blatantly destroying the fabric of our commitment to human dignity." By analogy, in cases of long-term hazards associated with market experimentation, regulation fills a need for a counterweight that makes up for the lack of consent or, more generally, for lack of an effective market mechanism.

The fairly strict model of legal control that the IND regulations present is indeed interesting in its area of direct application. It is just as interesting as a starting point in the effort to fashion standards for other, more elongated processes of experimentation, including those which involve the public at large. Thus, besides dealing with conventional medical and psychological experiments, this chapter will expand to treat cases of the market form of experimentation on which later chapters focus. It is useful in this connection to consider the argument that nontherapeutic experimentation on patients is generally impermissible, with the qualification that if one makes full disclosure, it is not degrading to propose to a hopelessly ill patient an experiment which it is hoped will aid in the treatment of other persons with that illness. It does seem that an extraordinarily strong case should be required to justify experiments on patients, even with "consent," that are designed in the service of projects unrelated to their illness.[29]

I suppose that in theory one might make a distinction between market experimentation with prescription drugs on the one hand, and chemicals in food or in the environment on the other, on the grounds that in the first case, at least society is likely to be acquiring information related to the particular health problem for which the prescription is made. But it must be stressed that a meaningful analogy between market experimentation with pharmaceuticals and drug experiments on patients would require full disclosure of risks to target consumers of the marketed drugs. This requirement is not fulfilled by the typical profile of information available to the prescription drug purchaser. Only recently did the extraordinary consumer labeling on birth control pills which I discuss below—the first case of direct provision of pharmaceutical information from the seller to the patient—begin to approach this standard.

Legal principles governing experimentation must guard against the use of psychological coercion to pressure people into entering or continuing experiments. Justification for concern on this point appears in a report of an experiment on pain, which utilized medical students wearing headbands with screws that could be tightened to press against the subjects' heads. The report mentions a subject who said that he could not endure the pain any longer, but was induced to continue to wear the headband for some time more after the experimenter told him that others had endured it much longer and employed various psychological threats to his masculinity and self-image.[30]

The case demonstrates the need for external standards rather than a simple reliance on the superego of experimenters. Moreover, though extreme, it leads us to reflect on more difficult cases of inducement to various kinds of experimentation. Calabresi provides a backdrop for analysis of market experimentation with his comparison of the role of consent in typical accidents and in medical experiments. He notes that the context of many experiments allows only "semifree" consent at best, which he compares with the unfree aspects of the "consent" to risk associated with driving cars or digging tunnels.[31] Yet the "dubious" nature of the consent in the latter activities is not so troubling to him; I have adverted above to his distinction between the relatively impersonal system of market control as a regulator for typical accidents and the imposition of more direct governmental control on experimentation. For him, the "beauty" of the market-based accident system is the way in which it conveys to individual decision makers "what society more or less wants without requiring an identifiable social statement."[32] Further, it is able to rely on self-interest rather than the conscience of the individual decision maker.

By contrast with events more properly called accidents, however, some kind of social intervention is needed with respect to experimental activity—of the sort involved in market experimentation as well as experiments of the conventional medical kind. Writing in 1969 of medical experimentation, Calabresi opposed "direct collective societal control" in favor of a "watchdog" role whereby government would impose higher standards in situations in which a "general control system, independent of government," had not worked adequately.[33] The present system, with its requirement that research grants be approved by institutional review committees, and ultimately by NIH, does embody some of the features of direct governmental control which Calabresi decried. It represents not simply a demand for standards, but for their closely scrutinizing application. Though formalized, however, it is at the committee level a quasi-official process at most. This informal side of its character may keep it from the vice, perceived by Calabresi, of flinging government into one balance against the lone subject on the other.[34] The system does facilitate a rather complex, polycentric, empirically derived statement of the conscience of society. When it works at all well, it requires more dissemination of information to potential research subjects, and thus more meaningful "consent." It also responds to concerns raised by the cases discussed above about the overawing influence of science and scientists on potential volunteers. If we decide that this kind of influence cannot be precisely assessed at the conscious level, nor effectively separated from commendably altruistic desires to do something for humanity through science, the administration of consent rules should nonetheless take into account its subtle effects.

I must emphasize that my approach to experimentation places considerable emphasis on the premise of individual inviolability, agreeing with Jonas that it needs "no justification itself."[35] I regard this premise as basic, entailing the general corollary that one who proposes to impinge on the physical or psychological intactness of another must justify his act. In taking this position, I am aware that one may make a strong case from a standpoint of mass welfare that society should permit experimentation on particular persons for the good of many others similarly situated. Yet given the importance of personal inviolability and the fact that experimenters can only hypothesize the good that their actions will bring to the greater number, they face a heavy burden in justifying experimental activity even if we focus on utility alone. This is clearly so when the benefits are unpredictable. Moreover, while my emphasis on personal inviolability does draw on an a priori belief in the sanctity of the individual life, it also carries ramifications for society at large, in the sense that a "publicly condoned violation, irrespective of numbers, violates the interest of all."[36] Such illegal experimentation is dangerous because of the implication that it is appropriate to use other members of the community as involuntary sacrifices to various kinds of goals that the majority deems important in its welfare. It is also undesirable because of the demoralizing effect it would have on the individual's views of his fellows generally and ultimately of himself. Again these remarks, while most easily applicable to experiments directly performed by medical and scientific investigators on selected persons, also are directed to the broader form of information gathering I have called market experimentation.

Analysis of the kinds of activities discussed in this book points up the importance of the concept of individual inviolability as a counterweight to arguments based on summed production totals. For example, it might be contended that, over the long term, the use of a particular agricultural pesticide will produce a net benefit in human happiness, although some random individuals will be sacrificed along the line to its cancer-causing propensities. This argument has a theoretically persuasive aspect even to physical injury, given the presumption that an increase in social capital will

have positive effects throughout society, including an augmenta-
tion of funds available for medical purposes. Indeed, simply by
producing broad marginal improvements in human health
through nutrition, or even by making millions of people happier
at mealtime, the use of such a product would effect social gains.
This line of argument has force if the victim understands the risks
to which he is being exposed. In that sense, the problem is only
one of supplying meaningful information, and it would be trivial
if one could cleanly separate the factor of communication about
risk from that of randomness of actual occurrence.

In practice, however, the matter is much more complicated.
Warnings are often general rather than specific, and those in the
danger zone do not always receive them anyway. Moreover—and
this is a point that, although it does not directly bear on the process of communication, does indeed affect the way that messages
about risk are received—each person who may be threatened is
likely to be infected by the hope that he will profit rather than lose
from the beneficial but hazardous product. Of course, when
prospects of quantifiable near-term lifesaving outpoint the perceived potential for loss, the case for experimentation becomes
stronger. But generally, the public law on uncertain risks should
be loath to permit the sacrifice of some life for even many personal satisfactions, at least for benefits not essential to life itself.

Therefore, in asking how society should respond to the threat
of long-term, uncertain risks, we must recognize that there is a
social commitment to preserving human life that goes beyond the
traditional valuations of welfare economics. The example of the
resources devoted to attempted rescues of trapped coal miners—
sometimes proportionally much greater than those spent to avoid
auto accidents—is a classic one.[37] As Calabresi has pointed out,
social attitudes on this question might change with a substantial
increase in the number of trapped miners,[38] but right now we
tolerate the disparity, in part because of the positive contribution
that the rescue of a desperately situated individual makes to our
basic values.

Further calling to mind social values in individual dignity
which reach beyond simple cost-benefit analysis are some examples of psychological research, particularly cases involving nondisclosure. Consider an experiment cited by the Ad Hoc Ethics
Committee of the American Psychological Association in a report
on which I draw several times in this chapter for examples of

sometimes shocking research designs. This investigation involved manipulation of the level of self-esteem by arranging a failure in competition for the attention of a member of the opposite sex; the researcher commented that he could think of no way to give advance warning without destroying the effect on self-esteem. Identifiable personal injury caused by such an experiment would theoretically fall within the conventional liability rules, including informed consent doctrine, applicable to charges of medical malpractice.[39] But often common law rights will remain theoretical in such situations. What merits emphasis is that the difficult problem in cases of psychological research, as it is with those involving experimentation with the body, lies in the possibility of destructive long-term consequences. The analogy is clear between psychological research and the cases of toxic substances and biological agents which are the principal concern of this book. Not only may the effect be long-term, but its mechanism may be unclear and not easily understood. This is precisely the kind of situation where regulation is necessary before the fact because of the difficulty of tracing causal chains afterward. This kind of regulation represents the judgment that, whatever the gains in social utility achieved by such research, we find it reprehensible to sacrifice values of individual personality to them.

My working principle, derived from what I have said already, is that a responsibly hypothesized possibility that an experiment will cause any type of long-lasting personal harm should be grounds for prohibiting it in the absence of a consent that expressly focuses on that hazard. In putting forth this standard, I reject the idea that it is permissible, except in cases of the gravest emergency, for the investigator unilaterally to make the choice of whether someone should participate in an experiment. There are of course many philosophical and behavioral shadings in the issue of what constitutes choice and what coercion. The APA's "Ethical Standards" document, for instance, asks what it means to "speak of the research participant's 'freedom of choice' when one considers that such choices are the logical psychological consequences of past and present influences in the environment."[40] Yet the nature of experimentation—use of one person's integrity for the furtherance of another's career as well as the general community's well-being—is such that the law should cut broadly in favor of subjects when it defines the requirements of consent. As with other aspects of my position, I should note that although I have outlined this argument with particular reference to conventional scientific investigation, it is generally applicable to market experimentation. Indeed, unilateral decisions to expose others to risk present much greater quantitative hazard when they are made in connection with the general marketing of goods.

If we proceed on the basis that consent is the principal legitimate basis for experimentation, we should note, with Calabresi, that the degree of consent that can appropriately be required will vary with the activity. The factors that must be weighed include available information, the possibility of psychological comprehension and external pressures.[41] And sometimes consent will not be enough by itself to achieve a solution. It may be necessary to require review both by experts and nonexperts, rationalized decisions on the record, and the advance provision of compensation for those injured in experiments.[42]

Yet the fact that consent is an insufficient vehicle to carry the complete social burden of experimentation should not obscure its centrality as a legal command as well as an ethical concept. The refinements that are introduced in consent requirements to accommodate factual variations should not blur the basic reason for requiring consent. In this connection we must note that social scientists have attacked the doctrine of "informed consent" as "unworkable in practice" because of the complexities of their research procedures, or because of the imperviousness of the subject to the explanation. Yet this criticism, coupled with the assertion that there is "very little evidence" to show psychological damage to social science research subjects, misses the point.[43] The dignitary interest protected by the law is one that does not require a showing of quantifiable injury to prove a violation. It is enough that the subject has not been told what is being done with his body, or mind.

Viewpoints current in social science research provide an interesting contrast to the law now generally evolving on research with the bodies of human beings. Generally illustrative is the report, to which I already have referred, of the APA's Ad Hoc Committee on Ethical Standards in Psychological Research. Running throughout this document is a theme of investigator responsibility as the first and final standard for psychological research. The report's focus is on calculations of costs and benefits. A recurrent motif emphasizes the investigator's primary responsibility in balancing costs—for example, those of "inadequate or misleading results against the moral costs of causing psychological stress to research participants."[44] Although the document articulates a requirement of informed consent, its general tone emphasizes the primacy of the investigator's decision. For example, at one point the document says, "We may find it necessary upon occasion to ask our human research participant to suffer indignities in the service of developing a meaningful science of behavior."[45] Again, the committee declares that a particular study would be "ethically unacceptable to the extent that its theoretical or practical values are too limited to justify the impositions it makes on the participants or that scientifically acceptable alternative procedures have not been carefully considered."

It is instructive, as we take a broad view of experimentation, to consider the enormous tension that psychological research creates with principles of informed consent, a tension that becomes well-nigh unbearable when one deals with experiments involving deception. An important question concerns the acceptability of a balancing standard. Although many psychologists consider deception impermissible at any time, other investigators think of it as "a particularly serious instance of the more general problem of informed consent," "to be resolved by the same responsible weighing of scientific and ethical considerations" applied to that question generally.[46] The pernicious possibilities in a balancing test for the use of deception are apparent in the APA committee's list of factors that it says "*may* make the use of deception more acceptable." These include the facts that the research problem is "of great importance," and that it "may be demonstrated that the research objective cannot be realized without deception." Because of the possible warping influence of self-interest, this is a defective theme. Investigators should not have the final decision on how to strike these balances; that is the province of law.

A particularly reprehensible example of deception with tragic aftereffects is a study, anonymously mentioned in the "Ethical Principles" document, in which investigators informed some subjects on the basis of false data that they had "homosexual tendencies." The report of this experiment, by someone who was not involved in it, mentions one student who, although "debriefed," was so seriously disturbed two years later that he was seeking advice on how to enter psychotherapy. The commentator laconically mentions that "the experiment ... was important and is commonly cited in the literature."[47] As a defense, this is at best superpaternalism, and it would not pass muster with respect to technical invasions of the body; equally it should not be considered appropriate to excuse interferences with peace of mind.[48] Indeed, with respect to any interests in personal integrity, it is unpersuasive as a justification for unilateral action in market experimentation as well as in limited laboratory settings.

Technically separable from issues of consent, but closely related to them, are questions concerning the volume of experimentation. It has been strongly argued that there simply is too much experimentation—too many people are being exposed to risks that should not be taken at all. In the 1960s, Food and Drug Commissioner Goddard estimated that only one in ten drugs that were investigationally studied would eventually be approved for marketing. He further estimated that in a five-year period, more than 1.4 million people would be used in clinical trials of products that did not get to the general market, with a million of these persons participating in large-scale clinical investigations. Assuming that one puts a premium on the dignitary interest of people subjected to experiments, this represents a serious social cost. Goddard asserted that there were "strong economic motives" to use "largely uncontrolled studies" employing rather large numbers of patients, despite the "usually equivocal" results that these studies produced.[49] The existence of these incentives reinforces the conclusion that when drugs are being used experimentally in a way that significant numbers of scientists would frown on, either patients have a right to know that fact, or government should intervene to require better research design and control.

Having described experimentation in terms of characteristic features and suggested a number of general principles for its regulation, I turn to comment on a number of issues involved in the actual conduct of the enterprise, analysis of which should aid in solution of the market experimentation problems that are the central concern of this book.

Serious distributional questions recur in the context of experimentation involving potential long-term risks. It is useful to approach these issues through an analogical question posed by the use of experimental technology—that of how to select the recipients of its first products. Paul Freund has tentatively argued for a randomness approach, or one based on mechanical principles such as age or priority in time. As an example of the dangers of basing selection principles on just desert , he mentions a Seattle plan for choosing recipients of renal dialysis treatment, which required a panel of laymen to make judgments of candidates on the basis of worth to the community. He reports that one member of a symposium on the subject announced agreement in principle until he heard that one factor on the panel's list of criteria was church attendance—at which point "he threw up his hands."[50]

This difficulty in the case of selection for benefits, which is a reversed image of the conventional experimentation problem, leads us into such questions related to the latter problem as who should be the subjects and what levels of information and consent should be required. With respect to the identity of subjects, one's view of the question may vary with the nature of the investigation. We would want to know, for instance, whether subjects of particular kinds of experiments are likely to be hospital patients whose illnesses are the random targets of nature, or whether they will tend to be members of disadvantaged groups whose vulnerability to experiment is a function of their social position. A major working principle here is that the law should discourage activity that effectively makes disadvantaged groups a prime subject of experimentation. In large part this principle rests on the assumption that persons in these groups will be relatively incompetent to comprehend explanations and to know their self-interest. But I refer also to an irreducible residue of belief that it is morally wrong to impose disproportionate costs of research on persons because of their social or economic status.[51]

At this point it is appropriate to refer specifically to the case of long-term risks in which it is the general market that is a vehicle for experimentation. It may be usual that the victims of extended market experiments will be random as to social status. Thus the problem is not one of potential unfairness to classes, but it may well involve injustice to individual victims whose welfare is sacrificed to those who receive benefits from a product or process. In such situations, it is important to know how much information about risk was meaningfully presented to the eventual victim, but the principle of inviolability provides the bedrock for both regulation and compensation after the injury.

Readjusting our focus for the moment to medical practice alone, we have come to realize that Holmes's aphorism that "all life is an experiment" applies to all phases of treatment, not only those generally thought of as experimental. The use of freshly graduated interns as the physicians for ward patients, some aspects of virtually every surgical procedure, indeed, every physician's use of his trained intuition in any patient encounter—all these have experimental aspects. And we cheerfully accept this, at least in those cases involving seasoned physicians, for the alternative would be the mechanical application of textbook principles.[52]

So it is throughout life in an industrialized society, with the constant introduction of new products on the market and of new processes in various environments. We are always at risk in some degree in our encounters with civilization as well as with nature. How much risk we willingly accept is related to general norms of social acceptability. But over the last half century we have grown somewhat less philosophical about accepting artificially created, avertible dangers, especially when information about them is or readily could be available to those in a position to avoid them.

It is in this sense that we come to recognize in the concept of experimentation a broader meaning than the one conventionally given to it. Life is an experimental continuum, running to greater and lesser degrees of uncertainty and predictability of risk, as well as potential gravity of harm. Our images of prisoners virtually compelled to submit to dangerous procedures or chemicals, or even having these indignities inflicted on their bodies without their knowledge,[53] are unpleasant ones. But it is only a series of gradations that separate these wretched victims from those persons who use food or drugs purchased on the general market, unaware that long-term effects have not been plumbed, and from industrial workers who are unknowingly exposed to products or processes with unrevealed dangers. It is because we are all perpetual subjects of multilayered experiments that we have come to think we are entitled to various protections. This principally means disclosure at the first trench, but lacking that shield, we resort to direct intervention, either regulatory or prohibitive. The considerations which determine how far government will intrude are related in large part to projections of the severity and incidence of risk, but they also include the predictable evenness of risk distribution throughout social strata. Yet it should be noted that the correlation between regulation and breadth of social risk is not exact: There is a certain irony in the fact that in some instances the broader the use of a product, the less "experimental" it becomes in the usual connotations of the word. The features of complexity and uncertainty of long-term risk may remain, but often, as the ambit of "experiment" comes to coincide with "all life," the more accepting we tend to become, and thus the "experimental" aura begins to fade. This may happen in part because experimentation implies culpably deliberate or careless exposure of others to risk, and the widespread nature of the product or process tends to cut against judgments of culpability, but it also occurs because the more frequent the exposure, the more it is taken as part of the "natural" background.[54]

The attitudes of psychological researchers demonstrate vividly the impossibility of controlling entirely the aftereffects of experimentation. These attitudes are especially telling as they relate to legal and ethical difficulties in withholding information about possible weaknesses that testing itself may reveal in a subject's psychological armor. The APA's statement of Ethical Principles declares that it is "the researcher's obligation to anticipate and ameliorate" stress reactions at the termination of a study. What is revealing is the assumption that there will be some stress reactions, and that the only way to carry on research, implicitly deemed worthy, is to allow them to occur. This document exudes at least a faint odor of *1984*; the implicit operating premise is that it is for the investigator to make these decisions. And it is not even a difficult case theoretically as grounds for legal action. Although our focus here is on regulation, it is appropriate to mention the potential application of private law: to anyone versed in the jurisprudence of personal injuries, the knowing creation of "potentially irreversible aftereffects"[55] sounds like tortious conduct.

We may broaden our perspective by a chain of comparisons involving three cases. First let us consider the birth control pill, the marketing of which involves an experiment, in close to the usual sense of the word, that is being carried on within a broad particular segment of the general population. Despite wide acceptance of the Pill, its use continues to generate intense and even increasing controversy, and this dispute significantly includes its potential to create hazards over the long term. One may compare the automobile as a risk-creating unit, whose collision-causing propensities are well known in a general sense to all who drive or walk the streets. It is true that each new model of an automobile embodies certain experimental features, as periodic recalls illustrate. Each dangerous feature of a new car model presents broad potential for side effects among users, including drivers and passengers, and innocent bystanders. These hazardous possibilities justify the degree of intervention represented by recalls. But the use of automobiles as a class of product has pretty much passed out of the experimental stage, at least in the popular sense of the term. Finally, one may contrast the case of asbestos as a component of automobile brake linings. Here is a product in widespread use over a long period of time, possibly carrying with it an insidious and deadly risk which by hypothesis was at first unknown to all concerned. During the time that knowledge about the potential hazards of the group of substances called asbestos was nonexistent or quite speculative, its experimental character remained—in the same sense that any new product is experimental when it is brought onto the market. But it was not until asbestos became widely established as part of the landscape of civilization, practically eliminating the possibility of removing it, that people came to realize that it in fact involved a large-scale experiment—a characterization which would not initially have occurred to them. At that point a thrust existed in favor of asbestos use which contributed to an acceptability that might not have existed had its risks been suspected at first. Despite its continuing experimental features, its place in everyday life had substantially negated the connotations of experimentation.

The fact that any risk from asbestos in brake linings is a risk to all, with the burdens of that use distributed ubiquitously, does give cold comfort—it is like "all life." Yet the continual outcropping of problems of this kind counsels us to identify more carefully and react more cautiously to the clusters of chemical development that have shown themselves most likely to produce unpleasant surprises, in a social setting where the perceptions of both unpleasantness and surprise are partly a function of rising expectations of personal security. In this regard, our development of principles for the regulation of experimentation in its narrow conventional connotation may give us guidance in deciding how to deal with it in its broader market aspects.

It is useful to refer in this connection to a problem which may generally be labeled as that of the idiosyncratic research subject. Let us begin with a case made easy by responsible conduct on the part of researchers. Psychological investigators conducting experiments with vibrating machines are careful to tell their well-educated subjects of the exact possible consequences of failure in the mechanism—for example that a malfunctioning machine may cause a broken back in persons with fused spinal vertebrae.[56]

Although research conducted with this kind of disclosure is defensible, it is clear by contrast that the law should not warrant psychological research which may cause damage to especially sensitive uninformed participants whose lack of knowledge is necessary for the success of the project. This reasoning carries over into research activities and market experimentation where the risk is chemical. We all have different tolerance levels for different chemical entities. Because of this, the marketing of products with uncertain risks becomes an elongated experiment in setting acceptable levels of idiosyncrasy. If a widely sold product affects one person in 500 in a seriously adverse way, this means 20,000 out of ten million. We may describe such cases as involving idiosyncrasy or hypersensitivity, but with that number of people unknowingly involved—none appreciating the harmful properties of the product, and the sensitive ones ignorant of their sensitivity—this seems an intolerable level of risk. It is the fact that persons serve unknowingly as experimental vehicles rather than the concept of idiosyncrasy which is crucial, and it is this which supports government intervention.

In this examination of different forms of experimentation with reference to possible techniques of regulation, I must underline a point inherent in the law now developing on medical experimentation. This is that the party who proposes to create the risk must make full disclosure of relevant dangers in a direct confrontation with the party who will bear it. In comparing the case of consumer goods generally, we see that there usually is no communicated understanding of their experimental features, unless one takes the position that a certain level of experimentation is implicit for purchasers of all new products. And where careful communication about the experimental nature of products is not the rule, or as a practical matter is not generally possible, the balance shifts toward regulation. An important reason for the amount of regulation that exists is that the image of such products projected to the general public is typically not an experimental one. "Try it, you'll like it" is not an invitation to take chances with one's personal safety. I should note that a bias toward regulation and risk-averseness in specific situations does not imply an adverse moral judgment on market experimentation generally. What it may reflect are rough, even inarticulate determinations that meaningful communication about risk is not standard procedure in a particular area, as well as the more paternalistic judgments which often are the basis for restrictions or even prohibitions on product sale or use.

An interesting comparison with a number of the problems we have discussed, and especially with the case of large-scale clinical trials, appears in the situation of widespread medical emergency. It should be remembered that the FDA's regulations for investigational new drug research make a "feasibility" exception to consent requirements in therapeutic research. The emergency question tests our tolerance for such exceptions. Consider the problem of an apprehended epidemic of swine influenza during the winter of 1976–1977. Fears that this would happen arose in early 1976 with a single outbreak of illness among soldiers at Fort Dix, New Jersey. Over the next months, Congress approved an appropriation for a nationwide campaign of vaccination and even a program effectively indemnifying vaccine manufacturers for injuries not caused through their fault. I have argued elsewhere that these actions were justifiable and even obligatory on government.[57] Yet is is useful to raise the question of whether the government could have conscripted persons to be injected with the vaccine during its experimental stage. On the surface the analogy of the military draft is compelling: one selects by lottery the citizens who must be regimented in order to meet a common enemy. Why do we react uneasily to this prospect in the context of testing a vaccine? It may trouble us vaguely that what the conscript is directly exposed to is not the enemy—the disease—but rather the vaccine. More to the point, combat demands bodies for known purposes. Even a peacetime draft envisions known dangers of war and requires that people undergo risks in training for specific protective roles against the identified dangers of enemy fire. By contrast, in the case of a vaccination lottery, the core of our unease lies in the singling out of random citizens for possibly injurious invasions of their bodies in order to experiment with defenses against a danger of unknown dimensions.

The case for compulsory vaccination of everyone presents a different profile. In the midst of an epidemic, it is an easy brief to write. But when there is no actual epidemic, but only a significant threat of one, the problem is somewhat more difficult. Yet courts have generally upheld the constitutionality of compulsory vaccination, and understandably so, given its universality. This element alone distinguishes it effectively from the conscription of volunteers for experiments.

The problem of securing volunteers for even a fairly risky experimental program will often be solvable in practice. Given the relatively small numbers of subjects who would be needed, a successful strategy probably would require reliance on a combination of altruism and the market—more on the market as risks increase. There will be some public-spirited individuals who are prepared to accept the risk entirely. In theory, others would submit to vaccination for payment, some perhaps with mixed motives not entirely divorced from altruism. Whatever combinations of behavior occurred, it should be stressed that generally the case of pre-epidemic experimentation is one in which the commonwealth should not compel service. The case for conscription would be stronger in a situation in which an epidemic was already in force, and there were responsible projections that a clear-cut saving of lives would be achieved by expedited small-group experiments aimed at determining dosages or selecting among vaccines. The military analogy would be rather apt in that case. Even here the mental image of randomly chosen conscripts being dragged away to vaccination depots seems intuitively more dreadful than military draft in time of war, but if there were an epidemic, we might reluctantly permit medical conscription. Nevertheless, the gravity of such a situation serves also to emphasize that involuntary experimentation is impermissible in ordinary times. And this prohibition applies generally to cases of market experimentation involving ordinary product innovation.

My emphasis in this chapter, as throughout this book, is on public regulation, designed to prevent unfortunate occurrences. At least brief mention should be made of another principal social concern with hazardous activity: how should the law respond when harm does occur? Liability rules are an important consideration at the point where government commands not that a product be banned but that it be marketed only for limited uses. One who employs a product in a way that departs dangerously from prescribed uses may be subject to private suit by those injured as a consequence, as he may be barred from pressing a claim if he himself is harmed. A variety of problems will arise from conduct of this sort, and the possibility of effective legal response will differ with the factual basis of the activity involved. For example, excess use of environmental chemicals that have complex effects over time may be so difficult to trace that there is no practical way to hold the offender responsible for identifiable harms. Thus there is a strong thrust toward regulation of things and processes which blend uncertainty and untraceability, for liability rules will not serve to vindicate personal interests nor achieve deterrent effects. One may compare the problem of physicians who experiment with drugs beyond the dosages approved by the FDA. A decade ago there was substantial debate about a suggestion that doctors who injured their patients in this way should be liable for it, and that perhaps liability should even be imposed on writers of medical texts who disagreed with FDA limitations.[58] The latter suggestion is dubious, but the idea deserves serious consideration in the case of clinicians. In this kind of case, the opportunities for effective regulatory intervention at the point where prescribing decisions are made are nil. Enforcement must be private. But given the premise that all doctor-patient relationships can and should involve at least interstitial experimentation, the imposition of liabilities in slavish imitation of regulatory rules might diminish patient welfare. A reasonable answer here lies in a conventional tort solution, which is that violations of agency regulations should be evidence, but not conclusive, of substandard conduct.[59]

In the context of parallel possibilities of private enforcement, public intervention with respect to the experimentation inherent in the general marketing of a product should be judged in large part by two factors: The ability to monitor the activity effectively, and the possibility that victims will be able to trace their injury to those who caused it. Sometimes requirements that facts and assessments be made public will facilitate private search for information, avoiding the need for more direct regulation based on fairness considerations. A controversial proposal made to publicize hitherto confidential information illustrates both problems and possibilities. The proposal involved the FDA's policy allowing New Drug Applications to be kept secret, the effect of which is that producers who wish to enter the market for a particular drug by reproducing it on a "me-too" basis must duplicate much experimental development, including human experimentation. Pharmaceutical manufacturers have argued that allowing NDAs to be made public would significantly diminish the incentives to do research.[60] But besides encouraging some potential market entrants to proceed, it would tend to cut down the number of victims of long-term, complex hazards in the experimental process by revealing to the "me-too" researchers problems that have occurred in human subjects in the original investigation. It is not

obvious that these economies would be outweighed by the benefits
from whatever increment of research is fostered by the secrecy of
NDAs. That is a subject for investigation and informed conjecture. In any event, the general point should be made that expan-
sion of public information provides an extra dimension in the
effort to keep regulation minimal and to maximize social utility.
As a matter of democratic values, there is a strong presumption in
favor of making public the facts about experimentation whose
subjects are the public. This presumption holds for information-
gathering constrained by the rules of formal drug investigations
as well as for market experimentation.

3 Personal Choice

IN THE PREVIOUS CHAPTER I presented the concept of experimentation as a principal focal point of our concern with regulation of scientifically created hazards. I explored several issues associated with legal response to experimentation, noting the centrality of the question of whether informed consent had been or could possibly be given in the circumstances. I referred particularly to the problems that arise when it is not possible to elicit consent in a meaningful sense. In this chapter, I maintain a rather broader focus on personal choice, exploring the boundaries of consumer understanding on one side and of governmental intervention on the other.

One of the principal problems in the regulation of uncertain product hazards concerns the public's capability to judge the evidence and to make its own decisions to encounter a product or to tolerate its use in spheres of possible contact. For in this society, individual freedom of choice provides the beginning point for analysis of issues concerning courses of personal conduct. It is the principal initial guideline for this chapter. As we progress into the analysis, however, we shall begin to inquire how much choice should be left to the individual citizen under legislative regimes which place the principal decision about acceptance of risk upon officials.

Increasingly, hazardous areas of activity have called forth legislative judgments that combinations of uncertainty and potential gravity require public intervention. Examples that come immediately to mind are the regulation of prescription drugs and food additives. But there are also areas in which it has been decided that no regulation is desirable even though hazards may exist, either because of their relatively low level, or because the market is capable of dealing with their uncertainties. The decision to keep choice individual rather than governmental may also take into consideration circumstances that guarantee the seriousness of the consumer decision even when overwhelming scientific opinion thinks it irrational. These areas where regulation does not

intrude broaden our perspective on the question of when intervention becomes necessary as risks ascend the ladder of complexity and uncertainty. They are in effect the other side of the picture
of market experimentation. For the social judgment concerning
such products is that either they are not truly experimental, or at
least that people should be able to conduct their own experiments.

An arena in which we approve the ability of ordinary citizens
to choose among goods is that of self-medication. Because of the
scarcity of physicians, and the fact that so much illness is transitory
or even psychological, there are often solid social reasons for encouraging people to select their own pharmaceutical treatments.

Moreover, there are some dangerous uses of self-medication,
or even self-abuse under the guise of medication, that the law
should not try to reach if only because it would be inefficient. To
take an extreme example, an upsurge in the use of a particular pill
as a vehicle for suicide presents more a matter for concern with
suicidal impulses than a call for regulation. Such an increase occurred with the analgesic Darvon after restrictions on the
availability of sleeping pills and codeine, and was partly attributed
to a misconception by many doctors that Darvon was essentially
harmless, as well as to "the situation that Medicare will pay for
propoxyphene prescriptions but will not pay for aspirin."[1] But
these factors do not incite suicide, and reducing the availability of
Darvon would not significantly affect the possibilities of substitut-
ing other vehicles for self-destruction. In short, the potential of a
drug for use in suicide attempts seems no more than a
makeweight for regulation in the total picture of drug abuse. If it
is seriously believed that there is insufficient public information
about the effects of 15 or 20 capsules of any drug, the answer lies
in providing that information, not in banning the drug.

For much the same reasons, it would be extremely difficult for
regulation to reach fad diets as they make their way across the
country. About all that can be done is to give wide publicity to the
opinions of experts, as with the National Research Council's warning against the "Zen macrobiotic" diet, which many people
adopted without knowing or considering the nutritional limitations inherent in an almost exclusive reliance on cereal grains.[2]

There is, moreover, a constitutional dimension to the problem. Given the notion that "[i]t is the glory of a free society that a
man can write a book contending that the earth is flat, or that the
moon is made of green cheese, or that God is dead, without hav-

ing to 'substantiate' or 'prove' his claims to the satisfaction of some
public official or agency,"[3] it would violate freedom of the press to
ban books that recommend physically harmful diets. Thus, for
example, the publisher of *Dr. Atkins' Diet Revolution: The High
Calorie Way to Stay Thin Forever,* could probably rely on the First
Amendment despite authoritative condemnation of the book's
advocacy of unrestricted protein and fat diets, excluding all carbohydrates, as "unbalanced, unsound, and unsafe."[4]

Yet the First Amendment's protection of ideas in books falters
when claims for those ideas—though presumably ideas them-
sevles—are advanced in advertising material. Hence the Government may seize booklets and vitamin compounds shipped by a
health food seller when the booklets and the products are part
of an integrated distribution program, even when the literature
goes in different mails than the compounds.[5] There is even some
authority that it may prohibit advertisements that make flamboy-
ant claims for an essentially sober and careful book.[6] The effect
of these rules is that people can choose their own diets and health
regimes, and publishers may communicate to them that there
exists literature presenting ideas about these subjects, but that it
is impermissible to misrepresent the ideas themselves or to make
false claims for specific products. The Constitution will not facilitate deceptive efforts to effect intellectual ingestion as a come-
on for physical consumption. With reference to the particular
concerns addressed here, advertisers are not permitted to oversimplify complexity when the results may be hazardous to the
health of consumers.

Drawing a linguistic line between those products which the
public should be able to sample on its own and those which require some government decision-making presents a difficult conceptual problem. An important solution appears in the definition
of statutory "new drugs," which effectively requires stringent government review of product data on therapeutic chemicals that
have not been shown to be "generally recognized as safe." This
provision constitutes the most significant practical roadblock to
sales of potentially dangerous products for self-medication. In
discussing the Laetrile problem below, I shall refer to its application in a context filled with legal tension. However, it is first useful
to mention another section[7] of the Food, Drug and Cosmetic Act,
which draws a line on self-medication by defining the kinds of
drugs that may be sold only on prescription. This provision re-

quires that a drug be put on the prescription list when it is safe for use only under medical supervision because of its "toxicity or other potentiality for harmful effect, or the method of its use, or the collateral measures necessary to its use." It is this clause that separates over-the-counter drugs from those available only through professional dispensation. Its application also provides useful analogical background for other questions concerning whether government should intervene to protect people from risks that require scientific definition.

The FDA recently has dealt significantly with the safety and efficacy of over-the-counter drugs, primarily using the vehicle of review by scientific committees, and the FTC has begun to confront the problem from a perspective defined principally by advertising. Only rarely has the issue arisen in the posture of litigation, in the context of an attempt to place a drug sold over the counter on the prescription list. It is instructive to examine one of the few reported cases, involving a product called Decholin, which was labeled as being for "indigestion . . . after-meal discomfort and fullness (particularly after fatty meals) . . . excessive belching . . . constipation."[8] The label of the drug also bore the "Caution" to "Consult your physician should symptoms persist or severe abdominal pain, nausea and vomiting appear."

The problem with Decholin, as the Government saw it in its effort to require prescription status, was that some of the symptoms for which the product might be used could indicate either obstruction of the digestive tract or an organic disease. But the opinions of the opposing expert witnesses on the question of the drug's "toxicity"—one of the crucial words of the statute—were in hopeless conflict. A Government witness's characterization of the drug as a choleretic—a whole bile-producing medicine—was met by the assertion of the manufacturer's expert that it was a hydrocholeretic and only increased the watery component of the bile. The frustrated district judge commented that it seemed "incredible that physicians of such stature cannot agree on the most rudimentary effect upon the bodily processes of the ingestion of 3¾ grains of dehydrocholic acid."

Compounding the court's problem in deciding on motions for summary judgment was the fact that the Government had not adduced a single case in which Decholin had done harm to someone who took it without consulting a doctor. To decide on the affidavits of the conflicting experts, the court would have had to

make an "educated guess," and in that posture of the case the trial
judge thought that guess would be that Decholin could be classed
as harmful in theory but safe in practice for use without a prescription. Medicine being a practical art, this sounded favorable to
a decision for the maker, but enough questions remained to be
explored that the court refused to grant summary judgment for
it. It is true, according to the court's reading of the legislative
history, that "Congress did not desire to proscribe self-
medication . . . just because under some set of circumstances, and
especially hypothetical conditions—the drug may be harmful if
taken without professional supervision." But although it was clear
that Congress did not intend to put aspirin or milk of magnesia on
the prescription list, even an extensive history of use of a drug
without reported harmful effects would not require a finding that
it could continue over the counter: "Congress never intended that
the Government must be able to document a Thalidomide-type
tragedy before it can obtain relief."

In the case of Decholin, an important concern was the seriousness of the possible effects of its use by over-the-counter purchasers. The particular question arose of whether life-threatening
conditions would occur only if someone kept taking Decholin past
the point at which a typical consumer would see a doctor. Echoes
and variations on these problems sounded in the court's response
to the issue of whether the "collateral measures" necessary to use
of the drug presented questions of fact needing further development of evidence. Again the court referred to the questions of
seriousness of delay and how much delay would be detrimental to
typical consumers. The court also asked whether the cautionary
statements on the label accurately identified the symptoms that
would signal the necessity of a visit to the doctor. There was one
further issue that wound around through all the others: Would
taking Decholin simply mask the symptoms of a profound problem so that the user would think he was cured, when in fact the
illness continued and probably was growing more dangerous?

The court thought that this parcel of questions would require
evidentiary development, and thus it denied the motions for
summary judgment offered by both sides. The decision seems a
wise one, fitting comfortably with an emphasis on both risk aversion and meaningful disclosure. Specifically on the risk-averseness
point, it seems important that the court refused to require partic-
ularized evidence of cases in which Decholin had in fact deterred

users from seeking professional attention. This highlights the case as one in which not only is the information initially available to consumers of questionable value, but information about injuries caused will be swallowed up in the consequences of caring for those injuries. We may better appreciate the court's decision if we ask some questions that might naturally occur as we visualize the patient with an obstruction who finally gets to the doctor. Is the intake interview likely to identify the brand name Decholin? Will that name find its way into a written report that will swim upstream to the Food and Drug Administration? One suspects that an affirmative answer to either question is unlikely.

This potential information gap is an important element of the reality that courts must consider under statutes which already embody a risk-averse point of view. Its existence counsels close scrutiny of products for which responsible opinion hypothesizes a long-term risk, even though no specific cases have been traced through the complex web of biological causation that surrounds us. In this regard, the problem of self-medication provides a useful benchmark with respect to the broader question of when unregulated consumer exposure to risk passes the limit of governmental toleration.

Recently the case of Laetrile, a chemical believed by its champions to be a cancer cure, has moved controversy about self-medication more dramatically into the judicial arena. Initially it must be said that there is much disagreement about the definition of the substance that has provoked so much public furor. Slightly different chemical formulations characterize "Laetrile" and "amygdalin," with the lower-case term "laetrile" being used interchangeably to describe both.[9] One medical definition of amygdalin—the name attached to the product in France in 1830—has called it glucoside in bitter almond and cherry-laurel leaves;[10] the substance also appears in the pits of peaches, apricots, and cherries. More than five thousand years ago it was used to treat tumors in China, and studies of various primitive tribes have reported correlations between a cancer-free existence and the use of diets rich in chemical compounds containing amygdalin.[11] Proponents of the anticancer hypothesis for amygdalin have argued that its chemical breakdown in the body, producing free hydrogen cyanide, triggers the action of the enzyme rhodanese—in which malignant cells are deficient. According to this view, rhodanese and sulfur combine with the cyanide ion in normal cells to form a harmless compound, but the cyanide ion will destroy malignant cells into which it enters.[12]

This version of biochemistry appears mythic to the great majority of cancer researchers, but it has gained a small core of advocates, who have litigated its effectiveness with varying results. These judicial decisions, and contemporaneous events, merit extended description because of the general problems they raise about personal choice. Representative of a successful prosecution of the drug was a government action in California, brought under the Food, Drug and Cosmetic Act, which produced an injunction against its sale. The branded amygdalin litigated in this case, tagged "Vitamin B-17" and made partly from apricot fruit and kernel concentrate, was labeled and sold as a food for special dietary use, and the court judged it adulterated and misbranded as well as holding it a drug under the act. The latter definition effectively sounded the death knell for the product, since it had not been cleared through the new drug application process and since the court found it was not generally recognized as safe by qualified experts—the statutory test used to determine whether a product is a "new drug" and thus subject to elaborate clearance procedures.[13] The court found that Laetrile lacked evidence of safety based on "scientific procedures, including original animal, analytical and other scientific studies and . . . an unprejudiced compilation of both favorable and unfavorable reliable information." The drug's sponsors had specifically advertised it as a cancer prevention agent and cure, and this provided extra support for the injunction because of the product's failure to bear either warnings or directions for use. Besides Laetrile's vulnerability with respect to its unproved effectiveness as an anticancer agent, it ran up against a recurrent obstacle in the law on self-medication: the danger that members of the public might delay in seeking professional medical treatment.[14]

A contrasting side of the picture—a portrait of judicial sympathy for a consumer willing to accept the risk of a product barred from the market on grounds of insufficient scientific support—appears in the extraordinary decision in *Rutherford* v. *United States*.[15] This case, though the Oklahoma district judge's original opinion allowing the plaintiff to get Laetrile had a rather credulous ring, had two distinguishing features. One was a specific dosage prescribed to the plaintiff by the Mexican doctor whom he consulted when the prospect of surgery for diagnosed cancer frightened him. The other was a report by that physician, with other unspecified testimony and exhibits, which convinced the court that Rutherford had been "cured" by amygdalin.

The nub of the court's legal view was that the FDA had denied the plaintiff his Fifth Amendment rights in failing to decide on the NDA status of amygdalin, although the agency had detailed an IND application's deficiencies to the sponsor, who failed to request a conference on the problem. The decision seems to sweep over the distinction between INDs and NDAs, and to exhibit confusion about the FDA's duty in the Congressional scheme, as it insists that the statutory provision on NDAs posed an impossible barrier for Rutherford and "those similarly situated . . . without means or resources to comply with the statute." Rough-hewn as the decision is from a technical point of view, the court does drive home its central point that such persons are "denied the freedom of choice for treatment by Laetrile to alleviate or cure their cancer." The court seems wrong in asserting that Congress intended the FDA to proceed on its own initiative to an NDA-type decision on a drug which had not passed the IND stage. But there is strong political appeal in its blunt statement that the agency had made it "impossible for the common man to have an application processed through FDA so that said agency would either approve or disapprove the drug known as Laetrile."

The court found specifically that the drug was "not a toxic or harmful substance if used in proper dosage." At least as to toxicity, this holding may be acceptable on the evidence, given its implicit requirement that there must be some form of dosage information and instructions. The court's reference to the drug as "an alternative treatment of cancer which can be used in lieu of surgery or radiation cobalt" is much more arguable, and indeed an incredible one from the point of view of the overwhelming medical majority. The preponderance of the state of scientific knowledge supported the strong objection of Government counsel that it was "not possible to make such a finding" under the evidence.

The Court of Appeals for the Tenth Circuit subsequently affirmed the *Rutherford* decision, saying that the FDA had not proved Laetrile to be a statutory "new drug." Characterizing the agency's record as consisting only of a "conclusory affidavit," and "grossly inadequate," the appeals court upheld the preliminary injunction granted by the district judge against interference with

Rutherford's access to a supply of Laetrile. Remanding the case, it said that the FDA must produce "an administrative record" to support the conclusion that Laetrile was a new drug, under statutory provisions which exempted from that category products marketed at the time of the 1962 drug amendments and recognized as safe, or recognized for the given use before the passage of the 1938 drug legislation.[16]

The appellate court's decision, though stated on more technical grounds than the trial court's, sent shock waves through the FDA, as well as provoking comments from outside the agency calling it "outlandish."[17] Given the statute as it is, it would seem that to require the FDA to show initially that any product over which a contest arises is a new drug presents an intolerable burden to the agency. But putting aside the technical requirements of the legislation for a moment, it would seem that the law should facilitate the affirmatively expressed desires of suffering persons to take risks—at least when they have gone through enough stages of conventional medical treatment to feel that they want no more of it—or that at the very least the law should not erect obstacles to this preference.[18] This should surely be the case were one reasonably certain that a Gresham's law of publicity would not operate to devalue the public perception of conventional medicine to the point that persons at the fork in the road between professional attention and self-medication would choose the latter to their detriment. The decision of the district judge in *Rutherford* in particular provides a striking example of a court, apparently unequipped to deal with scientific data, which sacrifices values of careful handling of technical information to assure primacy to what it perceives to be dignitary interests.

This view of the Laetrile problem places considerable reliance on freedom of choice. It suggests that the system of prescription-drug regulation should leave interstitial room for promoters of the radical hypothesis. Despite our belief that the kind of screening that the FDA requires is most in line with what we now know about reality, the history of many certitudes has been a melancholy one. On analysis of causal complexities we become less sure about what we do in fact know. The uncertainties and lack of knowledge of the scientific community may exist at a more sophisticated level than that of laymen, but they are uncertainties nevertheless. To be sure, the view of the medical establishment will be that it admits its desolate ignorance about what works in many cases, but that there is no uncertainty about the fact that Laetrile does not work. Yet although experienced practitioners may think the consumer choice lunatic, when their own knowledge about cures is itself primitive, sufferers should be able to decide on questions that have been publicly vented.[19] As minorities of citizens should be able to challenge an activity with potential long-term dangers that may harm a community whose majority ignorantly accepts the situation, so they should be able to choose risks *for themselves* when the situation guarantees that their choice is not a casual one. Though the publicists for the radical pharmaceutical alternative have the advertising advantage of a kind of religious appeal, the general legal framework of medical practice assures meaningful communication by those who represent the conventional wisdom. Given an opportunity for free dissemination of ideas, there should be leeway for private decision on matters of personal health, at least in cases like that of Laetrile, in which the situations guarantees that a full public discussion of the alleged merits and demerits of the product has taken place, thus assuring a relatively informed choice on the part of consumers.

As *Rutherford* progressed through the Oklahoma district court and the Tenth Circuit, a Minnesota district judge rejected an action against the FDA by Laetrile sellers, taking somewhat the same tack as the decision previously described which enjoined distribution of the product. In this case, *Hanson* v. *United States*,[20] the sellers had sought injunctive and declaratory relief in an effort to recover seized quantities of the drug and to establish their right to sell it in interstate commerce.

The *Hanson* court held first that Laetrile is a "drug," referring in part to promotional materials as showing that the use intended for it was the "diagnosis, cure, mitigation, treatment, or prevention of disease in man." Moreover, the court judged the product to be a statutory new drug, despite the "blizzard" of promotional materials, books, and articles offered by the plaintiffs "urging the curative effects of Laetrile." Even though some of the testimonials offered were alleged to be the opinions of leading experts, the court said that it had to hold the product to be a new drug because there was not a single statement in evidence that Laetrile was *generally recognized* as safe for the treatment of cancer.

The decision referred to the history of private litigation for products liability as "demonstrat[ing] the danger that new drugs may be released without adequate testing, too often with tragic consequences," and declared "that there is no shortage of peddlers who claim their miracle drug must be made available to the consuming public without further delay." This scathing characterization, however, does point up some sympathetic features of the Laetrile cases from the standpoint of those who wish to see the product marketed, implying the desperation of the prospective purchasers as well as evoking an image of face-to-face bargaining between purchaser and seller. There is a related peculiarity in the configuration of orthodoxy in this case: the conventional wisdom is lined up against the new product, and its proponents find themselves in the role of outsiders; this contrasts with the situation more typical of this book, in which the proponents of dangerous activities and products represent establishment interests and the opposition appears as radical challengers. The thrust of anti-Laetrile decisions is a conservative one in this sense. But the cases are not all alike, either legally or functionally. *Hanson* is easily distinguishable from *Rutherford,* because the plaintiffs in *Hanson* were only sellers of the drug who could not argue that they themselves needed it. The *Hanson* court also mentions that the plaintiffs did not allege that they were unable to afford the NDA procedures, a point touched by the *Rutherford* district court in the plaintiff's favor, although it seems doubtful that the *Hanson* claimants would have succeeded on their motion for an injunction even had they asserted this.

The Laetrile problem presents extreme difficulty if one considers the harm that would be done if the entire system of INDs and NDAs were eliminated and the consumer were left to the mercy of a market that has tended to push to the boundaries of responsible salesmanship even under the present system of regulation. But given the despair of Laetrile purchasers, and by hypothesis their failure to find medical aid within the orthodox system, it can be argued that marketing of the product should be allowed. This is not a conclusion to be reached lightly. Given the premises of the present regulatory structure, to allow the sale of a drug which few recognize as safe and effective might convey an appearance of cynicism, an Establishment grant of a last-ditch placebo as an alternative to the palliation of standard medical treatment. Yet this may not be cynicism, but rather recognition not only of the relative hopelessness of many episodes of disease but of the tendency of human nature to grasp at slender straws of salvation. To ask why suffering persons should not be able to make such desperate choices inevitably leads to the very broad question of why there should be a prescription list at all, or statutory requirements for drug review. The simple answer is that we perceive a balance of benefits as issuing from the present law; that in general it provides a sensible mediation of problems stemming from consumers' lack of information. But the Laetrile case indicates that there should be room within that statutory scheme for heterodoxy to have its innings.

Perhaps the best solution would be to create a category which allowed sale with strong and conspicuous warnings in cases where a given amount of time had passed after the filing of an unsuccessful IND, on petition from the maker and a showing that there was a probability of relatively intense demand from stricken consumers that would not likely be satisfied by established medical channels. By hypothesis, most physicians would not prescribe such drugs, under the gun of possible civil liability, and the flossiest pharmaceutical houses would shy away from them. Although such a law would open the way for small domestic entrepreneurs to enter a vacuum—Laetrile has been primarily sold from Mexico—it likely would be a vacuum that only exists at the edge of the market. Given the tools of persuasion available to the established medical community and the principal drug companies, one may assume that the negative public health consequences would be relatively limited, and in practice dispensation probably would be mainly confined to patients who could not receive help from conventional medicine. Moreover, even if Laetrile is chemically incapable of destroying cancer cells—as seems very probable—the widespread political support evinced for its sale would still pose the question of whether it is appropriate to prohibit the sale of placebos. Although there is no substantiated proof that cancer victims can will themselves back to health, we should not lightly legislate against even irrational attainment of mental comfort. In this regard, it is well to note the complexity of choice facing cancer sufferers. Chemical and radiation therapies often produce dreadful side effects, while producing only slight increases in survival rates.[21] It is difficult to contend that a government agency should arrogate to itself the choice between such consequences and the comfort of a placebo.

This proposal at least would permit the existence of a market, while preserving a risk-averse perspective against the introduction of new products alleged to carry serious risks. The greatest practical problem is one discussed in the Decholin case—i.e., that treatment will be delayed until it is too late. The question then becomes one on which admittedly there are no data, specifically, how many more persons would be drawn to Laetrile by its free availability than have been purchasing it on a black market. Even at the time when the politics of Laetrile became critical, presumably at a point when state legitimation of its sale had not had a chance to affect the market, the National Cancer Institute estimated that 50,000 people were using the drug per year.[22] Given the difficulty of getting a drug which is officially blacklisted, this seems a preference that should not facilely be dismissed.

This is hardly to ignore the danger that unscrupulous promoters will take advantage of human suffering of various kinds to reap large profits—a charge leveled at Laetrile promoters by various government officials and medical leaders. Moreover, this is not to deny that legalization of Laetrile may increase the number of needless deaths through delay, but to point out that it is not at all clear how many of those who have sought Laetrile on the black market are people who for one reason or another have not had access to conventional health care. The problem, indeed, may lie more in that lack than with fraudulent promotion of a quack remedy. Quite as significantly, I think we cannot sneer at the political meaning of the passage by several state legislatures of legislation permitting manufacture, sale, and use of Laetrile.[23] It is important to try to reconcile these statutes with the overall structure of the prescription drug laws. At least a partial accommodation might be achieved, given the complexities of life and politics, if marketing were permitted after a set period of time from the filing of an IND and under stringent requirements of disclosure and warning. The almost exclusive focus on Laetrile of the rash of state laws recently passed[24] suggests that the problem is not likely to become general and widespread, and that an exception to the general legal regime of prescription drugs can be limited to the facts presented by Laetrile—a dread disease, full-dress publicity and debate on the issue, and a general inability of prospective customers to get help through regular medical channels.

I should emphasize that what I have said here applies only to biochemical efficacy and to the safety issue as it refers to delay and diversion from presumably more effective treatment. There still exists, and should exist, the government's power to ban any drug because of positive toxicity. The Surgeon General has recently indi-

cated that versions of the drug may have serious microbial contamination, and that indeed it may cause cyanide poisoning,[25] as well
as pointing out the collateral dangers of fatality through improper
forms of administration[26] and even ingestion by small children—a
problem on which definitive legislation already exists.[27] A separate issue has to do with standards of identity and truthful labeling. Promoters of different forms of Laetrile-type remedies have
given their drugs different names and differ on their exact chemical compositions.[28] For those who believe that Laetrile is in fact
not useful as a cancer remedy, and who would prefer that suffering people not spend their money on it—a view to which I myself
subscribe—the toxicity, identity, and labeling approaches may
yield results more consonant with the ideas implicit in the widespread political support Laetrile has gathered. It would not be
surprising to find that products sold for purposes for which they
are not in fact effective have such other vices. From both a legal
and political point of view, this seems to represent a more satisfactory route of attack on Laetrile, and one that would command
more lasting respect, than a course of action that is perceived by
many as a grievous interference with personal freedom. A further
alternative for regulation of Laetrile promotion appears in prosecution for deceptive advertising, based either on failure to represent correctly the data offered by the promoters, or misrepre-
sentations of the beliefs of recognized experts. Bolstering this
form of regulation, for example, would be the FDA's recent, massive review of Laetrile in response to the demands of the *Rutherford* district court, concluding that there was "no evidence that the
drug works."[29]

The Laetrile problem may be pursued a step further by asking
what the likely results would be of continuing a nationwide ban on
the product, assuming that the more than a dozen state laws allowing its sale were held to be preempted. Besides the fact that there
would probably still be leakage onto the market of Laetrile labeled
as such, it is reasonable to suspect that it also would be marketed
under innocuously generic labels using the name of the distribut-
ing firm, and hawked only as that product—e.g., "Smith's apricot
kernel compound"—not as a specific. Given the amount of home
remedy uses for products like bicarbonate of soda, it would
stretch legal ingenuity and constitutional doctrine to prevent this
sort of sale so long as it was not accompanied by fraudulent representations.

There remains a final, highly controversial point. Press accounts of the lobbying activities of Laetrile supporters often convey the impression of a holy crusade. Because of this, we must
raise, at least argumentatively, the issue whether Laetrile promoters could successfully liken themselves to promoters of reli-
gion in an effort to gain First Amendment protection. We may
speculate that they probably would not be able to bring this off.
But the fact remains that the claims of freedom in this case are
made on behalf of the victims of disease and not the promoters.
And there remains the bothersome question of why we should
frown more on sufferers who submit to the ministrations of marginal physicians than those who seek cures at religious shrines.

A particularly interesting comparison to the Laetrile case, involving a judicial confrontation with unsubstantiated charges of
long-term hazards inherent in a product itself, appears in an action by the Federal Trade Commission to stop advertising for
weight-reduction clinics which used a prescription drug called
HCG (human chorionic gonadotropin). The clinics, adherents of
the "Simeons" method of weight reduction, used a radical diet,
medical counseling, and daily injections of 125 units of HCG,
which carried FDA approval on prescription for certain uses but
not weight reduction. The FTC argued that the clinics' advertising, which said that the Simeons method was safe, effective, and
medically approved, was untruthful and should be enjoined.

On the procedural threshold, the district court decided—and
the court of appeals agreed—that it must make an independent
examination of the need for the extraordinary relief of an injunction, rather than applying a standard based only on a reasonable
belief by the FTC that such a remedy was necessary.[30]

The central substantive problem from our present vantage
point was associated with the Commission's argument that the
drug was not safe for older men, because it might activate latent
prostate cancers. The Commission rested its case primarily on the
"opinion" of a medical witness that it was "entirely possible" that
the doses of HCG used in the Simeons program would stimulate
the secretion of the male hormone testosterone, and that this
"might be harmful" to someone with a latent cancer of the prostate.

It was true that the FDA had not cleared HCG—in 125 unit
dosages or any other amount—for use in obesity treatments.

However, it had approved its use in doses of from 500 to 5,000 units for other kinds of problems, including hypogonadism in males and in female infertility. Given the sex or the syndromes of the patients for whom these uses were approved, the assumption was that there was no danger of a potential carcinogenic effect related to HCG's propensity to stimulate the secretion of testosterone. By contrast, the FTC argued that the product presented a danger to older males who might use the Simeons method, because of its possible effect on the undetected incipient cancers to which this group was prone.

However, the case failed on this ground because of the speculative character of the Commission's evidence as well as some technical considerations of judicial review. The administrative law judge who had ordered the ban on advertising had not even addressed the problem of prostate cancer. Moreover, on review of the decision of the district court, which had refused to enforce the administrative judge's order, the test was one of whether the district judge had acted in a clearly erroneous way. Under this standard, it was not only the conjectural character of the FTC expert's opinion that dragged the agency's case down, but also the fact that there had been no clinical showing that HCG caused prostate cancer. In this connection the court of appeals emphasized testimony of the district court's own expert witness, who had said that he knew of no evidence either way of causation, and that possible side effects would not deter him from using the product in obese patients.[31]

The decision on this point is reasonably developed from existing law on FTC injunctions and is a justifiable one, particularly in light of the advertiser's First Amendment interest.[32] Yet if one views the question without the procedural overlay which attached to the case in the court of appeals, law-enforcing agencies might appropriately take a more risk-averse approach, based on the point of view advanced in this book. Arguably, a court could decide to ban the advertising; surely it could require disclosure of opinions concerning risk factors; and the FDA could withdraw approval of a labeling indication for weight reduction or forbid shipment intended for that use.

The speculative character of the risk makes us hesitate to muffle the market entirely; but the specter of even potential carcinogenicity would seem to require at least that the market be enriched with more information. Indeed, the case offered a chance to require more, but the court declined to do so. The opportunity lay in the FTC's contention that the Simeons were advertising in a misleading way, because they were disclosing neither the use of HCG nor the fact that the FDA had not approved the drug for obesity treatments, and were failing to reveal that the drug had not been scientifically proved to be more effective in weight reduction than diet alone. The court took note of judicial controversy on whether the test for misleading claims required that false public assumptions must be actively promoted. But it emphasized that there was no showing that the public exposed to the Simeons' advertisements had a belief either that "HCG was not used or that, if used, HCG had been approved by the FDA."

It is true, as the court also said, that "no single advertisement could possibly include every fact relevant to the purchasing decision." This, and the general ethic of advertising accepted in the law, certainly makes defensible the Simeons' failure to divulge that there was no scientific evidence to show the weight-reducing superiority of their method over diet alone. But as applied to the use of HCG and its FDA status, the argument seems ingenuous. As with many problems of this kind, the nettle lies not only in the fact that the public does not know about a product, but also that it does not know of its ignorance. For a substantial number of persons, the fact that a chemical formula is being used in a nonapproved way when prescription has been required for other uses would seem to be material. And on a point not specifically considered by the court, given the scope of public and regulatory anxiety about carcinogenicity, many people would probably consider some scientists' concern that a drug might cause cancer to be relevant to a purchasing decision.

When one considers that the Simeons case involved a responsible though conjectural allegation of a long-term risk, together with a deficiency in public information both about that allegation and about the lack of specific approval, the result seems unfortunate. If one takes as an ideal model a single consumer protection agency concerned comprehensively with all possible combinations of risk management and disclosure, it would appear that the consumer interest has not been well served, that metaphorically it has fallen between the FDA and the FTC.

The matter of alleged cancer cures provides an especially dramatic example of the competing interests that are involved in what I have termed the self-medication question. Triangulating among judicial and legislative responses to that problem, we can get an introductory fix on the social consensus now in a process of pluralistic evolution concerning the regulation of complex, potentially dangerous products. The case of potentially carcinogenic remedies for obesity presents overlapping problems, charged in a different way with public emotion about cancer. In a less desperate setting, analogous questions arise with respect to remedies for the common cold. Americans afflicted with colds ingest a great variety of drugs sold over the counter as well as on prescription, with ingredients ranging from vitamin C and caffeine to laxatives and antacids. Yet, as the sober Medical Letter pointed out in a 1975 survey, "aspirin is the most useful single drug" to relieve the headache and grippelike symptoms of colds, and can be bought for a fraction of the price of most combination-of-ingredient remedies. For those allergic to aspirin or suffering other undesirable side effects, both acetaminophen and phenacetin would do as well to reduce pain or bring down fever.[33] The publication did note that phenacetin had been associated with injury to the kidneys in cases of large-scale use of combination products over a period of years. Acetaminophen might also be a factor, but was probably implicated only because of its use with phenacetin. The only problem that precisely had been identified with acetaminophen was overdosage, a hazard more likely to occur with its syrupy forms. But this danger presumably could be contained by packaging,[34] at least in the case of children.

A startling hypothesis about aspirin itself as a palliative cold remedy was that it might cause viral shedding, and thus possibly enhance the spreading of colds.[35] This is information that presumably a meticulous consumer would want. In any event, one thing was clear to the Medical Letter's consultants: there was "no reason" to combine aspirin and another analgesic in the same product. Moreover, the amount of caffeine in cold remedies—to counteract sedation from antihistamine ingredients!—was too small to be effective for that purpose. Antacids as part of combinations probably provided no buffering effect that could not be achieved by food. And there was no evidence that the inclusion of Vitamin C in cold remedies, in much lower doses than recommended by its proponents for that purpose, was effective. All in all, the combinations were "irrational" medication offered at high cost.

This aspect of the problem is a substantial one in economic

terms, if one concludes that millions of Americans are paying for products that are worth little or nothing. A columnist's sardonic remarks that there were psychological justifications in the feeling of combat these medicines provide, as well as the distractions from illness inherent in "trying to get at the pills, in the child-proof pill bottle,"[36] offer comic relief but hardly rationalize the harm to the pocketbook. We should not minimize the economic impact of this injury, and it requires action under the heading of preventing deception. However, this concerns only mendacious advertising and not physical hazard, in contrast to our primary concern with complex and uncertain dangers.

The principal problem from the standpoint of safety is that of phenacetin, hypothesized as a cause of kidney trouble when taken over long periods of time. This, with speculation about the concurrent contribution of acetaminophen, brings the case within our area of central concern. The best solution, given the widespread use of phenacetin combinations and the fact that harm is associated with various degrees of overuse, would seem to lie in advertising and labeling requirements rather than outright prohibition. This would parallel the regulatory reaction to this historically nonprescription product with the governmental response to the promotion of oral contraceptives, which is discussed in Chapter 4. It is important that the advertising be forthright and blunt about possible hazards. As simple risks shade into complex ones, and responsible hypotheses are advanced about the existence of danger, public warnings should be explicit.

The theory of some pediatricians that even normal doses of acetaminophen might produce severely toxic effects on the kidneys of children presents a somewhat different problem.[37] Again, the widespread use of the product, together with the conjectural nature of the apprehension, makes the ultimate sanction of prohibition undesirable. Yet the severity of the hypothesized reaction, and the extreme vulnerability of the persons at risk, demand a public response. Possibly a sufficient sanction would be to require the issuance of bulletins to pediatricians, both cautioning them and calling for reports that raise warning signals of this problem. In theory, an acceptable halfway house, while the hypothesis remains only that, would be to require the posting of a compensation-fund bond, refundable if the association is not proved. Although many reactions to various kinds of chemical product dangers may be characterized as idiosyncratic, in the case of adults the problem of kidney damage from acetaminophen seems more quirky than most, given the speculative character of the evidence mentioned earlier. With respect to children, we are perhaps more concerned despite the lack of hard data. On balance, the conjectural elements of concern and the undeniable usefulness of the product combine to keep regulation at a moderate level. To make provision in advance for random victims may not be an adequate remedy in itself, given the difficulty of establishing causation after the fact, but it seems sufficient in conjunction with a decision to require warning notices and to push for increased information-gathering.

In 1976, the FDA announced a panel recommendation that was lukewarm on the value of cold remedies, simultaneously with a proposal to allow the over-the-counter sale of several previously prescription drugs. This combination of events may seem logically curious at first blush, but is understandable in terms of both common sense and politics.

The panel emphasized that there was no "generally accepted treatment which can prevent, cure or shorten the course of a common cold," in the words of its chairman, Dr. Francis C. Lowell, at a press conference. The panel stressed that no marketed remedies could provide more than symptomatic relief, saying that though antihistamines had been widely advertised for use against colds, their effectiveness was not established. It therefore declared that products should be selected for specific symptoms, and cautioned that combinations might be counterproductive, as for example when expectorants loosen phlegm while antihistamines combat runny noses.[38]

At the same time, the panel found that a number of cold remedies did not achieve symptomatic relief at the dosages then permitted, and it recommended that ten prescription drugs be converted to over-the-counter status, and that four previously nonprescription drugs be allowed to be sold over the counter at prescription strength. The FDA accepted the panel's recommendation on ten of these products—the first time the agency had changed prescription drugs to over-the-counter status on the basis of an external recommendation—but reserved judgment on the other four.[39]

The panel's report, associated with the acting FDA commissioner's announced intention to remove many combination products from the market, provides a useful reference point for the problems principally dealt with in this book. Although the report did find some products to be lacking in evidence of safety, its principal thrust was not directed to insidious, long-term harm growing out of product complexity; by hypothesis the action of these drugs was relatively simple. If there is to be government intervention in this product area, it must be based largely on grounds of saving consumer dollars. Speaking of combination products, the panel's chairman declared that consumers "don't need" such remedies. His statement that "individuals should not consume drugs they do not need" possibly had a tinge of safety considerations, but the gist of it was that people would be "better off in the pocketbook" without these formulas.

Given this premise, it is useful theoretically to consider the question of whether there should be an outright ban on nostrums that people "do not need." The case for prohibition is a hard one to make. Viewing self-medication as a necessary aspect of health care, and personal experimentation as something to be encouraged, we are generally slow to accept regulation for economic reasons alone, especially given the possibility of placebo effects. Even a showing of toxicity or collateral-measures problems along the lines alleged by the Government in the Decholin litigation— and typically there would be no such proof in cases of this sort— would presumably compel no more than a placing of the product on the prescription list. To be sure, deception deserves regulation, but less urgently when it relates to short-term effectiveness against the symptoms of nonemergency illnesses than when it concerns uncertainty about long-term safety. As a general matter, even if there is strong scientific evidence that products have little value, when there is any room for argument about economic worth alone, there is much to be said for leaving the question to the market subject to constraints against fraud in advertising and labeling.

An analogous question of how far government should intervene in consumer choice has received judicial consideration in the context of regulations which classified high-potency dosages of vitamins A and D as prescription drugs. Promulgating these regulations, the FDA reacted to medical literature which showed serious toxic effects associated with the use of large dosages of the vitamins, against the background of "widespread promotion" of these dosage forms for various diseases and disorders. The gravity of the problem as perceived by physicians was manifest in a warning statement about large dosages of Vitamin A sent to the media by the American Academy of Pediatrics.

The Food and Nutrition Board of the NAS/NRC had established as a recommended daily allowance (RDA) a figure of 4,500 to 5,000 IU of Vitamin A for older children and adults, 6,000 IU during pregnancy, and 8,000 during lactation. It set an RDA of 400 IU of Vitamin D for all groups. The agency's response to these figures was to classify as prescription drugs all Vitamin A preparations of more than 10,000 IU per dosage form, and all Vitamin D dosages of more than 400 IU.

It could have been argued that this kind of regulation was not only an unwarranted interference with freedom of choice but also foolishly ineffective, since someone who wanted to consume, say, 20,000 IU of Vitamin A could simply take two pills. However, the agency contended that experience had shown that availability of the larger dosage forms tended to increase the risk of excessive ingestion.

Among several problems faced by the court of appeals reviewing these regulations, the most important from our substantive standpoint involved the question of whether the agency had acted legally in classifying the higher dosage forms as drugs. The answer embodied a mixture of technical administrative law and judicial estimation of the FDA's motives. The vitamin manufacturers had argued that the pills fell within the agency's other principal product mandate, namely food, rather than drugs. The Commissioner contended that except in the case of a few people with poor Vitamin D absorption, there was no evidence that the higher dosages were used for nutritional purposes, and that therefore their use must be therapeutic. The court recognized that the Commissioner had not gone the last mile and submitted proof fulfilling the statutory requirement of intent that the product be used therapeutically. However, the court was willing to hypothesize that the Commissioner had not articulated his reasons fully; it conjectured that he might have had information showing that the higher dosages were used almost exclusively in that way. Almost lugubriously, it further speculated that because of the small percentage of high dosage forms used nutritionally, the Commissioner might have concluded that those dosages fulfilled the statutory definition of "drug" as "intended for use in the 'cure, mitigation, prevention or treatment of disease.'"[40] If one granted this to the FDA, its classification of the high dosages as drugs would not be arbitrary and capricious and the court should not tamper with it. Additionally, the court was able to divine that statements on the labeling to "Take one a day or as directed by a physician" would indicate a therapeutic use.[41]

Although much of this analysis of the Commissioner's possible reasoning had support in the record, the appeals court's reading of the technical profile of the case required it to remand to the district court to rule on the rationality of the "drug" classification. The tone of the court of appeals opinion did suggest a prospective disbelief that the district court could find the regulations irrational. But the court was especially sensitive on the question because of a decision which had just been published in a case involving the FDA's power to set standards of identity for vitamin supplements sold as foods. In that case the imposing figure of Judge Friendly had interposed itself in the agency's path with a holding that there was insufficient evidence to show that the preparations were intended for therapeutic purposes. Judge Friendly had noted that a significant number of consumers—principally women using oral contraceptives—were taking the higher dosages for nutritional purposes and declared that evidence of therapeutic intent required more than "demonstrated uselessness as a food for most people."[42]

However, Judge Mansfield emphasized for the court in the vitamin pills case that there was no "mere possibility" of occasional misuse but a situation in which "the actual way in which the product is apparently used on a normal basis by many persons presents serious risks of toxicity."[43] Taking this cue, the district court found on remand that the high-dosage tablets were drugs. Emphasizing the "widespread promotion" of the preparations as specific cures and cure-alls, it also declared it a "relevant and important datum" that these doses had "no demonstrated usage as a food," except possibly for an "extremely small percentage" of the population.[44]

On a further appeal, the court of appeals reversed the district court, finding that the Commissioner's regulations were "arbitrary and capricious." Keying on the statutory language requiring that the FDA show intention for therapeutic use to bring the product into the "drug" category, the court said that toxicity evidence only presented an indication that excessive intake of the vitamins "may not be nutritionally useful and does not provide the objective evidence of therapeutic intent necessary to support" the regulations. Although there may have been promotion by third parties of large doses of A and D to treat disease, there was no evidence in the record that manufacturers and vendors of the preparations made these kinds of representations. The court said that the Commissioner's selection of the levels at which he declared the products drugs was "solely related" to his "fear of potential toxic effect and his belief that the ingestion of vitamins at levels above the U.S. RDA is not nutritionally useful." No evidence had been produced on the remand, said the appellate court, to support the Commissioner's argument that therapeutic use of the vitamins at the prescription levels so far outweighed their use as dietary supplements that it "showed an objective intent that these products were used in the mitigation and cure of diseases."[45]

This reading may be technically as reasonable as the one given on the prior appeal, but viewing the question more generally from a standpoint of governmental incursions on individual choice, it would seem that the situation is one of producers protesting too much. The argument that it is foolish to force vitamin fanatics to take two pills instead of one is at once revealing of the triviality of the inroad on personal freedom and of the justifiability of that limitation, given a record of demonstrated overuse and scientific evidence of toxicity.

The freedom-of-choice point made by some consumers who commented on the FDA proposal as well as by proprietors of health food establishments, who argued that consumption of desired dosages was an "individual right," does deserve serious consideration. This case is distinguishable from that of medicines being used for market experimentation, and from that of food additives whose carcinogenic properties are hypothesized but unconfirmed. Here the definite knowledge of the toxic properties of the product, consumed in certain quantities, may easily be communicated to prospective purchasers. At least for adult consumers the vice of manufacturer-initiated experimentation gives way to no more than the possible folly of experimenting on one's self. However, a contrary and perhaps dispositive argument, favoring the agency, arises from the concern of pediatricians. Children whose parents want to stuff them with excess vitamins have no say in the matter; they cannot choose on the basis of information disseminated either by the government or by private physicians. This point alone might support the regulations, given their rather limited restriction on freedom to choose. Analogous to the position I have taken on Laetrile, the dosages approach allows consumer choice but effectively requires that it be a somewhat considered one.

We should refer specifically here to one other aspect of the case, and this concerns both the information available to consumers and the quality of their understanding. It may be that a product with even the "scientific" aspects of vitamins exudes a sense of complexity sufficient to discourage analysis by many purchasers. The promotion factor enters importantly in this regard, for example in the use of advertising which deals one-sidedly with the biological effects of products. In defining the product only in terms of its advantages, advertising which obscures its complexities by failing to disclose its risks is sufficiently distorting to merit regulation.

The vitamin controversy may have had aspects of a tempest in a teapot. However, the resources committed to the litigation—the substantive issue as well as a bitter struggle over FDA rule-making procedures had sent the agency and a group of makers and sellers of vitamins thrice to the appellate mat—served as indicia of its symbolic as well as economic importance. A coda to the story is that the "freedom of choice" argument finally won at least qualified political approval. In 1976, the same year the district court held the high-dosage pills to be drugs, Congress passed a law prohibiting the establishment under certain specific sections of the Food and Drug Act of maximum limits on the potency of synthetic vitamins or minerals in foods for special dietary use.[46] It defined this category of foods as supplying a special dietary need existing by reason of a "physical, physiological, pathological, or other condition." It further defined the classification of conditions to include a list, inter alia, of disease, convalescence, pregnancy, weight problems, and the need to control sodium intake, but said specifically it was not to be limited to that list. The legislative history indicates that the limitation of the prohibition to certain sections of the legislation leaves unimpaired the FDA's authority to regulate vitamins and minerals as food additives when questions arise about their safety,[47] a point on which Judge Friendly provided the FDA balm in yet a fourth appellate treatment of the vitamin problem, while announcing "with regret" a finding that the agency had not met its procedural obligations in rule-making.[48]

Most directly on the prescription point, Congress prohibited classification of a vitamin or mineral as a drug "solely because it exceeds the level of potency which the Secretary determines is nutritionally rational or useful."[49] This presumably would leave room to regulate products for which the Secretary could prove that promotion actually led to ingestion of toxic ranges of vitamins. Besides this interpretative possibility, the legislation was specific that this prohibition did not apply in the case of products "represented for use by individuals in the treatment or management of specific diseases or disorders, by children, or by pregnant or lactating women."[50]

It should be noted that the exception concerning advertisement for use by children and pregnant or lactating women relates to our specific concern with long-term harm from uncertain risks. A House committee report on the conference substitute bill referred to the possibility that drugs not intended for use by these groups could be "taken by or administered to them inadvertently." Noting that the fetus could be affected by excessive doses of "some food supplements," and that too much vitamins or minerals could affect the normal growth and development of children, the committee declared that "such possibilities of unrecognized or unanticipated harm" were a predicate for giving regulatory authority to prevent "unsuitable or inappropriate ... preparations" from being "inadvertently administered to individuals in these vulnerable groups."[51] There still exists, of course, the possibility of irrational attempts at therapeutic use by those who are persuaded by general advertising that more of the same means better, but the statutory exception significantly reduces the chances that this will happen.

Clearly, a core element of the problem lies in product representation, the initiating event in marketing. While responding to this reality, Congress evidently was prepared to permit consumers irrational economic decisions, but undertook to empower the agency to make it more difficult to make dangerous medical choices. It could be argued that given the evil at which the statute was aimed, it was an overreaction to set up the general ban on classification as a drug. Driving those who seek high dosages without medical supervision to the two-pill alternative may be a relatively small price to pay to keep a certain number of vitamin enthusiasts from poisoning themselves. Yet with latitude for the Secretary to prove use at toxic levels and the assumption that the agency may regulate vitamins and minerals as food additives, it may be argued that the statutory mix is a sensible one: sellers are prevented from irresponsible advertisement; in order to regulate, the Secretary must show at least a question about safety, if not prove genuine danger; and only when a safety question has been raised, consumers who want to overdose themselves must give at least some extra consideration to the consequences. With the articulated exception for products advertised for children and pregnant or lactating women, the legislation seems satisfactory on balance. We can only ask whether Congress significantly advanced personal freedom by prohibiting restrictive classification of certain product configurations, considering how closely the same functional result may be approximated by what presumably remains permissible as a matter of regulating deceptive advertising.

One other interesting feature of the vitamin amendments of 1976 was a ban on advertisements for foods for special dietary use which gave prominence to ingredients that were not vitamins, minerals, or "represented as a source of vitamins or minerals." It reflected a concern that consumers should "not be led into a belief that such substances have nutritional value."[52] Moreover, the legislation authorized seizure and condemnation of foods whose advertising misbranded them because it was false and misleading, if the advertising was disseminated in places where the food was held for sale, and if the owner was responsible for the dissemination or paid for its cost. This provision represents a rather standard constraint on false advertising, confirming that a seller cannot raise claims of self-medication or freedom of choice based on beliefs he has deceptively engendered.

Diet-linked advertising presents an unusual version of the problem of dealing with long-term risks in the Federal Trade Commission's assault on the content of advertisements for eggs, generating litigation in that context with a rather different focus than that of the vitamin cases. The Commission claimed that the National Commission on Egg Nutrition (NCEN) had engaged in deceptive advertising about the relationship between the eating of eggs and the risk of heart disease or heart attack, thereby raising issues concerning both advertising for self-selected products and scientific evaluations. Pending completion of the Commission's administrative proceedings, the Court of Appeals for the Seventh Circuit upheld the agency's request for a temporary injunction against advertising statements to the effect that there was "no scientific evidence" of a relationship between dietary cholesterol from eggs and risks of heart disease. Construing Section 13 of the Federal Trade Commission Act, the court said that the Commission did not have to support its demand for an injunction on the basis of a balancing of the equities and the likelihood of ultimate success. Instead, it declared that it would be sufficient if the agency could show "a justifiable basis for believing . . . that such a state of facts probably existed as would reasonably lead" it to believe that the defendants were disseminating false advertising. Chief Judge Fairchild thought the First Amendment required a higher standard to justify an injunction, but went along with the result because he thought that deception had in fact been shown.[53]

The FTC focused on the problem of conflicting scientific opinion in its subsequent decision on the barrage of advertising claims for which its complaint counsel had attacked the NCEN.[54] The Commission concluded emphatically that it was false and misleading to claim that there was no scientific evidence that eating eggs would increase the risks of heart attacks or heart disease. It took note of a range of expert testimony, including that of witnesses who had helped prepare a British report which stated "[W]e have found no evidence which relates the numbers of eggs consumed to a risk of [coronary heart disease]." Detailing the testimony of one of the experts, the agency spoke of "the fine line between 'no evidence' and 'the evidence does not persuade me.'" For example, it cited a statement by one of the English physicians at the end of a long colloquy that "my opinion is that this evidence does not demonstrate that eating eggs increases the risk of heart disease." In this sense, the Commission admitted, one could not dispute the egg industry's "use of the term 'no evidence' to characterize the evidence relied upon by proponents of the diet/heart disease hypothesis."

But the Commission concerned itself with the meaning of the term "scientific evidence," which it said "as that phrase is reasonably understood, means precisely those competent and reliable scientific studies of the sort summarized by the administrative law judge which, in the view of a body of well qualified experts would lend support to the proposition." The "no evidence" claim might be a respectable way to describe the situation in one regard, but it was deceptive if what the industry really meant was, "we, along with one segment of the relevant expert community, do not believe that the existing evidence supports this hypothesis."[55] It was misleading, the Commission said, to make the "no evidence" claim in a context which lacked any mention of the "substantial scientific controversy" on the subject, including assertions by "many well-qualified scientists" that the literature incriminated dietary choles-terol in heart disease. Thus, although the industry's claim argu-ably had a truthful aspect, the judicial precedents permitted the Commission to call on the proposition "that where an advertise-ment conveys more than one meaning, one of which is false, the advertiser is liable for the misleading variation."

On this point, as well as with respect to the administrative law judge's determination that the respondents must possess a rea-sonable basis in competent scientific studies to assert that eating eggs would not increase the risk of heart disease, the Commission emphasized that many if not all consumers would be inclined to trust dietary claims without further challenge. Concerning the NCEN "no evidence" claim, the agency said that some people might believe that it meant that those who argued that eggs con-tributed to heart disease had not based their beliefs on a mass of "competent and reliable scientific studies." This claim discour-aged independent review, said the Commission; the organization was effectively representing "that there is no need for the con-sumer to go beyond their advertisement, because in this case there is simply 'no evidence' to warrant further inquiry."

Yet the Commission was willing to bend a little on the remedy with regard to the positive assertion that eating eggs would not increase coronary risks. It stressed that safety representations re-quired "a high degree of precision and care." But it had to con-cede that to require a "reasonable basis" for the industry claims, given the evolving nature of scientific opinion on the subject, would force it to resolve a disagreement between well qualified experts. The Commission's "simple solution" to the respondents' deception was partly borrowed from the injunction ordered by the Seventh Circuit: The respondents must indicate "clearly and conspicuously . . . that the claim they seek to make for eggs is sub-ject to substantial disagreement by qualified experts within the scientific community." This would not place a damper on the respondents' ability to publicize new developments, and yet it would prevent them from making broad assurances of safety without stating the "substantial contrary opinion."

This Solomonic resolution, however, should not obscure the force of the Commission's dictum that "claims involving scientific judgments necessitate careful scientific evaluation before they may be made, and the difficulty and possible uncertainty involved in making such judgments should normally be no bar to requiring them." In light of the uncertainty of the evidence on the egg-cholesterol problem, one may rationalize the Commission's decision on grounds that no more was required than the advertiser's disclosure that it was presenting one "side of a complex, unresolved scientific debate," restricting this reading on the facts of the case to a background risk that has been part of the dietary landscape. When the scene shifts to prevention of hazards in synthetic products which are not the focus of advertising, the need for regulation generally will become greater. Yet a comparison of this case with the problems of drugs, food additives and environmental chemicals addressed in this book makes clear a certain commonality of the issues. In significant ways, the case of eggs and cholesterol may turn out to be very close to that of suspected carcinogens in pharmaceuticals, for example. It is true that the fact that eggs have been there all the time—in common sense a risk of life—argues that we should keep regulation at a low profile. But when there is respectable scientific assertion that a hazard exists, advertising which implicitly involves controversy on that question reasonably provokes government intervention, at least to a point of compelling disclosure of the uncertainty that is involved. The case contrasts somewhat with the problem of cold remedies discussed above, in which as noted the problem at its worst is one of whether the product will give short-term, symptomatic relief against a relatively trivial ailment.

It bears emphasis that it is the factors of hazard, uncertainty, and complexity that make regulation necessary in some form, be the subject matter a food, a drug, or the chemical fallout of an industrial process. Whether government's role is limited to requiring disclosure or involves direct restrictions on marketing will vary with the subject matter. Whatever the form of regulation, we generally seek to match intervention with reasonable apprehension of potential welfare costs, which have many similarities across the range of disease-caused death and disability. Often, personal choice will coincide with welfare costs, and regulation will thus respond to both considerations simultaneously. Sometimes social and personal interests will diverge, requiring difficult political judgments. In either event, the point urged with particular force here is that regulation should give special consideration to the amount of personal choice that is possible in practice.

4 The Pill

A STRIKING ARRAY OF EXEMPLARY PROBLEMS in the control of scientific progress appears in the development of the oral contraceptives known as the Pill. The symbolic value of the Pill as an illustrative case is obvious. Intensity of desire must be balanced against several serious risks for a relatively small number of people over the short term, and growing uncertainty about risk for larger groups of the population over the long term. Complicating the problem is a special consideration incident to all prescription medicines, the role of the physician as an intermediary. The model of an individual consumer assessing risks and benefits for herself requires modification when the primary target of seller information is a third party, the physician. The doctor's role will significantly affect both the allocation of liabilities in private lawsuits for drug injuries and the rules of the system of public regulation which controls promotion and sale.

It is worth stating a truism at the outset: Effective contraception provides significant social and individual advantages. It stems the drain placed on national resources by population increase and it enhances personal choice. The problem for a large majority of the population is not one of ends but of chemical or mechanical means. Accompanying these perceived advantages and the resultant demand is the interest of unorganized consumers in avoiding the stochastic consequences of large-scale experimentation.

As we review the scientific developments related to the Pill, it is well to keep in mind an element that is significant in any study of products that may embody long-term hazards: the marketing scheme. In the case of oral contraceptives, that scheme is one peculiar to prescription drugs. Crucially, it involves the use of detail men—salesmen who visit individual doctors to make pitches for particular products. Reports of instructions used to inspire detail men reveal the point of view that companies wish to inculcate in them, and through them in the prescribing physician. Company sales manuals for one drug, a cholesterol reducer which became notorious for causing cataracts, told detail men, "You owe it to yourself—to your company—to the millions of people who need MER/29—to be enthusiastic!!!"[1]

In addition to personal contact by detail men, drug firms utilize an array of media. Reflecting regulatory concerns about the use of these varied channels, as well as the natural tendency of manufacturers to push drug prescription past the limits of medical acceptability, is an FDA official's recent accusation that advertising presentations are "consistently tilted" toward persuading doctors to prescribe drugs that patients do not need. Using this language, Dr. Richard Crout, director of the agency's Bureau of Drugs, gave as an example a videotape distributed to hospitals by Pfizer Laboratories. The tape mentioned an estimate that 4 to 8 million Americans suffer from depression, but asserted that under a definition of depression as "the absence of joy," the figure would be 20 million.[2] Can anyone dispute Crout's conclusion that Pfizer wished to create the impression that depression was "everywhere and being underdiagnosed"?

Beyond the videotapes, slides, and various printed materials that are the staples of pharmaceutical advertising, there stands a considerable promotional structure, a source of international machinations. G.D. Searle & Co., a leading Pill manufacturer, allegedly purchased advertising space in a Lebanese magazine in order to ward off editorial criticism.[3] There is also evidence that Searle representatives inspired a letter to the editor of an Irish publication responding to critical comments about the safety of the Pill.[4] Perhaps symptomatic are remarks of a Searle official, who praised a World Health Organization report which discounted the connection between the Pill and blood clots as "pretty good . . . from our point of view in terms of whitewashing the Pill."[5] Such remarks may be more indicative of a viewpoint prevailing among sellers than many firms would like to admit. Much of this conduct may be discounted as normally aggressive merchandising or colorful corporate confidences. In the present climate of marketing ethics, even an admission that "[o]bviously we have to pay for . . . 'impartiality'" in a medical journal is not surprising. The point is, simply, that the merchandising of oral contraceptives is a bruising business, at home as well as abroad, for firms must compete not only against other marketers of the Pill but also against other forms of contraception. Significantly from our standpoint, this involves competition in the marketplace of ideas and information, and analysis of that competition requires assessment of the growing literature generated by research on the Pill.

The problem of consumer information is indeed at the core of social concern with the Pill. Manifesting the problem in a light vein is a report about a man in Heilbronn, West Germany, who complained that his wife had had six children in seven years despite the Pill—that is, *his* use of it. Because he did not trust his wife to take the Pill regularly, he had been taking it himself—and then complained that "modern medicine is no good."[6] Our intuition that most people are better informed about Pill use and misuse should not obscure our view of the broader information problem: Scientists have found numerous negative effects related to the use of these chemicals in the years since they have been generally marketed, and public knowledge of these developments has lagged considerably behind scientific theory and even clinical findings.

The following review of the history of oral contraceptives proceeds on the basis of a justice-oriented premise concerning the kind of injury with which this book principally deals—physical harm caused by trauma or disease. The premise, significant in the background of public regulation, is that this sort of injury cannot easily be quantified in dollars in the way that consumers assign values when they conventionally trade off one form of economic goods for another. Implicit in social judgments in this realm is a notion that there is a qualitative feature of pain and death, particularly the kinds of pain and death caused by the sort of products discussed in this book, that our humanity refuses to balance nicely against marginal gains in welfare. Associated with this is the perception that it is unfair to impose these special costs on unsuspecting individuals—or even on those who cannot adequately take precautions although information about risk is generally public—in order to benefit others. A related set of considerations concerns information deficiencies—both the dearth of raw facts about the effects of goods, and ignorance resulting from the inability to assess data. These factors are indivisibly entwined with issues of fairness. We should not fail to ask what individuals want and what is efficient; and government intervention often represents an effort to compensate for market inefficiencies related to information costs. But public regulation also embraces questions of what society desires in the way of justice.

The story of oral contraceptive regulation has been checkered by confident assurances of safety, cries of alarm, and decisions

under pressure to issue public warnings mixed with soothing reas-
surances. A distinguishing feature of this history, generally symbolic of the problems of regulating the products of scientific advance, has been the consecutive outcropping of new areas of concern about the effects of the Pill on various organs and systems of
the body. The Babel of messages reaching the public has resulted
from the great variety of transmitting agencies that have involved
themselves in public discussion and debate, ranging from officials
and scientists of the FDA to manufacturing executives and researchers, and including Congressional critics of drug marketing
and regulation.

The development of the chemical technology of the Pill illustrates the compromises which occur in all efforts to respond to the
demand for contraception. Convenience and aesthetic satisfaction
primarily motivated the decision to utilize hormones for this purpose; however consciously, the developers of chemical contraception were trading against uncertainty and problems of consumer
information. They were trying to find a better substitute for the
older mechanical methods of the condom and the diaphragm, as
well as for the rhythm method with its particular frustrations and
constraints. Contemporaneous research efforts yielded new
mechanical methods, including the intrauterine device (IUD), a
contraption of varying configurations designed for insertion in
the uterus.

The development of oral contraceptives provides an instructive example of the way scientific discovery requires consecutive
revelation of discrete pieces of knowledge. The lines of investigation that culminated in the original application for approval of
Enovid in 1957 include research published in 1922 on the influence of gonad-stimulating hormones in bringing on ovulation, the
identification in 1929 of progesterone as the corpus luteum hormone, and the discovery in 1931 that ovarian hormones would
prevent conception in animals.[7]

The maker of the first Pill, G.D. Searle, began testing it as
early as 1956—perhaps revealingly in Puerto Rico and Haiti. Having secured approval in 1957 to sell Enovid as therapy for
menstrual disorders, the firm received the go-ahead in 1960 for
large-scale clinical testing of the product as a contraceptive.[8] At
that point in the experimental years, members of the medical
community voiced substantial reservations. An FDA questionnaire sent to 61 professors of obstetrics and gynecology asking

whether Enovid should be put on the market could not command a majority in favor. Of those who did not respond affirmatively, 14 said that they did not have enough data to reach a conclusion. Yet the FDA decided to allow trials involving thousands of women even though the drug had been continuously tested for more than a year on only 132 women.[9]

Through the first half of the 1960s, as the Pill proceeded to the general market, accounts of serious side effects began to trickle in. Reports specifically related to thromboembolic episodes prompted the FDA to appoint an ad hoc committee to investigate the subject. The committee's conclusion typifies the profile of the Pill's bumpy history. It could not find a statistical association between the Pill and thromboembolism, but it was unsure enough about the matter that it recommended further study.[10]

An unwitting early pioneer of market experimentation in these years was Mrs. Sarah Lawson of Illinois. Her case illustrates the alternative of private litigation for personal injuries, exemplifying the complexities and uncertainties of common-law decision-making as well as, to an extent, its legal possibilities. Mrs. Lawson was in good health, except for being overweight, when she saw Dr. Richard Neely for menstrual pain in July 1962. Dr. Neely prescribed Enovid to relieve her suffering. The next month, on August 20, Mrs. Lawson appeared at a hospital emergency room with pain in her upper abdomen, but after several days of examinations she was discharged on August 29, with no symptoms. Only three days later, however, she returned to the emergency room, and this time she did not leave the hospital alive. By the third day of this visit a massive swelling had developed in her left leg, attributable to obstruction of the main vein, and she went into shock.

Pulmonary embolisms developed that resisted efforts by specialists to break them up. After two more days of intensive medical efforts to save her life, Mrs. Lawson died. According to the pathologist's report she was a victim of thrombophlebitis with complicating pulmonary embolism; the age of the clots was reported to range from a few days to six or eight weeks. She was twenty-five, an age at which this kind of death is uncommon.

If Enovid was the culprit in Mrs. Lawson's case—a point of considerable dispute—one could at least reasonably conclude that she was a victim of experimentation that regulation permitted, even if one could not categorically state that regulation failed. In any event, the lawsuit that her administrator brought later against the maker of Enovid reflects the fact that private litigation for products liability necessarily involves an unprevented injury. First filed in 1971, and litigated to decision by an intermediate appellate court of Illinois in 1975[11] and the state supreme court the next year,[12] the case also presents a melancholy example of justice delayed.

It is useful, in a book primarily focused on regulation, to refer to some of the testimony and judicial findings in that private lawsuit, in which the jury found for the defendant manufacturer. The answer to one important question in the case turned on the plaintiff's ability to show a causal relationship between the Pill and blood clotting. As a general matter, the establishment of this relationship was not difficult: The appellate court cited the defendant's own literature referring to the association between ingestion of the pill and abnormal blood clots, and quoted a 1970 FDA regulation which emphasized the need to warn users about this statistic.

Obviously the more difficult problem was the one of whether Enovid had caused Mrs. Lawson's death, and the divergent views which the two appeals courts took of this evidence showed the difficulty of unraveling such causal relationships. One of the defendant's experts suggested that the clots could have been due to obesity and bed rest in the hospital on the first visit. The intermediate appellate court focused on the evidence of blood clots six to eight weeks old in finding this theory effectively rebutted, but the supreme court pointed to the fact that some of the clots were only a few days old. The appellate court rejected a hypothesis that the clots resulted from prior pregnancies, saying that on the evidence Mrs. Lawson had had no problems with previous pregnancies and no prior blood clots. But the supreme court found that there was evidence to support the jury verdict on this score, citing the fact that the autopsy showed recanalized blood clots in the pelvic region—indicators that Mrs. Lawson suffered clots before she took Enovid. Thus, while the appellate court thought it an "inescapable" conclusion that Enovid had caused Mrs. Lawson's death, the supreme court thought there was enough evidence to sustain the jury's verdict for the defendant. If we view the two results together, we are impressed with the after-the-fact uncertainty on scientific matters incident to such litigation. If we view the supreme court's decision as correct, we can agree that justice was done in Mrs. Lawson's case, despite that court's agreement that the "manifest weight" of the evidence supported the general causal relationship. But it is interesting to view the appellate court's decision as representative of successful conclusions to lawsuits brought by women who were in fact stricken by blood clots attributable to the Pill. For it emphasizes the point that "successful" in this sense means as success goes in lawsuits. Even if the appellate court's view of the facts were correct, it would be necessary to count the costs—the ultimate sacrifice of Mrs. Lawson, the suffering of her family, and the expense to the judicial system. To emphasize the tragic aspects of this occurrence, we should conclude this brief summary of a private action by noting how veiled the future was on the day in 1962 when Mrs. Lawson first took the Pill: these events all then lay before the parties involved, including manufacturers and Pill-takers, as well as the various government officials concerned with defining and responding to uncertainty as market experimentation proceeded.

By the mid-sixties, concern about various side effects had inspired sharp inquiry from congressional overseers quizzing FDA officials. An exchange between staff members of a House committee and agency representatives in 1966 underlines the uncertainty of the Government's representatives, as well as the exasperated curiosity of their inquisitors. At issue were limited studies with a combination of two chemicals—the progestational agent ethynerone and the estrogen mestranol—in a compound labeled MK-665 by the pharmaceutical house Merck, Sharp & Dohme. The MK-665 symbol principally described ethynerone, which was used in the studies both by itself and in combination with mestranol, and the colloquy summarized below focused in part on the fact that the FDA had allowed clinical trials of the combination without having required animal studies to demonstrate its safety as a combination.

Mr. Gray, the senior investigator of the Intergovernmental Relations Subcommittee of the House Committee on Government Operations, interrogated Dr. Sadusk, the FDA medical director, on the agency's approval of first-stage clinical trials. Dr. Sadusk testified that the agency's pharmacologist had decided it would be "sound" to go ahead though there had not been animal studies to demonstrate the safety of the combination. Gray next asked whether there could be a synergistic reaction between the drugs when they were combined that would not have become apparent when they were tested separately. Dr. Sadusk demurred on grounds of lack of knowledge, suggesting that the inquiry be directed to other physicians. But Gray pressed on, citing concerns that MK-665 caused cancer in animals. There had been reports that MK-665 might cause hyperplasia, an increase in tissue bulk, in the breasts of rats, and canine carcinoma *in situ*—a cell configuration whose definition is a matter of some medical controversy but which may fairly be described as a form of cancerous condition.

Gray then cited a report from Merck to the FDA, which included the statement that the firm could not be "certain" whether MK-665—that is, ethynerone—was responsible for the hyperplasia or the carcinoma *in situ*, or "whether the combination of drugs is responsible." Gray commented, "Apparently Merck thinks that is a possibility." Dr. Sadusk agreed that it was: "They are expert scientists, and that is their opinion." Now Mr. Gray's questioning took on a sharper edge. Citing another controversial drug for which the FDA required a new Investigational New Drug application because of a proposed combined use, he said, "I don't see for the life of me what is so different about this case." Sadusk and Gray then fenced about the policy of the agency concerning combinations, a policy which had come to require new INDs for drugs that included progestational agents. Now Gray pushed to the question of whether a general policy requiring pre-clinical studies on combinations had existed before the adoption of the criteria then current for oral contraceptives. Answered Sadusk:

> I think one can say in general we have always required animal experimentation as well as the individual components of that examination. But here is where the pharmacologist, by his best judgment and experience, believed that tests initially on the combination should not be required.

A further exchange brought out that although the pharmacologist had written a memorandum on the subject, he apparently had not provided what Gray called a "rationalization" for his conclusion.[13]

Gray next turned to the matter of thrombophlebitis, asking if tests had been performed on the association of that risk with oral contraceptives then being sold. Dr. Goddard, the Food and Drug Commissioner, replied that there were then "studies . . . going on in humans" of the thrombophlebitic effect of marketed versions of the Pill. Gray inquired about the revelations of research on this issue in both humans and animals; taking a lead from one of Gray's questions, Sadusk termed the results "conflicting." Specifically referring to changes noted in coagulation blood tests, he said that no one knew whether they had a "correlation with the production of thrombophlebitis in the female." But, retorted Gray, the "effect of blood clotting . . . on thrombophlebitis" was not the question; the issue was "the effect of these drugs . . . on blood clotting." There followed a colloquy about the existence of studies on this question, with the FDA's Dr. Hodges finally saying they had been done and that they showed almost all of the factors under consideration to be "affected by the administration of the oral contraceptives," but remaining "within the limits of normal." He then referred to the "difficulty of interpretation" that arose from the fact that women who were not taking the pill also had "variations within the normal limits."[14]

At the time of this confrontation between Congressional investigators and agency officials, 1966, the clouds were gathering on the blood-clot issue. This hearing was only a way station on the road to the 1968 publication of the first authoritative conclusions linking use of the Pill and clots. But the fencing and the frustration evident in this Congressional investigation—with the FDA officials finding some of their inquisitors' questions impossible, and the investigators irritated by the difficulty in pinning down the officials—reflected the scientific uncertainties surrounding the use of these drugs by millions of American women.

Yet it did not require definitive studies for the early warning signs evident in 1966 to affect the FDA's approach to the pill. That year, the agency published guidelines for the labeling of oral contraceptives, which included a contraindication for patients who had had a current or past bout with thrombophlebitis or pulmonary embolism. The document further noted, under the heading of "Precautions," that physicians should be "alert to the earliest manifestations of the disease." The contraindications section also included "known or suspected carcinoma of the breast or genital organs" and "undiagnosed vaginal bleeding."

The "Warnings" section of the guidelines mandated immediate discontinuance of medication, pending an examination, upon sudden losses of vision or the occurrence of certain specified symptoms including migraine headaches. If examination then revealed papilledema—inflamed heads of the optic nerves—or retinal vascular lesions, the "Warnings" section said the medication should be terminated. The guidelines also included a list of about twenty adverse reactions which had been observed in Pill users "with varying incidence," ranging from nausea and vomiting to breakthrough bleeding, loss of scalp hair, and depression. The document concluded with a cryptic further reference to thrombophlebitis and pulmonary embolisms, saying they had been "observed in users of oral contraceptives," but with the notation that a "cause and effect relationship has not been established."[15]

These guidelines were intended for use in relatively technical labeling. There remained the problem of advertising. Because it is aimed at physicians, prescription-drug advertising usually is a somewhat more sophisticated kind of puffery than that aimed at persuading laymen to buy mundane products, but still it utilizes a colorful array of techniques and media, ranging from advertising in medical periodicals to slide presentations at specialists' meetings. Indeed, a 1967 FDA proposal to regulate promotional labeling of oral contraceptives[16] dealt with categories including "brochures, booklets, mailing pieces, file cards, similar pieces of printed matter, and audio or audio-visual presentations."

The FDA's definition of "labeling" in this document was interesting. Naturally, it included presentations used in a promotional setting by detail men or those "associated with product promotional pieces." But it also embraced matter that was "promotionally slanted through use of information that is false or misleading," or that was "lacking in balance" in its presentation of products' advantages as opposed to their side effects and contraindications. The proposal generally was premised on the idea that material intended for use by doctors, nurses, and pharmacists was labeling, and that it thus must contain "full disclosure" information including mention of hazards, contraindications, side effects, and precautions.

This promotion-focused document did not limit itself to communications directed at practitioners, but also addressed the problem of patient labeling, concerning which the Pill came to present a particularly interesting history. In the case of patient labeling which contained only "simple instructions or simple dosage information" but said nothing about safety or effectiveness, the proposal did not seek to require disclosure of information on side effects or other warnings. By contrast, it demanded information about side effects, presented "in laymen's language," when labeling referred to safety or effectiveness. Yet this relief was literally only symptomatic: for example, the document named certain symptoms, including severe or persistent headache or dizziness, as requiring a report to the physician, but explicitly said it was not necessary to mention that thromboembolic episodes had been associated with the Pill. Given the existing information in 1967, the date of this proposal, this was perhaps understandable; the most disturbing findings about blood clots lay just over the horizon. Moreover, the agency was engaged in only its initial exploration of the legality, as well as the wisdom, of requiring labeling specifically directed at patients. Even at that time, however, the unknowns about the pill were significant enough to raise the question of whether the FDA should have prescribed a general warning to this effect: "Anyone who takes this medication must realize that it is being experimentally tested on millions of people, and that its potential long-term dangers have not been confirmed, and in some cases not even hypothesized."

In the same year that the FDA proposed this regulation, a doctor working for the Armed Forces Institute of Pathology reported what a lay person might have thought a disturbing finding. The physician, Dr. Herbert B. Taylor, discovered a "striking" association between ingestion of oral contraceptives and "atypical polypoid endocervical hyperplasia"—an increase in the number of tissue elements in the cervix. Dr. Taylor noted the "resemblance" of these cells to adenocarcinoma, a form of cancer noteworthy for its tendency to recur, but his tentative conclusion was hopeful—that "the available data point to a benign interpretation."[17] Whatever the intermediate judgment, it was not a matter to treat lightly, and indeed Dr. Taylor continued his research. Two years later, responding to a request from me for further information, he wrote that subsequent investigation had revealed both that the change was associated with the Pill and that it was benign.[18] This was the technique and the language of science, reporting only facts and loath to engage in panicky speculation. Should a public regulator infer from these facts—or artifacts— that a hormone product, regulating the age-old cycle of human life, might be producing latent conditions that would lead to a less happy eventual conclusion? That remained a question in 1967, at the same time that a survey of obstetricians and gynecologists indicated an "overwhelming" acceptance of oral contraceptives.[19]

The next year, 1968, British investigators led by W. H. Inman and Martin Vessey published the first concrete statistical indication of the kind of problem that not only causes scientists to pause, but produces a ripple effect of concern in the general public. These investigators reported a "strong relation ... between the use of oral contraceptives and death from pulmonary embolism or cerebral thrombosis in the absence of predisposing conditions." Comparing Pill users and nonusers among healthy married women, they estimated that the death rate per 100,000 was 1.5 for users in the age group 20–34, as compared with 0.2 for nonusers, and 3.9 for those who took the Pill in the age group 35–44, contrasted with 0.5 for nonusers. The report is sprinkled with indications of the researchers' caution; for example, their statistical methods tended to overestimate the use of oral contraceptives among members of the control group. Taking into account admitted uncertainty about the risks of thromboembolism in childbirth, Inman and Vessey posited that "On balance, it seems reasonable to conclude that the risk of death from pulmonary embolism during one year's treatment with oral contraceptives is of the same order as the comparable risk of bearing one child."[20]

The investigators' cautious tabulations and careful comparisons now approached judgment. In characteristically measured terms, they noted that British women bore only two or three children on average during their lifetime, "that other means of contraception are reasonably effective, and that birth control may be practiced during most of a woman's child-bearing years." Along with these observations and their statistical tables, Inman and Vessey offered a striking example of the imperfections of information flow about product hazards: despite widespread publicity about the Pill both in medical journals and the popular press, just 8 of 53 deaths of known users of oral contraceptives were the subject of independent reports to the Committee on the Safety of Drugs. Moreover, the reports of only two of those eight deaths came from the respective patients' general practitioners, even though all these doctors were aware of the patients' use of the Pill.

Serious infighting over labeling for the Pill began in 1968, the year of the publication of the British thromboembolism studies. In February of that year, doctors of the medical advertising branch of the FDA's Bureau of Medicine, who had advance notice of Inman and Vessey's data, approved labeling for the Pill which contained the following language under "warnings": "A cause and effect relationship has been established for the following: Thrombophlebitis and pulmonary embolism." The FDA's Advi-

sory Committee on Obstetrics and Gynecology gave its blessing to
a draft with this wording on March 1, but in the following weeks
the drug firms began to apply pressure to soften the labeling. In a
May meeting rent by bitter disagreement, the companies argued
that the British studies had not necessarily shown a cause-and-
effect relation, but only a "statistically significant association."
Within a couple of days of this noisy session, the FDA had
changed the labeling in a way significantly more favorable to the
drug makers.

The story of the agency's relaxation of its position was related
several years later, in 1968, by Dr. Robert McCleery, an FDA
official in charge of scrutinizing the labeling. He was called to
testify about the matter in the charged context of a personal injury suit brought by a woman who had suffered a stroke in her
mid-twenties after taking Searle's Pill, Ovulen-21. This plaintiff,
Anita Lee Vaughn, claimed that she had taken the Pill several
months after the watered-down warning was promulgated by the
FDA. McCleery testified that the chairman of the FDA advisory
group, who had first supported the originally proposed labeling,
drew back after criticism by the manufacturers. Eventually, FDA
Commissioner Goddard approved labeling which omitted a clause
that read, "[b]ecause of the increased risk," replaced "cause and
effect" phraseology with the words "a statistically significant association," and suggested that data on British populations could
not be "directly applied" in other countries. The tensions that the
Commissioner must have felt were further reflected in the fact
that in his own "Dear Doctor" letter to physicians at-large, he used
the term "a definite association"—stronger than "statistically significant" although weaker than "cause and effect."[21]

These events set off an extraordinary public debate over the
merits of the Pill. Probably unmatched in the history of prescription drugs, this controversy has few parallels even in the era of
intense public interest in medical matters that is currently reflected in the news media. Not only was the work of Inman and
Vessey widely reported, but other studies revealed possible correlations between the Pill and other disorders. In fact, in the year
before the landmark article on thromboembolism, researchers
writing in another British journal said they had found adverse
psychological effects in 28 of 50 women who used the Pill. However, this had to be balanced against beneficial effects reported by
11 patients, including "feelings of increased well-being and

'vigour,'" as well as the somewhat more specific finding that 4 women experienced a lessening of premenstrual tension.[22] The uncertainties in the press, both medical and popular, were magnified as adverse reports washed through the population. Reflecting what must have been a general feeling of unease among many Pill users was a complaint to a magazine by a young sociologist, whose girl friend had read an article describing various risks associated with the Pill. His relationship, "a very serious [one] but not yet a marital one, was upset, physically, but most of all, emotionally," he wrote, asserting the "incompetence" of the article. The author, a respected journalist, replied in kind.[23]

As we summarize this history, it is important to emphasize the role of advertising with respect to products which pose uncertain future risks. A letter sent by Searle to its detail men, comparing clotting deaths from the Pill favorably with the risk of deaths in traffic accidents, raises serious issues about techniques used in pharmaceutical promotion.[24] Is it appropriate to draw such a parallel across such diverse risk categories? Indeed, would not the comparison between fatality rates from the Pill and risks from conception or other forms of contraception be the only relevant one? Knottier problems present themselves with respect to another Searle comparison—that of the rate of 22.8 deaths per 100,000 from all risks of pregnancy with the 1.3 rate of clotting deaths from the Pill. The testimony of Dr. McCleery of the FDA in the Vaughn trial mentioned above provided a corrective to this statistic. For him, the more relevant comparison involved the death rate for women whose attempts at contraception had failed, rather than all women. Selecting the diaphragm as a comparative contraceptive method, he noted that its failure rate was 2,000 per 100,000. He then argued essentially that in order to derive risk figures per 100,000 users, one should figure the death rate only on the 2,000 births that occurred following the use of diaphragms, a calculation that would yield only 0.45 fatalities per 100,000 users.[25]

However, the subject is complicated by the perceived benefits to women and their spouses from the lower failure rate and the aesthetic advantages of oral contraceptives over diaphragms. The risk of death or serious disability from thromboembolism is a grim one; but for many couples the risk of pregnancy is quite serious in itself, perhaps serious enough to outweigh that of severe bodily injury resulting from medication. The advertising episodes I have cited illustrate the subtlety that characterizes salesmanship in an area in which the prescribing consumer—the physician—is presumably sophisticated; and to recite the advantages of the Pill is to emphasize the difficulty of the choices to be made in light of the complex motivations of the ultimate consumer.

Despite the FDA's 1968 resolution of the labeling question, the controversy created by the thromboembolism study continued to embroil the agency, augmented by suspicion and concern about other possible effects of the Pill. By 1969, the FDA's Advisory Committee on Obstetrics and Gynecology had appraised the current research on several problems. On the matter of blood clots, it found a relationship established, with use of the Pill "adding slightly less than three percent to the total age-specific mortality in users of these drugs."

The committee's conclusions on the cancer risk were much more tentative. Noting that animal experiments with long-term estrogen use had produced evidence of cancer in five species, it said that these findings could not be "transposed directly to man." Yet—and here the problem on which this study focuses is explicitly defined—"Suspicion lingers . . . that the results in laboratory animals may be pertinent to man." The problem in drawing firm conclusions on this subject lay in that special bugaboo of cancer prediction—the long latency period between administration of carcinogens and the development of cancer in human beings. The committee could only conclude that carcinogenicity of the Pill was "neither affirmed nor excluded." It urged continuance of "clinical surveillance" of all women taking the Pill, and proposed a "major effort" to find out whether or not the Pill caused cancer.

The need for continuing "clinical surveillance" posed questions of its own, including some broad ones about the role of regulation. Besides serious doubts about the effectiveness of that surveillance, there existed the question of how useful the vigil would be if the Pill were a long-term time bomb operating in millions of women. Most vexing was the issue implicit in the understated phrase "suspicion lingers." How much suspicion on the part of how many experts should be required to justify government action with respect to assuring both quantity and quality of consumer information—and indeed as to more direct regulation of the production and sale of potentially hazardous products?

The committee also surveyed the effects of oral contraceptives on metabolism. No definite alarm signs had appeared in this area, but it was clear that the Pill produced "systemic effects" that were "fundamental and widespread," and that "basic information" was "lacking" about their significance. Again, the committee's call was for "continued medical surveillance and investigation."[26]

Do not these statements effectively confirm that marketing such drugs constitutes experimentation on a very large scale? And does this not force us to ask how meaningful the information was that was communicated to the women who were taking these pills in 1969? To exaggerate the point, how disposed would they have been to continue this medication had advertisements appeared on television and in mass-market magazines saying: "Participate in one of the great medical adventures of our day. Previous experience with oral contraceptives on the market has shown that the Pill increases the risk of fatal blood clots for healthy women. Now, join the millions of American women who are using their bodies in the quest for the answer to the ten billion dollar question: 'Does the pill cause cancer?'" Of course, the FDA did not, indeed could not, go to the lengths of mandating such notices. Perhaps, given that "all life is an experiment," it should not be allowed to do so. The agency did continue on the course of "Dear Doctoring" the thromboembolism risk, and the government also granted a $585,000 contract for a five-year study of the Pill, to determine "once and for all" whether or not it was safe.[27] But these events themselves indicate that the sardonic suggestion above, though offered with full recognition of its political infeasibility, has a very serious side to it.

The 1970s did not bring a rosy dawn for either the makers or consumers of oral contraceptives. On January 12, 1970, manufacturers acting under FDA instructions sent revised labeling for the Pill to all American doctors, emphasizing the risk of thromboembolism with references to the studies of Vessey and his colleagues. Hearings held by Senator Nelson of Wisconsin produced considerable impact upon users of the drugs. Nelson attacked pharmaceutical firm literature with such vigor that an estimated 18 percent of the women taking the Pill stopped using it, and another 23 percent seriously considered doing so. But the AMA's Council on Drugs found no medical imperative for this consumer behavior, declaring that no change should be effected "in the present availability of oral contraceptives."

This propulsion of the Pill into the political arena produced further feedback to the FDA. By March, the agency had taken the extraordinary action of proposing a "patient insert" for oral contraceptives. Never before had it been required that packages of prescription drugs must contain information about their potential effects. But the widespread concern about the Pill drove the FDA to consider requiring the inclusion of a 600-word leaflet with each container of the drugs. This proposed document would have contained a "warning about blood clots," with a mention of specific symptoms. It also listed eight or nine other health problems, ranging from heart disease and high blood pressure to diabetes and depression, with the possibly optimistic statement that for patients with any of these illnesses "Your doctor has indicated you need special supervision while taking oral contraceptives." The draft leaflet also mentioned other possible risks to health, and then added a "Note about Cancer." Implicit in the lay language in this note was a point now becoming conventional wisdom, namely that continued surveillance of the drug on the market was necessary: "Scientists know the hormones in the Pill (estrogen and progesterone) have caused cancer in animals, but they have no proof that the Pill causes cancer in humans. Because your doctor knows this, he will want to examine you regularly." In closing, perhaps somewhat lamely, the document urged women who noticed "unusual changes in your health" to report them to their physicians, and urged that those taking the Pill should have "regular checkups and your doctor's approval for a new prescription."

However, less than three weeks later, the FDA's bold 600-word document had shrunk to 96 rather vague words—evidence of the speed of reaction of the drug firms and organized medicine and their ability to bring pressure to bear. The only hazard mentioned in this bobtailed version was blood clots, and there was no indication of the magnitude of the risk. The Food and Drug Commissioner commented, "We decided it wasn't our role to play doctor or to scare people away from the Pill."[28] This philosophy also informed a proposal that the agency published two weeks further into the controversy. That document listed five symptoms that should be reported to physicians, but referred only to blood clotting as a specific risk, and qualified this warning with a reference to "rare instances."[29]

Yet even this proposal did not end the agency's zig-zag course across the complex terrain of politics and scientific uncertainty. On June 11, the agency opted for a two-level documentary approach. First, it decided to require a 150-word package insert for patients, which referred to "abnormal blood clotting which can be fatal" as the "most serious known side effect," and which said that safe use of the Pill required "careful discussion with your doctor." This leaflet also announced that the manufacturer had prepared a more comprehensive document written for consumers, which was available from the doctor on request. The longer document was an 800-word pamphlet, written by a disapproving AMA, which had responded reluctantly to the developing regulatory situation. The chairman of the AMA Board of Trustees said the organization was still opposed to providing this kind of document to patients, but characterized its willingness to issue the pamphlet as a form of *noblesse oblige*. The AMA's view, he said, was that it was better for the professional physicians' organization to publish and distribute such pamphlets than for either the government or the drug companies to do so.[30]

FDA Commissioner Edwards found this resolution of the problem heartening, describing it as an example of "how public and private sectors can work together" despite a "basic difference of opinion." But the president of the Pharmaceutical Manufacturers Association indicated that the PMA might publish a pamphlet of its own, which would refer to recent studies showing that the risks of the Pill were not as great as the AMA brochure said. An interesting feature of this round of infighting was an AMA official's expression of concern that many women were getting the Pill from friends rather than by prescription. Presumably, the publication of a brochure available only from physicians was related to the AMA's goal of assuring that all Pill users were seeing a doctor. "There's only one person who can judge if the Pill is safe for an individual," the spokesman said with an obvious backhand at Senator Nelson, "and that's your physician—not your Senator."[31] He did not explain, however, how keeping more comprehensive information under the control of physicians would encourage office visits by people who already were acquiring the drug outside the prescribed stream of medical commerce.

One party was prepared to litigate the question of whether or not the more comprehensive document should be placed directly in the hands of patients, at least of prescription users. James Turner, a member of Ralph Nader's team of consumer advocates, sought a preliminary injunction directing the FDA to require that the AMA pamphlet be included as a package insert with the Pill.

His arguments on a motion for that purpose, however, failed to convince Judge Gesell that he had a substantial likelihood of prevailing on the merits. Noting the elaborate nature of the rulemaking that led up to the FDA's June 11 regulation, and doubtless cognizant of the fever of political argument that attended the agency's two-tiered resolution of the problem, the judge found that the labeling required by the regulation was sufficient to withstand the claim of irreparable injury necessary to support a preliminary injunction.[32]

The flurry of regulatory activity that made 1970 a dramatic year for oral contraceptives was only a part of the picture. Below the noise level of the pushing and shouting in Washington, the engines of research were gathering steam, and their early output was not entirely encouraging to those relying on the Pill. In January of that year, it was reported that the Pill might be implicated in an increase in coronary problems in women under 45,[33] although the disturbing formal studies on this problem were not published until 1975. Moreover, there came advance news of a problem with the Pill that might affect not merely women using it, but fetuses they were carrying if for one reason or another they were taking the Pill while pregnant. This was the revelation that Enovid, G. D. Searle's pioneer birth control pill, had caused serious abnormalities in almost two-thirds of mouse fetuses whose mothers were given the drug during gestation. More precisely, deaths of mouse fetuses of mothers given the chemical during late pregnancy were five to eight times the normal rate, although fetal deaths were infrequent when the chemical was administered earlier in the gestation period.[34]

Just as apprehensions about heart disease would be confirmed in five years, the animal data on birth defects would find its tragic human counterpart in research published in 1974. In the meantime, other research results coming to public view made it apparent that the 1970 compromise on patient labeling would not be the end of the matter. The years ahead were to add lists of precautions to documents transmitted to both physicians and patients; indeed, even by 1970 it was beginning to appear that some medical hazards might be so great that more stringent regulation would be necessary. During the period of intense public debate about the patient insert, test results on beagles receiving high doses of certain oral contraceptives had begun to reveal a correlation with breast nodules. Like many other test animals used in tumor research, beagles were especially prone to such growths, and the FDA stressed that the nodules had not been found to be malignant. However, the *Washington Post*'s crack reporter on prescription drug news, Morton Mintz, wrote that the FDA found the situation "extremely delicate." There was conflict among scientists on the significance of these results for humans. Moreover, the background provided by the Nelson hearings and the controversy over the patient insert must have made the agency particularly nervous.

In this tense setting, it was reported on October 18 that FDA officials were holding quiet conferences with two manufacturers of the pills associated with the beagle nodules, discussing the possibility of revisions in labeling and instructions.[35] However, even as these discussions were being publicized, a combination of factors was pushing the agency and these companies further toward the extreme alternative of withdrawal, although this effective result was achieved in a strange masque. On October 23, there came an announcement of a joint agreement between the FDA and the two firms—Eli Lilly & Co., manufacturer of C-Quens, and Upjohn, the maker of Provest. The statements given to the press reflected continuing tension and ambivalence. FDA Commissioner Edwards said there was "no cause for patient alarm," and the agency commented that women taking either drug "should continue until advised by their physicians of a change." At the same time the two firms announced that they had decided to stop production of these pills. They emphasized that this was a "course of extra caution," and Upjohn asserted that all its evidence indicated that Provest was "completely safe for human use."[36]

Rather full publicity followed this action, including press releases and "Dear Doctor" letters sent out by the firms to all physicians. The episode raised interesting questions concerning patient access to information in a market featuring product choices of increasing complexity, as well as growing uncertainty about latent risks. Had fewer alternatives existed, the firms' insistence that their products were safe might have seemed persuasive to a sophisticated patient who had studied the public record and viewed the concept of safety rather relatively. Knowing, for example, that the test beagles had received 10 to 25 times the normal dose of synthetic progesterone—the apparent cause of the breast growths—she might well have chosen to continue this method of contraception if the other chemical means on the market presented similar profiles of risk. Yet a greater variety of oral contraceptives was beginning to be marketed. Several models were available, though most consumers could not know which ones were Cadillacs and which Chevrolets, which Continentals and which Volkswagens. Given this availability of other versions of the Pill, even a moderate risk aversion in the consumer might have produced a decision to turn away from C-Quens or Provest if she had a realistic opportunity to consider the beagle evidence in light of a statement in the patient-directed pamphlet that "large doses of female sex hormones have produced cancer in some experimental animals," and also of the long latency period for cancer. Some skepticism about consumer ability to work this kind of medical calculus seemed inherent in the curious compromise that produced the exit of these two pills from the market; the event also seemed to suggest the beginnings of a countermarch by the FDA, apparently motivated by developing caution about long-term risk.

A subissue of the general controversy emerging over the Pill around 1970 related to the amount of synthetic estrogen hormone in particular brands. All oral contraceptives then contained estrogen, but its content was greater in some, including those labeled "sequential" pills—drugs requiring patients to take tablets that contained only estrogen during most of the menstrual cycle and pills with both estrogen and progestrogen, another synthetic hormone, the rest of the month. In December 1969, the chairman of the British Committee on Safety of Drugs urged Pill users to switch to low-estrogen brands containing only 50 micrograms of that hormone. Although around the beginning of 1970 the FDA approved a 100-microgram pill, Estalor, it was anxiously awaiting British data on correlations between estrogen content and blood-clotting rates.[37] By spring, the agency had evaluated the British studies sufficiently for the Commissioner to recommend that doctors prescribe pills with the lowest amounts of estrogen. On April 24 it announced the immediate mailing to physicians and pharmacists of a special bulletin containing a review of data on the estrogen problem, as well as the Commissioner's recommendation.[38] This episode, which occurred simultaneously with the battle over patient literature, emphasized not only the need for government intervention in a market whose complexities outran consumer capacity, but the desirability of a risk-averse agency position in situations of developing anxiety about hazards.

Adding to dim fears of cancer as a possible by-product of chemical contraception, as well as increasingly firm evidence about blood clots, other concerns arose about the effects of the Pill on the quality of molecular life. Another study reported in 1970 dealt with chromosomal abnormalities associated with ingestion of the pill. In a group of women using sequential mestranol and mestranol with chlormadinone for extended periods, researchers found both an increased percentage of chromosome breakage and also the appearance of an unusual chromosomal aberration known as satellite association, which previous research had implied was passed on from parents to children in a form of Down's syndrome. The study revealed that the percentage of satellite association in this group of extended-period users was three times that of a previously analyzed group of four families with Down's syndrome children. As is often the case with such research, this finding in itself did not set off alarms, but it did cause concern. With typical reserve, the investigators commented that "An increase in satellite association may suggest that the person's chances of producing Mongoloid children are much greater but still leaves the question as to the cause of this atypical condition undefined."[39] The abstract of their study suggested that "[f]urther cytogenic studies are indicated." Again the situation recurs: shadows of possible danger materialize; no definitively horrible conclusions may be drawn; more research is needed. Meanwhile, consumers continue to use the product, for the most part unaware of the sophisticated investigations being carried on in the background. The distinctive feature of this case is that the shadow reaches beyond the direct consumers to their unborn children.

For the moment, however, the principal focus of scientific concern remained on the generation taking the Pill, and on the blood-clot problem. A full-scale attack on the allegation that the Pill caused clotting appeared in early 1972 in articles by Dr. Victor Drill, an official of G. D. Searle & Co., the maker of Enovid. Writing in the *Journal of the American Medical Association*, Drill criticized studies which had reported increased risk of thromboembolism because the research was retrospective rather than prospective, and thus did "not measure the incidence of disease." Because these studies always selected both patients and controls after the patients had suffered a thromboembolic episode, they could only compare the frequency of use of the Pill between persons who did and did not have clotting diseases. Drill thus argued that retrospective studies could never provide more than a hypothesis; they could not show cause and effect. By contrast, he cited prospective studies which involved administration of the drug, followed by measurement of the incidence of disease, as showing that the Pill did not "increase the incidence of venous thromboembolic disease of the lower extremities."

In addition to these quarrels with methodology, Drill registered some other complaints against the studies reporting increased clotting risks. These criticisms were of varying power. Perhaps most plausibly, he attacked the Inman-Vessey data for "the degree of variation in such a study" because only 10 deaths turned up in a control group of nonusers when 21.8 were to be expected, "a twofold variation." Drill further noted that Inman and Vessey had excluded from their study the deaths of 49 women who had not been married and 18 who were widowed, divorced, or separated, and advanced the less than convincing assertion that "few, if any" of these women would have been using the Pill. Though this hypothesis might understate present reality, he said with some persuasiveness that the addition of even some of these women to the sample would have a "definite effect on the calculation." He concluded generally that "the hypothesis of a risk derived from this retrospective study [was] not confirmed by any of the other studies" he had researched. Drill also emphasized that Inman and Vessey had found no statistical significance in the comparison of user and nonuser deaths in women with predisposing causes, suggesting that if the hypothesized relationship existed, the increase in risk should be greater in users with such conditions.[40]

A further study by Drill concentrated critical fire on the Inman-Vessey findings with particular reference to the alleged increased risk factor of mestranol as the estrogen in the pill, as compared with the substance ethinyl estradiol.[41] With respect to one drug, Enovid, which combined mestranol and norethynodrel, Drill claimed there was actually an indication that the Pill had a protective effect against thromboembolism. But beyond such "discrepancies and incongruities," he noted that ethinyl estradiol was a more pharmacologically potent contraceptive agent than mestranol, and suggested that it was therefore improper simply to compare the two estrogens on a milligram-dose basis. He declared that when one assessed the two chemicals on a potency rather than a dosage basis, "there is no direct correlation of estrogens to risk." Yet this argument lost some force, given that the drug firms were typically putting higher doses of mestranol in their combination pills. Considering the generality of the literature available to patients, the situation appeared to call for increased regulation even if "absolute dose" was not a proper measure of risks. The problem presented itself as one about which laymen typically would be unable to understand the scientific debate, indeed one as to which most laymen were never exposed to that debate even at a level of sophisticated journalistic summary; and it even showed a forbidding face to the busy, nonspecialist physician who might not have a realistic chance to weigh the technical data. How should regulators react to a situation of such complexity and controversy? At this point, we may venture that they should display extreme caution when responsible experts make a case for the existence of risks that will fall heavily on unsuspecting consumers.

By August of 1972, wariness of the Pill characterized the respected *Medical Letter*'s review of the literature on blood clots, including the Inman and Vessey studies and Drill's article in the AMA *Journal*. The review noted, as Drill had done, that the British studies and some others were retrospective and "did not actually measure the incidence of the disease in users and nonusers." But it also criticized one of Drill's studies for "the use of heterogeneous data from uncontrolled prospective studies." The *Medical Letter*'s consultants refused to consider this data valid, "especially since the studies were not designed to determine the frequency of adverse effects." The report also found fault with a 1971 study which discovered no difference in the incidence of clotting disease between Pill users and women who employed other contraceptive methods. It said the conclusions were difficult to assess, in part because the study was not blind.

The *Letter* advised that it was desirable to keep estrogen content low, but it also took note of an advertisement by Ortho which said it was unwarranted to imply that any of the low-estrogen (0.05 mg) pills were superior to any of the others. This reference incidentally reflected another weapon in the FDA's regulatory arsenal, for the ad had been published at the agency's behest.

The regulatory scheme thus prohibited deception about drug effectiveness as it also did concerning safety. The Pill having passed the initial statutory hurdles on both requirements, this left the choices between them to the more or less educated decisions of the market. In its continuing effort to provide information, the *Medical Letter* reached a conclusion identical to one it had previously announced. Its consultants thought it clear that the Pill caused "an increased risk of clotting disorders." For this reason, besides advising that there should be no more than 0.05 mg of estrogen in each tablet, the *Letter* suggested that "women who can satisfactorily use topical contraceptives or an intrauterine device should be advised to do so."[42]

Medical research is not a pushbutton affair. The start-up costs are substantial, and a single project may take years. This is especially true with respect to what I have termed market experimentation. In cases of this kind, regulatory establishment of acceptable levels of risk must consider the substantial lag time between the introduction of a product to consumers on a broad scale and the flow of research results. Such a lag occurred with the marketing of the Pill, and it was one not fully hedged by the early regulation of the product. But by the early 1970s, the studies were beginning to tumble out of the laboratories. Though not all of this research concerned diseases with the most awful medical connotations, it generally involved painful and disabling conditions. And when combined with the accumulating data about possible side effects, some of the reports of Pill correlations with less deadly illnesses were enough to give regulators further pause. For example, among these discomforting, if not terrifying, reports was the finding published in 1973 that Pill users could expect twice as many attacks of gall bladder disease as nonusers. Investigators who retrospectively studied gallstone surgery predicted a rate of 158 per 100,000 for users, and 79 for nonusers.[43]

In 1974, a disturbing finding was added to the catalogue of intergenerational effects. A retrospective study of cases of limb defects in newborns revealed a statistically significant association between these defects and the ingestion of oral contraceptives during pregnancy or just before conception. The reasons for administration of the drug and the circumstances of conception were various, and included the use of the hormones in pregnancy tests and supportive therapy. Several women who gave birth to deformed children had "breakthrough pregnancies" while using the Pill. A particular feature of the findings in this study was the predominance of male babies in the affected group, a fact which technically suggested a causal association between the Pill and the defects.[44] Yet the investigators appeared to think that the association was more probably secondary than causal, related to an underlying predisposition in the mother. And some characteristics of the mothers of the affected babies, including high fertility and the ability to conceive very quickly after discontinuation of the Pill, suggested that these women had hyperactive reproductive systems. The fact that most pregnancies involving use of oral contraceptives did not eventuate in deformed babies lent strength to the theory that the problem lay in maternal predisposition. The investigators therefore suggested further research on the reproductive and endocrine systems of mothers who bore deformed children, and discontinuance of the use of hormonal pregnancy tests.

This article, published in the *New England Journal of Medicine*, was accompanied by substantive editorial commentary from Colorado researchers who referred to several studies then going on, both prospective and retrospective, probing the relationship between the Pill and birth defects. Their reference to this work in progress emphasizes a recently mentioned point concerning the lag time for research—or in this case monitoring of clinical experience—on complex medical questions. They noted that prospective studies of the problem required "large numbers of patients" on whom it would take three or four years to accumulate data. Pending the collection and analysis of this information, these commentators offered tentative support for the conclusion that the Pill formulations under study caused a "low frequency rate of defects probably acting on predisposed persons." As a matter of prudence, pending more comprehensive results, they opposed the use of hormonal pregnancy tests and emphasized the necessity of showing that a woman was not pregnant before she began a regime of oral contraceptives.[45]

The unfolding of these reports, wrested from months and years of research, evoked the picture of a parade of troubles accompanying the very real and continuing benefits of the Pill. It was as though the observer was standing just past a corner as the parade rounded it, and hence he was unable to see all of the problems that ultimately would march by. But by the mid-1970s enough potential problems had appeared, however heavy their masking and doubtful their identity, that increasing regulatory caution seemed fully justified. The experimental nature of the product was brought home more forcefully each month, as was the fact that the consumer patients of the nineteen-sixties had only the vaguest notion that they were acting as guinea pigs.

Exemplary of further potential for intergenerational mischief was a more alarming if more uncertain hypothesis publicly advanced by a New York psychologist as early as 1969, in a paper published in 1972 and given press publicity in 1975, to the effect that ingestion of the Pill might adversely affect the intelligence of children born years later. The psychologist, Dr. Jean Jofen, had been led to this idea by the results of intelligence tests on small children in a Hebrew private school, which showed significantly diminished I.Q.s in children whose mothers had suffered through the Nazi concentration camp at Auschwitz. Under the explicit label of "sterilization experiments conducted on Jewesses," the Nazis had poured daily doses of estrogen in the soup eaten by Auschwitz inmates. The use of this hormone stopped menstruation in the women, and depressed the sex drive in men. Despite the sequence of hormone ingestion in mothers and relatively low intelligence in children, one might well ask whether the result might not be due to many other factors related to imprisonment. But on this question Dr. Jofen confidently held to her postulate, noting that she could find no I.Q. effects in children whose fathers had been imprisoned in Auschwitz but whose mothers had not.[46]

It must be noted that Jofen's results are vulnerable in other ways. She has revealed that her formal statistics include an important control group, composed of children whose mothers were in concentration camps other than Auschwitz as well as in Russian camps, which is much smaller than the experimental group. She attributes this disparity to the fact that she discarded I.Q. tests when she was told that no drug was involved in these camps, as well as to the fact that members of this group were the hardest to find.[47] As an interesting sidelight to this problem, her research was conducted on a mere $6,050 in private grants.[48]

But if one puts aside evident statistical weaknesses, and judges that Jofen's conclusions make a prima facie case for the causal effect of estrogen administration at Auschwitz, one must then consider the hypothesis that children of the sixties and seventies with learning difficulties might have these problems because their mothers took the Pill. There are strong grounds for skepticism about this theory. Oral contraceptives, after all, use relatively small amounts of measured estrogen, whereas the chemicals used at Auschwitz were poured indiscriminately into the inmates' soup. An HEW official wrote Jofen that he found her paper "interesting but scientifically unsupportable." Yet the hypothesis did seem to merit further investigation, because of its genesis in cases of children born some time after the administration of estrogens, and an official of the National Institute of Child Health and Human Development promised exploration of the question.[49] Standing alone, the Jofen theory did not make a case for regulation. But because of its relationship to other data, it raised the issue of how to respond to a conjecture about risk, developed from relatively obscure research, which was piled atop a number of disturbing results and disquieting hypotheses about side effects.

In this connection it is well to note the need for sensitivity to warning flags that do not bear the stamp of Establishment research. Jofen's 1972 study does not convey unvarying statistical rigor. It mixes some statistics with generalized research conclusions and with primary documents concerning the Nazi decision, approved by Himmler himself, to use the estrogens at Auschwitz. But there are many sources which may shed light on problems of long-term risks. I have referred, for example, to the suggestion that a survey of veterinary literature on limb deformations would have brought the problem of thalidomide to light earlier.[50] Research in such areas does not always follow a straight line, and regulation should give consideration to plausible hypotheses despite some inelegance in the presentation. It seems especially necessary to be alert to the imperfectly developed theory in a context of developing evidence of serious associated risks, and in cases where the tracing of consequences is particularly difficult.

But while we must be careful not to block out faint danger signals, we should not be content with reflexive response to possible hazards viewed in isolation; it is necessary to weigh the risks and advantages of a number of competing alternatives. This necessity is implicit in a 1974 issue of the *Medical Letter* that published a general review of contraceptive methods. By then the clotting dangers of the estrogen-progestin combination were considered established, and other effects had also become manifest: for some patients high blood pressure was an unfortunate fact; others experienced changes in the metabolism of lipids and carbohydrates, the long-term consequences of which were unknown, that were similar to changes appearing in pregnancy. With respect to cancer, the effect of the Pill "remain[ed] undetermined." The report cited studies finding no relationship between the Pill and the risk of either cervical or breast carcinoma, as well as data suggesting that the Pill actually protected against functional ovarian cysts.

Along with this review of what was and was not known, the report provided examples of the balances that must be struck with other methods of contraception. The estrogen-progestin pill was undoubtedly effective, and more reliable than the progestin-only "Minipill," for which the rate of pregnancy was 2.5 per 100 woman-years, as compared with 0.1 to 1.5 for the combination. The performance of intrauterine devices varied, but they were marginally less effective than the combination pills, with pregnancy figures ranging from 2 to more than 10 per 100 woman-years. Moreover, about 20 percent of women using IUDs had to give them up because of bleeding, uterine cramping, and infection. The Pill did avoid these consequences, but by 1974 it was evident that it carried some unwelcome baggage of its own. Besides the clotting and other systemic effects mentioned above, several other problems had appeared. Some were reversible on discontinuance of the Pill, including headaches, bloating, nausea, and vaginal yeast infections; others, such as amenorrhea and anovulatory cycles, would sometimes continue to plague women after they stopped using the drugs.[51]

Thus the debate carried on, parallel to the ongoing, large-scale public experimentation. In the same year, 1974, a study by the Royal College of Practitioners "concluded that the estimated risk at the present time of using the pill is one that a properly informed woman would be happy to take."[52] And assuming consumers with a mild sense of adventure, the Pill arguably was a reasonable choice—especially if one also assumed that all prescribing doctors read the *Medical Letter* or other publications which summarized the continuing gush of new evidence on this multifaceted question.

The story was indeed a continuing one. Through 1974, the only major side effect reasonably confirmed by statistical evidence was the blood-clot problem. But information was now surfacing about other killer diseases possibly related to the Pill. Two 1975 articles in the *British Medical Journal* stimulated anxiety about heart attacks. Let by Dr. Mann, a veteran of the original thromboembolism investigation, a group including Dr. Vessey examined the use of oral contraceptives and other risk factors in women under the age of 45 who had survived myocardial infarctions. It was important, in the view of these researchers, to investigate the Pill as it related to other health hazards or physiological problems associated with heart attacks. To the surprise of few, a by-product of the study was the conclusion that people who want to avoid heart attacks should not smoke, for cigarette smoking is clearly associated with myocardial infarction. The Mann group also surveyed several other risky conditions associated with heart attacks. These included the now well-known coronary peril of high blood pressure, the acute form of hypertensive disease known as pre-eclampsia, diabetes, and obesity.

From their study of the interaction of this complex set of factors with oral contraceptives, the Mann team concluded that the "combined effect of the factors is synergistic," that is, the number of heart attacks increased disproportionately as risk factors were combined. This finding underlines a point that will recur throughout this book—namely, that the synergy problem in product and process hazards is most insidious when it layers one set of risks unknown to consumers upon another which may or may not be recognized by them, causing an even greater increase in risk into the bargain. Specifically, the Mann team found that in comparison with women not known to have any risk factors, "the relative risk increased from 4.2 to 1 in women with one factor to 10.5 to 1 in women with two factors and 78.4 to 1 in women with three or more factors." The researchers thought it a difficult question "whether the association is causal or reflects the association of oral contraceptive use with some other factor." Yet they felt assured that such an association was not due to bias, because of the strict methods they used in the selection of cases. Moreover, the "significant relative-risk estimate" seemed to "argue in favour of a causal relationship," especially given 1970 findings demonstrating a relationship between frequency of reported cases and estrogen dose. The investigators gently suggested the practical conclusion for physicians: Consider prescribing other means of contraception for patients for whom the other risk factors exist. In this regard, it was a matter of particular concern that "in Britain oral contraceptive use is associated with cigarette smoking, and cigarette smoking is associated with myocardial infarction."[53]

The Mann group's labors also concerned the possibility of death from heart attack. In a separate report on that subject, they presented figures quite as worrisome as those on survivors of myocardial infarctions—and particularly disturbing for women over 40. This report resulted from a retrospective study conducted by Mann and his co-worker Inman, also a veteran of the thromboembolism research. They found that the death rate for Pill users in the 30–39 age category was 5.4 per 100,000, as compared with a rate of 1.9 per 100,000 in nonusers. Among women in the 40–44 age range, the respective figures were 54.7 per 100,000 for users and 11.7 for nonusers. Thus, it appeared that the increased risk of death from heart attacks associated with use of the Pill was 2.8 times in the 30–39 category, and 4.7 times in the 40–44 group. It also appeared that the subjects of this study—women who had died in 1973—had taken oral contraceptives for a longer time than the women in a control group who were currently using them. Mann and Inman found the year of these deaths significant in light of the threefold increase in the use of oral contraceptives since 1966, when the Committee on Safety of Drugs first received a report on myocardial infarction in a Pill user. However, Mann and Inman warned that their risk calculations required cautious interpretation because of the number of assumptions involved in figuring them out. Illustrative of their wary view of their own research was their statement that the data were "helpful" in giving a "crude estimate of risk."[54]

An editorial comment on the two studies in the *New England Journal of Medicine* reflected both light and shadow. Samuel Shapiro, of the Boston University Medical Center, found the statistics actually "reassuring" from a "public-health perspective" with respect to the 30–39 group. He said it was "a matter of opinion" whether the risk was acceptable in women over 40, but the synergism point was clearly disturbing to him. Shapiro thought it "striking" that the Mann group had found only 1 of 17 women using the Pill at the time of her heart attack who had no other identified risk factor. With respect to causation of myocardial infarction, he thought the data "strongly" suggested a synergistic rather than merely additive action of the Pill with other risk factors. Moreover, evidence associating oral contraceptives with hypertension, as well as with such other problems as abnormal glucose tolerance and high blood cholesterol, indicated that clinicians "would be prudent" to keep an eye on Pill users, and to consider discontinuance if other risk factors appeared. Shapiro's concluding paragraph defined the then recognized shadow of risk. There was now "convincing evidence," he wrote, "that oral contraceptives cause thrombosis throughout the vascular tree." The heart attack data, he said, "cannot but add to the current uneasiness."[55]

Compounding that sense of unease, it had come to appear that concern with synergism must take extra account of the traditionally recognized risk factor of diabetes. In a public interview, a Harvard researcher declared that use of the Pill by women with "very mild" diabetes would "unmask" that illness. Carefully indicating that this problem was one for personal balancing, he said that if there were diabetes in his own family he would advise its women members not to take the pill.[56]

The heart attack studies were obvious catalytic agents in the FDA's decision in the fall of 1975 to initiate a major change in the labeling of oral contraceptives. In August, the agency notified physicians of the recommendation by its Advisory Committee on Obstetrics and Gynecology that "patients over 40 be made thoroughly aware of the increased risk and be urged to utilize other forms of contraception." It was reported that a draft of new physician labeling would also declare unequivocally a connection between the Pill and clotting disorders, repeat that the cancer question was not settled, refer to studies on birth defects in children whose mothers had used the Pill while pregnant, and mention the increased risk of gall bladder disease.[57] In soliciting comments on this draft, the agency said it had decided to revise the physician labeling first because the wording of new patient labeling would depend in part on the revision of the physician insert.[58] It should be noted that at this point the patient package information was the same statement that the FDA had approved in June 1970, with the addition of a sentence telling patients to notify their doctors if they noticed "any unusual physical disturbance or discomfort."[59]

By the end of the year, as the process of labeling revision ground forward, mounting public concern about the Pill coincided with a TV interview of the Food and Drug Commissioner, Alexander Schmidt, on "Face the Nation." Schmidt's responses to the reporters' questions, when evaluated with comments emanating from his agency, are revealing with respect to the politics of regulating uncertain dangers. He declared that the agency would "take pains" in revising the labeling to document the increase in risk of heart attacks as age went up, and an FDA spokesman said

later in the day that new guidelines would "probably" contain a
warning to women over 40 that because of this hazard they should
use another method of contraception. Should a specific warning
about heart attacks be given to women under 40? Agency officials
had said that because of the substantial increase in risk above that
age, they preferred to direct the cautionary notice to the older
group.[60]

Still another thread was woven into the complex picture six
weeks later, when Mann himself revealed via transatlantic tele-
phone that a broader study had shown a somewhat smaller degree
of risk in the 40–44 group. He said that the new study yielded a
figure about three times normal for heart attacks in Pill users,
compared with the 4.7 number reported previously. Mann also
said there was no change in the figures for the 30–39 group.
Speaking to *Washington Post* reporter Morton Mintz, Mann emphasized his own operating conclusion: that no woman, whatever
her age, should use the Pill "in the presence of other risk factors
for heart disease." The same report characterized Schmidt as
wishing to assess the data with caution, especially because of uncertainties about the role of cigarette smoking.[61]

A number of implications for regulation may be drawn from
this episode. Certainly one should not overreact to partial studies.
And one must be careful not to overemphasize the risk from one
factor that is risky primarily because it interacts with others. But a
central point to remember is this: as new breakers of information
washed through the media, along with various cross-tides of opinion, a gigantic experiment was being conducted on the public. It
was being carried out with products whose long-range effects
could be documented only by extended investigation, and could
be confidently assessed only after the passage of long periods of
time and the use of millions of human beings as experimental
vehicles. This reality bears importantly on the posture that legislators and regulators should take with respect to long-term risks,
and suggests that this stance should be an especially cautious one
when a trend of suspicious data becomes established.

Indeed, grounds for suspicion were increasing even as the
FDA began to publicize its own concerns about the risk of heart
attacks. In the same month that Commissioner Schmidt "faced the
nation," December of 1975, the specter of cancer materialized,
although it appeared fuzzy and hedged with scientific qualifications. A California study reported a twofold increased risk of

breast cancer in users of oral contraceptives for periods of from two to four years—a finding the investigators said might have been due to chance—and a 6- to 11-fold excess risk of breast cancer in women with a history of breast biopsy who had used the Pill for more than six years. The researchers, although saying that these "curious" findings might "represent a bias due to earlier detection of breast cancer" because of greater alertness in Pill users, also declared that the results might "anticipate a true increase in risk." They concluded that "surveillance for long-term oncogenic effects of oral contraceptives should include extended observations on any association of type-specific benign diseases with use of these hormones."[62]

Also hedged, but still disturbing, were two reports on estrogens used not for contraception but for relief of menopausal and postmenopausal discomfort. In one of these studies, which appeared together in the *New England Journal of Medicine,* Dr. Donald Smith and associates reported that there was a "completely unadjusted relative risk" factor of 4.5 that cancer of the endometrium would develop in women who underwent estrogen therapy as compared with those who did not. After the statistics were adjusted for year and age of diagnosis, this figure became 7.5. The researchers emphasized that certain variables required testing—dosages, the specific estrogens used, and treatment schedules. They also noted evidence, rather surprising intuitively, that the risk for estrogen administration was highest for women who had no "'classic' predisposing signs" for cancer. Trying to explain this result, they speculated that perhaps contributing factors "had a kind of upper limit" for each woman, with each having a "maximum but limited risk." More generally, although they were properly cautious in drawing conclusions and emphasized the need for more research, the Smith group found a "credible argument for a causative role of exogenous estrogen in the development of endometrial cancer."[63]

At the same time, the *New England Journal* published an article by Drs. Ziel and Finkle reporting the results of a study of 94 matched triples, each of which included one patient with cancer of the endometrium and two controls. They found as a basic figure that the risk in users of estrogens was 7.6 that of nonusers. Because of other experimental associations of estrogen use with endometrial cancer, Ziel and Finkle thought there was "some biological credibility" in a "[c]ausal interpretation of the association."

This reading drew support from the fact that the reported incidence of endometrial cancer had increased "dramatically" over the time when the Pill had begun to be prescribed, allowing for the relatively high frequency of hysterectomies among American women. In general, Ziel and Finkle thought the evidence for a linkage "rather persuasive," although they also urged further study.[64]

These disturbing findings left numerous questions in their wake. One editorial commentator in the *New England Journal*, Dr. Noel Weiss, listed several inquiries that should be made, including whether different estrogen preparations presented variable risks with respect to the risk of endometrial cancer, and whether the long duration of use that appeared to increase the hazard of that disease might not yield benefits by reducing other forms of cancer as well as arteriosclerotic disease. Dr. Weiss also pointed out that no endometrial cancer was found annually in more than 99 percent of postmenopausal women who used estrogens, and speculated that there must be women for whom estrogens would not increase cancer risk, although noting that it was not yet possible to identify this group. In any event, although many puzzles did remain for research, Dr. Weiss thought there was "no question" that menopausal and postmenopausal estrogen users with intact uteruses should be checked "quite closely" for the development of endometrial cancer.[65]

The problem, of course, was not limited to this one form of malignancy, nor were the overall effects of the Pill fully defined by then existing data. Emphasizing the breadth of the spectrum of risk in the same journal issue, another commentator somberly opined that when the "putative" risk of endometrial cancer was combined with the hazards of thromboembolism, heart disease, and stroke, estrogens entered "a category of pharmacologic agents that must be used with extreme care."[66] And with respect to the incomplete character of the evidence, it is worth quoting a general description of the problem principally addressed in this book, offered by Dr. Weiss in the editorial first quoted: "Unfortunately, questions regarding long-term drug safety can rarely be resolved in a short time. Despite the urgent need for answers, there is little choice but to remain in the dark for a few years more."[67] At that point, however, it might have been added that the margin of that choice could be broadened by further education of consumers.

Still another parallel development near the close of 1975 sounded echoes of an issue first publicized five years previously concerning the sequential birth control pills. Toward the end of December, FDA medical officers urged the Obstetrics and Gynecology Committee to ban the sequentials in the wake of data suggesting, although not proving, that they produced a risk of endometrial cancer not associated with other versions of the Pill. Studying 27 randomly reported cases of cancer of the endometrium, Colorado investigators had found that the "overwhelming majority" had been taking the sequential pills. None of these women had been taking the estrogen-progestogen combinations, although these were prescribed nine times as often, and there seemed to be no predisposing causes in the sample. Dr. Stephen Silverberg, one of the authors of the study, was careful to note that controlled studies had not been done. But he was quoted as saying that he had "the feeling" that the risk of cancer from the sequential pills came from the use of estrogen "unopposed" by progestogen. Bolstering the case against the sequentials were some reports that they were implicated in clotting episodes slightly more often than the combinations, as well as assertions that the sequentials were a little less effective. On the other hand, some advisory committee members reportedly opposed a ban because the sequentials seemed to cause fewer complications while preventing conception in certain young women.[68]

The problem of the sequentials, particularly given the uncontrolled retrospective nature of the studies, squarely confronted the FDA with a recurrent issue treated here: Under what circumstances should government move to prohibit sale of products shown to have reasonable efficacy for their advertised purposes on the ground that they provoke statistical suspicion among qualified scientists who cannot yet nail down their case? The agency's answer was just two months in coming. At the end of February, Commissioner Schmidt announced that the three domestic makers of the sequentials were "voluntarily" discontinuing sale of the products—after a request by the agency—because of what was described as a higher risk of clotting and a "potentially" higher risk of endometrial cancer. The Commissioner rationalized the agency's request on the ground that the sequential pills posed "an unnecessary potential risk compared with other marketed birth control pills."[69] Thus, even though the sequentials were shown effective, the theoretical alternative of informing consumers about their comparative risks was insufficient to save them. Government had stepped in to say it would not permit consumers—even small subgroups of them—to prefer a generally more risky product.

I have suggested that the case of the Pill is especially instructive for a society confronting the continuing problems of uncertainty posed by scientific progress. By early 1976, quickening events suggested that in the future, regulators of dangerous products and processes might profitably base their foresight on hindsight of this increasingly disquieting story with its growing evidence of statistical risk, and act more expeditiously to assure better public information or even less public exposure to products shadowed by similar suspicions.

At this point clouds building for at least three years[70] became perceptible over new physiological territory—the liver. Suggestive of the problem of information-gathering about previously unknown associations between drugs and disease was an informal report to the *Journal of the American Medical Association* that revealed an increase in liver tumors in the practice of some Kentucky physicians who had virtually never encountered the disease before. Particularly troubling, the writers of this communication said, were scattered reports from all over the country of such tumors being discovered after the Pill had begun to be marketed. Moreover, they observed that significant changes in liver function had been associated with the Pill, including impairment of bile secretion in 10 to 40 percent of users. They also declared that "the increasing occurrence of hemoperitoreum [the effusion of blood into the peritoneal cavity] in young women of childbearing age is alarming."[71]

More troubling because of its depth and formality was a study reported by Dr. Hugh Edmondson of the University of Southern California, which defined a significant correlation between the length of oral contraceptive use and the development of liver-cell tumors called adenomas.[72] Edmondson and his associates reviewed the histories of the 36 women who could be contacted, of a total of 41 for whom they had recorded surgically removed adenomas since 1955. These women were compared with a group of others—generally neighbors—who were closely matched as to age, age at the onset of menstruation, and number of pregnancies, but who had not had liver-cell adenomas.

Notably, Edmondson and his associates reported that the

mean number of months of use of the Pill was 79.7 in the patients, and 37.8 in the control group. They found, more specifically, that the "relative risk increased dramatically with duration of use, particularly after 60 months." Their data also revealed a "highly significant" difference between the contents of pills used by the patients and by the control group. Every oral contraceptive at the time contained one of two synthetic estrogens—mestranol and ethinyl estradiol. Of these two, it appeared that ethinyl estradiol was by far the more benign compound, for it was used more than half the time by the controls and in only about seven per cent of the pill-months for which the drugs had been used by the patients. The Edmondson group formulated a technical hypothesis for this, concerning the biochemical necessity for the liver to metabolize mestranol to, ironically, ethinyl estradiol. They theorized that the increased risk to users of mestranol-containing drugs resulted from the "attempts of the liver to demethylate this compound." Unhappily, it appeared that even ethinyl estradiol might be a culprit, for several patients with tumors evidently had taken a brand that contained only that estrogen compound. Still, the investigators recommended that ethinyl estradiol should be the preferred synthetic estrogen in the Pill, and emphasized that doctors should prescribe oral contraceptives with low doses of estrogen and progesterone.

With conventional scientific sobriety, Edmondson and his co-workers recommended "further clinical and experimental research" on oral contraceptives. Specifically as a matter of clinical necessity, they declared that all women taking the pill "should have palpation of the liver as part of their routine physical examination"—a precaution they called "especially important after five years or more of use." Beyond this, confronting the problem of consumer information, they suggested that all users of the Pill "should probably be informed of the risk" of liver tumors, and that patients should be urged to tell their doctors of pain or palpable enlargement in the upper right quadrant of the abdomen.

Taking this case as illustrative of the information problem, it is useful to consider some further questions raised by the Edmondson group's suggestion. If users of the Pill are to be informed of this risk, how should this be done? Should the medical significance of the risk be specified? Or is it enough that the doctor simply mention the symptoms that should trigger notification? How far should regulation go to deal with the case of the doctor who mentions either symptoms or risk very casually? How much of the decision practically rests on the doctor's perception of the strength of the patient's desire for contraception at the expense of a certain amount of increased risk? Given that the Pill will continue to be sold—at this writing some brands are marketed with mestranol—it must be remembered that the FDA has no power to tell a doctor what he must say. It can only dictate to the manufacturer what it must tell the doctor in the labeling, although this does exert some indirect control on the physician.

Requiring a physician to communicate such information to consumers may make him antagonistic. He may sincerely believe that to catalogue a warning on liver-cell adenomas as well as blood clots and perhaps also cautionary references to several other risks which presently appear minor or conjectural, will scare a significant number of patients away from a medicine which he thinks will serve them well on balance. Is there a convincing response to his argument that the FDA is indirectly "playing doctor," and that this kind of regulation is counterproductive? The answers may not be entirely satisfactory to conscientious physicians who share this point of view. They are that science that serves the public must ultimately be responsible to the public, and that free enterprise in both experimentation and clinical practice must entail the widest possible dissemination of information. As a counterpart to the principle that those who invoke the reputation of scientific discipline must rely on scientific method,[73] the controlling axiom here is that one who employs the market must rely on the consumers.

It was in this spirit that in February 1976, the *Medical Letter* recommended that patients for whom the Pill was prescribed should be "informed as specifically as possible about risks associated with [its] use." In saying this, the publication referred not only to the literature on blood clots—later studies had confirmed generally the findings of Inman and Vessey—but to studies on heart attacks and liver tumors. It also mentioned inconclusive data on breast tumors, including evidence that certain progestins had been "shown to increase the incidence of breast cancer in animals." Manifesting the uncertainty about that subject were reports that the Pill could lower the incidence of benign breast tumors, set off against the suggestion that it simultaneously might "increase the incidence of breast cancer in women with already established benign breast disease."[74]

This review outlines part of the informational profile confronting physicians as potential prescribers of the Pill in early 1976. It was over a span of four months bridging this period that the problem of endometrial cancer in users of estrogens for menopause triggered an unusually quick regulatory action. Within three weeks of publication of the articles reporting statistical associations on endometrial cancer, the FDA's Advisory Committee on Obstetrics and Gynecology recommended warnings both to doctors and to patients taking estrogens for menopause. The committee emphasized the need to inform doctors that the pills were to be used only for conditions for which effectiveness had been proved, that lower doses should be employed, and that the drugs should be periodically discontinued to check on the need for further use. It also recommended that a warning about endometrial cancer be placed in a leaflet with every package of pills going to users.[75]

The FDA struggled with the question of how to respond to these developments. Commissioner Schmidt implied what would be the minimum tolerable amount of regulation in a statement to a Senate subcommittee that the use of estrogen for menopause problems was "currently beyond what many physicians would consider wise" in light of the association with endometrial cancer.[76] On this basis, Schmidt said that the agency would require physician labeling that stressed that estrogens should be used only for "hot flashes" and warned about the association with endometrial cancer. But the complexity of the problem, including the many uses of estrogen and its several dosage forms, continued to vex the agency.

In early March it was reported that the FDA was still considering the matter. By that time, the AMA's Department on Drugs announced that it had received "numerous calls from anxious physicians" concerned about possible personal liability. An AMA attorney said that the organization could not answer the question of whether doctors were legally at risk for cancers developed after estrogen therapy. He simply cited the now established rule that doctors could be liable for "not keeping abreast of the literature on the dangerous effects of drugs and not fully informing patients of the dangers."[77]

At the end of March, the FDA issued a warning to doctors about the risk of endometrial cancer. It also specifically criticized the manufacturer of the estrogen preparation Premarin, the American Home Products Corporation, for what it called "irresponsible" inaction in not advising doctors of the risk.[78] Immediately, subsequent developments emphasized the interim nature of all regulation of scientific progress. A study published in the *New England Journal of Medicine* in August 1976 reported that while the risk of breast cancer for women with benign breast disease diagnosed before estrogen use was "about twice" that among women generally, "the risk among women with disease diagnosed after they started taking estrogen is seven times greater." These investigators speculated that "benign disease and breast cancer are part of one response to an estrogenic stimulus—at least among some women." Moreover, they suggested that certain long-term trends of increased relative risk of breast cancer in estrogen users, such as women who had had their ovaries removed, "could be highly relevant."[79] The FDA reacted to this further identification of risk by approving a new labeling for menopausal estrogens which recommended use only for moderate to severe vasomotor symptoms. This labeling contained a new, boxed warning which emphasized that the hormones should not be used by patients with known or suspected breast cancer. Besides also contraindicating use by women with thrombophlebitis, thromboembolic disorders, cerebral vascular disease or coronary arterial disease, this rather somber document also contained warnings on endometrial cancer and the benign liver tumors.[80]

Taking as a touchstone the idea that the government should only warn about clearly defined statistical associations, this FDA response may have represented the practical limits of regulation had it incorporated a direct warning to patients. By then prevailing standards, the agency had moved swiftly in the circumstances as they then existed. From a historical perspective, government had at least two principal alternatives. One, especially drastic, would have prevented the general marketing of estrogens as regulators of the female cycle at the time of their initial clearance, withholding approval pending smaller-scale clinical testing over a much longer period. Because of the built-in dilemma of market experimentation—one finds out more about hazard only by exposing more persons to risk—this might have prevented the endometrial cancer problem from surfacing as quickly as it did. As the existence of these drugs became known, it would also have generated insistent public demand, perhaps furor, from those who wanted to purchase them. The FDA's other alternative would have been to require, from the beginning, much broader cautions to physicians and patients about the functions of these drugs in a delicately balanced system within the female body; these warning notices would have included statements indicating the range of uncertainty and disagreement, even among experts, with respect to possible long-term consequences. Given our commitment to experimentation, including market experimentation, and our reluctance to choose the prohibitory alternative, this would have been the politically more acceptable choice. In retrospect, one may at least argue that it ought to have been the agency's minimum response. More generally, as we approach other areas of biochemical suspicion in the future, the cases of the Pill and its chemical siblings should provide especially helpful instruction.

I have summarized in some detail the progression of medical reports on the consequences of estrogen use, both for contraception and menopause, because I think it is useful to view the problem as it was unfolding. At the time the Pill arrived on the general market in the mid-1960s, many of the concerns mentioned here were only hinted by government documents or were embodied in complaints by people whom prescribing gynecologists called Nervous Nellies. As these problems have taken on urgency, the question occurs of whether the government should have reacted sooner and more positively. Fashioning social responses to doomsaying is a very difficult business. The FDA's position on the matter, which is hard to quarrel with in the abstract, is represented by the premise in its proposal of new regulations in December 1976 that it contraindicate only proven risks.[81] Certainly no one scientific problem is quite like any other, and we should not use previous experience on one matter to jump to conclusions about another. But lines of problems and lines of research do exist, and the story of oral contraceptives teaches that such novel scientific developments call at least for substantially augmented public information about uncertainty, and perhaps even an increase in the authority for and exercise of direct regulation.

Reports on still other problems provided more developing breakers in the waters of research even as the endometrial cancer issue came to a head. The effect was one of wave after wave of new concern about the drugs. Importantly illustrative of both concern and uncertainty is a Stanford study of blood triglyceride and cholesterol levels as well as blood pressure. Briefly, the Stanford researchers reported that among white women in a survey sample, users of either combination pills or pure estrogens had higher plasma triglyceride levels than nonusers, with systolic blood pressure being higher in women who took combinations. They observed no statistically significant differences between those who did or did not take estrogens with respect to diastolic blood pressure or plasma cholesterol concentration, although they reported "somewhat lower" levels of plasma cholesterol in women taking the combinations. Tabulating results for a group of Mexican-American women separately, the study found that those who used estrogen-progestrogen combinations had significantly higher levels of triglycerides and higher systolic and diastolic blood pressure than those who did not take any estrogen compounds. Among Mexican-American women who took pure estrogens, triglyceride levels were higher, but not to a point of statistical significance, and their blood pressures were not higher. In both groups of women, the ingestion of combination compounds was associated with lower cholesterol levels, but these were not statistically significant.[82]

This study, with its differential results both among agents and effects, exemplifies the need to examine research findings with care and to avoid reacting to them with alarm. Yet these results appeared as the fruits of the first analysis of a random sample of a defined population against a background of other disturbing data about the effects of the Pill. In the general area with which the Stanford research dealt, two studies had reported that users of oral contraceptives were two to six times as likely to develop hypertension as nonusers.[83] As of early 1976, one might question whether these findings represented a few random threads of discovery or were part of a developing tapestry of cardiovascular diseases. Yet it was this very uncertainty that created the problem: Scientific endeavor had produced a boon to human welfare, but at the time of discovery was incapable of tracking down all its possible consequences. Some associations were impossible to perceive at the outset, and some of the risks had not yet crystallized.

Each new development concerning the effects of oral contraceptives on a specific organ or body system fueled the broader controversy over how risks from the pill compared with other means of contraception. On one side of the question, research emerging from the Population Council, and published in the Planned Parenthood journal *Family Planning Perspectives*, offered detailed comparisons between deaths from childbirth and from Pill use. These studies gave the Pill a comparative advantage of 1 to 2 deaths per 100,000 under age 30, against 5 deaths per 100,000 women under 25 who used no contraception. The comparative figures gave the Pill a continued advantage of 5.2, as against 12.3 childbirth-related fatalities from 30 to 34, and 7.3 as against 15.5 from 35 to 39. However, at age 40, the Pill death rate rose to 25 per 100,000, compared to 12.6 for deaths consequent on childbirth.

An immediate dispute arose from an assertion by a Population Council researcher that women under 30 using the Pill had "little reason to switch to other methods out of concern over the risk of mortality." The limitation of the study to fatalities inspired critical comment from Dr. Herbert Ratner of Oak Park, Illinois, a public health physician who had been a critic of oral contraceptives generally. Referring to various illnesses which had been found to be associated with the Pill, including blood clotting and heart disease, he said that "to brush off anything less than death as a 'side effect' is scandalous language," and asserted that the cumulation of effects made the Pill "one of the riskiest drugs ever put on the market." One point that Ratner emphasized was that gross mortality rates had "no relevancy" to individuals, such as the "young girl who is seeking birth control information."[84] Even given that personal choice is facilitated by statistical comparisons, Population Council researchers themselves would presumably agree that an important lesson of the developing research on the Pill concerned a point implicit in the FDA's 1966 guidelines—that a crucial need was for the maximum individualization achievable by physicians dealing with their patients.

That need obviously made the contents of physician labeling of great significance. But it also implied the importance of the labeling given directly to patients, then still attached uniquely to the Pill among prescription drugs. In turn, this raised the payoff question of consumer understanding: How helpful is the package insert for patients? A study published in the midst of the continuing debate about the Pill yielded mixed results, but concluded that the document had a "positive impact on patient education." This research included both present and past users of oral contraceptives as well as women who had never used the pill. That the patient insert does not communicate to everyone is evident from the fact that only 64.4 percent of users even know about it; however, of those who were aware of it, 91.2 percent said they had read it and 86.4 percent found it helpful.

Perhaps the most discouraging statistic was the finding that only 64.4 percent of all the respondents to the survey knew that the Pill could cause clotting abnormalities, a fact that seemed "somewhat surprising" to the investigators in light of both the explicit, boxed warning in the package label and the "extensive publicity in the press." In this connection, the study also found that patients from low-income families and with low levels of education were less likely to know about the association of the Pill and blood clots. Rather puzzling was the fact that 32.6 percent of present users, 57.9 percent of past users, and 56.1 percent of nonusers disagreed with the statement, "I believe the benefits of preventing unwanted pregnancy by taking the Pill outweigh the risk to my health." These answers were interpreted by the investigators to mean that the women who gave them "did not consider the benefits of oral-contraceptive use to outweigh the risk to their personal health." However—a point that perhaps common sense or a preliminary test of the questionnaire might have revealed— the researchers speculated that "perhaps some women did not understand the question." Even if they did understand it, other interpretations of these answers seemed plausible, including the hypothesis that many women "found it difficult to make a decision on this issue." Most anxiously, the investigators commented that it was a "worrisome possibility" that some women were taking the Pill "in a sense against their will, either because other contraceptive measures are not available or are not realistic alternatives."

Inquiring whether the fears of many respondents were "justifiable," the researchers took note of what appeared to be "a substantial discrepancy in attitudes regarding the safety of oral contraceptives between the scientific and lay communities." For them, this discrepancy—apparent from a comparison of the consumer responses with general conclusions drawn by studies commissioned by both the Royal College of General Practitioners and the FDA's Advisory Committee on Obstetrics and Gynecology—raised the question of whether their respondents were "adequately informed." Women who found their information inadequate and the ratio of benefits to risks unfavorable frequently complained that conflicting information confused them, or that information was too general or that not enough of it was available. The theme of "insufficient information" was repeated by the investigators in their assessment of the patient package insert. Noting that the insert and the booklet about the Pill dealt "primarily with adverse reactions," they asked rhetorically why only one side of the story was given. They mentioned decreases in various illness patterns associated with use of the Pill, and concluded that "[t]he good as well as the bad should be available for those struggling with the decision of whether or not to prescribe or use" it.

In general, despite the deficiencies in knowledge or comprehension revealed by the survey, the researchers thought the impact of the patient labeling was positive enough to deserve "more widespread use," and concluded that it would "promote the better use and understanding of medications."[85] These conclusions are not at variance with the evidence; nor do they conflict with the view that control of long-term risk requires an approach that blends positive regulation, as in the negotiated termination of the marketing of the sequential pills, with enhancement of consumer information. Still open are questions of precisely how much government should intervene—what amounts of information and opinion it should compel sellers to provide, when it should fund research or require it, and when it should impose prohibitions on products that are relatively more dangerous than their competitors.

A good illustration of the difficulty in choosing among regulatory alternatives appears in the FDA's preliminary announcement of its decision to recommend, both in physician and patient labeling, against use of the Pill in women over 40. Based on the heart attack data, this decision provoked an alternative suggestion by the American College of Obstetricians and Gynecologists, which the organization advocated as "more balanced" and which favored simply urging doctors to give careful scrutiny to the trade-off between risks and benefits.[86] Although the agency's proposal was not one for prohibitory regulation, it exhibited a much blunter edge than the position of the ACOG. The FDA's preliminary decision to go beyond a simple recitation of data reflects a problem implicit in the ACOG's assumption that the choice of using the Pill does, and principally should, lie with the doctor. The decision suggested a belief that the consumer's share in that choice should increase and that more specific information should be provided to her to aid her deliberations.

In the FDA's later formal proposal of a regulation in December 1976, its resolution of the problem of patient information about heart attacks was to repeat in the patient labeling its recommendation to physicians against use by women over 40.[87] That result may have been the best one that the politics of regulation could produce in that context, and indeed the agency's formal adoption of regulations in 1978 reflected these pressures when it discarded the recommendation in favor of an informational approach emphasizing the risk of Pill use by women who smoked, especially in the older age categories.[88] But when we survey the possible range of legal responses to the variety of dangers associated with the Pill, we remain obligated to ask what the level of consumer understanding is. Consideration of how data on this question might affect private litigation provides an interesting analogue to our examination of public regulation. Illustratively, for judges confronted with common-law suits arising from injuries allegedly caused by the Pill, a 64.4 percent level of consumer understanding would counsel substantial liberality to claims of defect and stringent oversight of defenses based on warnings. Moreover, because of the extreme difficulty that usually would be associated with showing causation, such a statistic would suggest a need for continuing regulatory scrutiny before the fact, because it would indicate that post-injury litigation was a doubtful control on long-term danger.

A potential problem even more troubling because of both its long-term nature and its uncertainty is the possible carcinogenic effect of the Pill. Given latency periods for cancer running up to thirty years and even longer, perhaps no better general summary can be made than the FDA's language in its 1978 regulation. Referring to findings that the estrogen used in the Pill caused cancer in some animals, the "brief summary patient package insert" said, "These findings suggest that oral contraceptives may also cause cancer in humans. However, studies to date in women taking currently marketed oral contraceptives have not confirmed that oral contraceptives cause cancer in humans."[89]

Questions do present themselves about how many people read and understand this caveat. By 1978 one might have been persuaded that this language represented a reasonable solution to the problem. Yet if regulators of future products look to the history of the Pill for guidance, they may well query whether the previous requirements for consumer information were sufficient.[90] And given our present knowledge of consumer understanding about the Pill in the context of continuing uncertainty about long-term consequences, including synergistic consequences, the present mixture of uncertainty and potential gravity of risk may yet appear acute enough to justify an increased government role. This might take the informational form of warnings placed conspicuously on each package of pills. Even more direct regulation might be justified—for example, the prohibition of pills containing more than 50 micrograms of estrogen.

Difficult questions of comparisons across categories of risk now arise with respect to the propriety of various levels of intervention. Would it be more inappropriate to require conspicuous warnings on pill containers than on cigarette packages? Would a prohibition of pills of more than 50 mcg estrogen be more destructive of personal freedom than many regulations of working conditions promulgated under the Occupational Safety and Health Act? To ask the questions is not to imply the answers, but only to suggest that in the balance between preserving safety and freedom, regulatory choices of this kind must reasonably be considered.

Among the possible responses, one that commends itself in theory would be to require a conspicuous general warning on the outside of the patient package about the dangers of the specific Pill formula it contained. With respect to first purchasers, this would have no practical effect on consumer behavior; it is hardly point-of-sale advertising. But over time it arguably should have the effect of stimulating patients to ask their doctors for more information, resulting eventually in a rational choice of brands by the patient, aided by her physician. A complementary alternative would require that manufacturers provide doctors with a simple comparative information sheet for the express purpose of showing to patients before the prescription decision is made. Although the FDA could not compel individual physicians to follow this procedure, a formal regulatory requirement of this kind would put considerable pressure on them to do so because of the implications of civil liability if they did not. This document might track the FDA's 1978 revision of detailed patient labeling by detailing the comparative contraceptive power of various pill formulas and other techniques as well. For example, it could report that tablets of 50 micrograms estrogen or more have better than 99 percent effectiveness, comparing this figure with 98 to 99 percent for pills with 20 to 35 mcg estrogen, and 97 percent for the "mini pills," which contain only progestins.[91] In theory, consumers should be able to make choices among figures this precise; in practice, there are questions about how much they will or can read and absorb.

Equally difficult, and perhaps unlikely to receive satisfactory answers, are questions of how closely consumers are able to distinguish risks among different forms of contraceptives, and how rationally they may make comparisons with other physical hazards associated with a variety of everyday activities. Presumably a conspicuous package warning and a summary of principal risks would provide more protection than consumers receive in many other areas of their lives. Yet the FDA's action effectively barring the sequential pills implies that the presently marketed higher estrogen tablets walk a fairly thin edge of comparative risk, bearing a track record which with the addition of a few more adverse reports would rationally justify prohibition.

We may yet face the issue in the future of whether the government should ban a version of the Pill that has been shown to be clearly associated with a high rate of cancer in women who had used it two or three decades previously. Should such statistics confront us, the question may not be a close one. A harder issue is whether the prospect of such events is sufficient to stop the marketing of these drugs, or to require warnings that place much more emphasis on the uncertainty factor than the FDA's proposal did, if present data do not show an increase in risk, but are accompanied by an articulated need for "further study."

A relevant example of a risk-averse posture based on intuitive suspicions, rather than grounded in hard data, appears in the agency's reference to the risk of breast cancer in its proposal of revised regulations. The document points out that women whose mothers had breast cancer are four times as likely to develop that disease as those who do not have this history. It does note that there is no "adequate" evidence that use of the Pill would further increase this risk. Therefore, it refuses to contraindicate its use for such patients, because contraindications should "properly relate to known, rather than speculative hazards." Yet it emphasizes the need for "particular care" in monitoring women with a family history of breast cancer. It says this is necessary because estrogen use "may very well cause rapid progression" of any hormone-

dependent breast cancer that develops.[92] But it also seems that
close to the surface is an undocumented fear that the disease itself
may in some way be associated with use of the pill. Given the
history of the drugs, this cautionary notice would appear the least
the FDA should require. More generally, the agency's position on
this matter teaches that when consumers are confronted with multiple risks through a multiplicity of potential causes, at least informational regulation on the basis of educated conjecture may be
appropriate.

As an afterword to problems of heart disease and cancer, it is
interesting to compare the FDA's reactions to these problems with
its enforcement of a risk-averse viewpoint on a peripheral issue.
This is the agency's decision to require a statement both in labeling and in the patient brochure that the Pill has no value in the
prevention or treatment of venereal disease. The Commissioner
elected to impose this requirement even though he had no factual
evidence showing a relationship between an increase in venereal
disease and the absence of such warnings. The mere prospect that
Pill users might be misled into thinking that it could prevent VD
was sufficient to galvanize the agency. However, the Commissioner rejected a suggestion that would have required the warning
to mention related physiological effects of the drugs, including
the possibility that they might make the genital tract more susceptible to infection. He opined that VD prevention programs were
the business of clinicians and other experts in health care.[93]

The venereal disease question illustrates both the multitudi-
nous nature of the issues associated with Pill and the necessity
for setting priorities. Even given the possibility that a few Pill users
might think they were protecting themselves against syphilis, it
seems fair to say that the VD warning dealt with a matter of less
concern than the others we have discussed, especially considering
the state of both research and consumer knowledge. The agency's
alacrity in responding to a collateral problem, involving no demonstrated risk, contrasts with its caution about imposing regulation concerning suspected direct side effects. The caution was
understandable, but these issues would not go away, and the reason lay more in uncertainty about subtle biochemical events rather
than in consumer conduct.

The subtlety of these life processes, as well as the complexity of
the social and economic problem, provide background for the
continuing search for new contraceptive methods. This analysis of

the regulatory issues posed by the Pill requires mention of the continuing efforts to find substitutes.

Concurrent with the initial discoveries of serious side effects associated with market experimentation on the Pill, a 1969 report described a line of research on biochemical substitutes being conducted in female monkeys, utilizing a kind of released-time capsule implanted under the skin. These pellets contained tiny amounts of ovulation-inhibiting hormones which would be released into the body on a constant basis, preventing conception over a period of years.[94] By 1975, an intrauterine device that released small doses of progesterone received FDA approval. Its developer claimed a pregnancy rate of 1 to 2 percent for the device, which had to be replaced by a doctor after a year's use.[95] The next year, as publications about problems with the Pill crested in a worrisome wave, it was reported that safety tests were being conducted with an antipregnancy "vaccine" on "small numbers of women in at least six countries." The biological effect of this product was to block the action of human chorionic gonadotropin, a hormone essential to the maintenance of embryo life.[96]

Work proceeded, meanwhile, on chemical and hormonal contraceptives for men, but at best the hope revealed by published reports lay in the future. A 1973 study of ten men found that the drug danazol caused "slight and variable reduction in sperm concentration" when used by itself, but that when it was employed with increasing doses of testosterone, there was a clear "synergistic suppression" of sperm formation.[97] Yet although further studies confirmed the ability of the combined agents to decrease spermatogenesis, those conducting them found it "disappointing" that the combination was "not more effective."[98] And while other experimenters found encouraging reductions in sperm-producing levels using testosterone alone, they also discovered side effects which gave them pause, including the propensity of the hormone to increase blood fat in some men.[99] A practical indicator of the level of development was the fact that no one was willing to propose commercial use despite the optimistic inferences that the press drew from some reports. Perhaps part of the reason lay in the ignorance of basic processes reflected in a statement in the 1973 study that "[t]he mechanism by which danazol results in decreased sperm concentration is not clear."[100]

A survey of studies on male contraception, published during the growing surge of concern about the Pill in 1976, reflected the range of possibilities but also the relatively primitive state of the art. The article reviewed efforts at hormone suppression and attempts to inhibit the production of sperm by direct effect on the testicles. It also discussed inhibitory experiments directed at the epididymis, an organ which in effect serves as a gateway from the testes where sperm may be said to ripen, acquiring their ability to move forward in the female genital tract. The sum of this research was that several chemicals and hormones had been shown to cause decreases in sperm counts, but there had been only one study of whether such an agent would prevent pregnancy, and even it did not seem to count for much, because the investigators had stopped other contraceptives only when there was a showing of no sperm count. The conclusion was not encouraging for the short run:

> It remains to be demonstrated that any chemical or hormonal agent, given singly or in combination to large numbers of men over a prolonged period, at dosages low enough to avoid unacceptable side effects, will reliably prevent conception during otherwise unprotected intercourse.[101]

In other words, there were no male contraceptives ready for the market. Indeed, despite 70 years of research directed to that goal, no method was yet available for large-scale human testing.

It was reasonable to assume that experimentation on various methods would continue, and that consumer demand would exert pressure for early marketing of chemical contraceptives for men. The history of female oral contraceptives defined the issues for regulators who would confront the powerful biological agents that will be the male "Pill," and which will bring new uncertainties about their effect on another set of endocrine systems. At what point should these drugs be permitted on the market? What warnings about uncertainties as well as established side effects should accompany them? The answers to these questions awaited further research developments, but it seemed sensible to advocate that extreme caution should prevail and that at the very least, direct consumer information should be much fuller at the outset than it was with the female Pill. Indeed, the argument on regulation of the prospective male Pill closes the circle, for equal sexual protection requires that the same degree of caution be applied to the present marketing of the Pill for women. Even more profound questions of sexual justice with empirical content may remain, but these require extended treatment elsewhere.

Whatever the choice of methods for reversible contraception, we have noted that when the means is risky, an alternative to regulation is litigation after a personal injury has taken place. We have encountered the case of Mrs. Sarah Lawson,[102] representing the mixed bag of compensation possibilities in "products liability" actions for insidious dangers created by scientific progress. But even when plaintiffs in such lawsuits are ultimately successful, it is worth reiterating that the remedy is after the fact; money serves as a kind of substitute for normal life, or even life itself. And the payment of money is ordered only on a finding, after an individualized trial on particular facts, that the medical evidence demonstrates causation. Thus, in taking note of this alternative, which has proved in some contexts a reasonably effective agent of social control, we must also emphasize its limitations—and the consequent need for public regulation.

Regulation, although its adoption manifests a social judgment that the market is inadequate, must itself account for the public's perception of its own good. Interestingly, there is evidence that the public's valuation of ease of contraception ranks it relatively low as compared with disease-fighting pharmaceuticals, not to mention other consumer products. Asked to list benefits derived from science, with the opportunity to mention more than one benefit, 34 percent of respondents to a 1971 Harris poll named medical research generally, and 11 percent specified penicillin. Twenty-two percent mentioned major appliances, 8 percent named longer life span, and only 1 percent listed birth-control pills.[103] The lack of parallelism in categories may be subject to criticism, and it is not clear how directly the respondents were comparing penicillin with the Pill; nor can one determine how many considered oral contraceptives simply a subset of "medical research." Yet it does seem striking that as many as 11 percent would specifically name penicillin, a drug which has been generally available for a quarter century, whereas so few thought to mention a newer product whose benefits were so well and so recently publicized. Whether or not this relatively low polling priority mirrors growing public information about possible hazards of the Pill is a matter of speculation. The findings at least counsel us against a facile assumption that high sales figures represent enthusiastic public acceptance of the potential that some products present for long-term risk.

Finally we must respond to the argument that life holds many risks, and that one cannot hope to shut them out through regulatory prohibition, through government provision of cautionary information or through the kind of continuous personal deliberation that would occupy one's life exclusively with thoughts of physical hazard. There is much to this point, and from different perspectives. When the cost of warning outweighs the probable costs of the danger sought to be publicized, it would require a very strong case on policy grounds to justify regulatory action. And whether our general outlook is one of optimism or of philosophical resignation, we do accept a certain amount of risk in all our everyday living. But there seems an unspoken premise in the "risks of life" argument, a premise of a naturalness that does not exist in the case of the Pill and similar products. Regulation in this area is not an extraordinary effort to stave off dangers normally presented by the environment to a population of cave dwellers. Oral contraceptives and estrogen therapy in menopause are not natural background risks. They are artificial introductions into civilized human existence. Thus, they must be judged by standards of scientific investigation and risk assessment that are appropriate to the artificial effects desired by their marketers and their consumers as well. And this judgment should embody a societal commitment to risk avoidance that might almost be said to be natural to a modern level of existence, where it is assumed that conventionally sold products are not concealed time bombs.

5 The Delaney Amendment: Rough-Hewn Regulation

THERE IS MORE TO THE STORY of legal regulation of the hormones used in oral contraceptives, and it will appear shortly. First, however, it is necessary to discuss the policy problems associated with an unusual piece of legislation which attempts to resolve scientific uncertainties in an extremely risk-averse way. This law, enacting a legislative decision to avoid substances with cancer-causing propensities even at great cost, is the Delaney amendment.

The original Delaney amendment imposed a ban on carcinogens in food additives. A statement of Congressman James Delaney to the House in 1958, supporting his proposal of that first clause bearing his name, reflects the concern that led to the amendment's passage. He focused on the case of a pesticide, aramite. The FDA had first published a zero tolerance for this chemical, meaning that it was impermissible to leave any at all in marketed products, but later backed up to a tolerance of one part per million for residues, despite evidence that the chemical had caused malignancies in test animals. Excoriating the agency's advisory committee, Delaney declared that the establishment of the permissive tolerance in conjunction with suggestions for further study of the problem were "strange recommendations for scientists to make." He emphasized that the advisers had admitted that their data were "insufficient and incomplete" and that more information was needed about the product's carcinogenic potential. In the terms used here, the amendment was designed to prevent what I have called market experimentation: Delaney declared that by allowing a tolerance of one part per million for aramite, the FDA had created a situation in which "once again, as so often in the past, the public became a guinea pig."[1]

The Delaney amendment must be understood in the context of the food additives law of 1958 of which it is a part. The legislative history is instructive. The Senate committee report on the original bill, asserting that most food processors were already behaving responsibly in testing additives but that a few were not,

142

proposed to require premarketing investigations of food additives as a prerequisite to regulations allowing "safe use." The committee specifically referred to the fact that one could sell an untested additive without pretesting on generations of mice, "for as long a time as it may take for the Government to suspect the deleteriousness" of the product.

A House committee report described the proposed law's "safe use" concept as requiring "proof of reasonable certainty that no harm will result from the proposed use of an additive." Concerned that requirements of animal testing might permit findings of hazards on the basis of administering "inordinate amounts" of substances, the committee emphasized that it would be unwise to require proof "beyond any possible doubt" that an additive could cause no harm under "any conceivable circumstances." Thus the law provided for the setting of "tolerance limitations,"[2] describing precise levels of additives that could be used in specified products. Those determining the safety of additives were to consider the "probable consumption" of the additive and its "cumulative effect," taking into account other related substances in the diet.

Importantly, the bill required the Secretary to consider other factors "generally recognized as appropriate for the use of animal experimentation data," in the opinion of experts "qualified by scientific training and experience" to judge the safety of food additives. Thus the proposed law mandated the use of scientific expertise, and required the exercise of judgment by the experts. The Senate committee emphasized the notion of "informed judgment based on educated estimates," with a balance thus struck between protection of the public health and "sound progress in food technology."[3] This balancing presumably would protect the public from the entire range of harms to which it might be exposed. One among these was the specter of cancer, for the investigation and data required included information about carcinogenicity, thus shielding consumers from "possible harm on this count."

But Congressman Delaney, to whom the Senate committee gave full credit for his persistence in shaping the legislation over a period of six years, was not satisfied. When the report spoke of protecting the public from "possible harm" evidently it was dealing in probabilities, and that was not enough for a man whom the committee made a point of commending for the "amount of time and energy" that he had devoted to "the fight against cancer."

Delaney's proposal of his amendment established a proviso to the general rule of "safe use" based on scientific judgment. Under the amendment,

> No additive shall be deemed to be safe if it is found to induce cancer when ingested by man or animal, or if it is found, after tests which are appropriate for the evaluation of the safety of food additives, to induce cancer in man or animal.

The Senate committee piously applauded the Congressman for taking this, as well as "every other opportunity," to focus on the carcinogenicity of "various substances." But it stressed that in its opinion the original bill was aimed at all substances "the ingestion of which reasonable people would expect to produce not just cancer but any disease or disability." Ingenuously, the committee added, "[W]e believe the bill reads and means the same with or without the inclusion of the clause." Arguably, this was wrong. The strenuous opposition of the producer community only served to indicate that the Delaney clause potentially possessed a potent independent meaning: If the agency were governed only by a general safety standard, at least in theory it might be disposed to approve a weak carcinogen for use. The Delaney clause, however, removed the judgment from the agency and deemed it unreasonable per se to take any chance with a long-range danger of carcinogenicity.

The Delaney amendment of 1958, later to be joined by another principal "Delaney clause" and a third, technical amendment with the same language, became the subject of political fire and scholarly dispute. As we analyze the subsequent history of the provision and the arguments about its wisdom, it is well to remember that at the time of its original passage, as now, scientists were quite ignorant about the process of carcinogenesis.

Since this ignorance about how cancers occur was such a direct trigger for passage of the amendment, it is useful to examine the model-building approach that scientists have taken in their assaults on the problem. One of these models posits a process of biologically active substances—"effectors"— reacting with organic constituents labeled "receptors." A complex set of principles and equations leads to the conclusion that "as dosage is increased, all reactions of the effector will be increased and the effects produced will be augmented."[4] In this view, and taking causation in the scientific sense as a quantitative definition of relationships, a carcinogen would be no more than a substance that "increases the incidence of cancer in exposed animals."[5]

Another hypothesis, analogized from experimental induction of cancer in mice with ultraviolet light, posits that chemical carcinogenesis is "a cumulative process which begins with the first dose of the cancer-inducing agent." Following this argument, a National Cancer Institute specialist theorized that there was a "threshold dose" below which no cancer could be produced. However, it was "very difficult" to determine what the threshold was, and there was no basis on which to generalize with certainty from test animals to human beings. In the effort to fashion a system of regulation, problems also arose from the facts that while single doses of certain agents could result in detectible cancers if they were large enough, there was no "adequate knowledge" about the effect of repeated small doses. In general, the uncertainty surrounding the subject caused this expert to say that he could not see "how we have any sound basis for assigning tolerance doses or tolerance levels for cancer-inducing agents." The practical counsel, he declared, was to keep "any substances known to induce, or suspected of inducing cancer at as low levels as feasible."[6] Lack of knowledge, including the impossibility of knowing the relation between cancer in test animals and in man, was a factor in similar views put forth by others. A scientist quoted by Delaney opined that "[a] conservative position would . . . be to limit artificial food additives to as small a list as possible sufficing to meet actual needs for production and distribution of food."[7]

Passage of the 1958 legislation did not end debate on the merits of these hypotheses and opinions. Hardly a year later, a storm of discontent had broken around the Delaney amendment. Representative Henry Dixon of Utah, a former president of an agricultural college, described the feeling of many members of Congress that to oppose the amendment would have been "voting for cancer."[8] Speaking of the legislation's implications for farmer and processor behavior, and its ramifications for the economy, he listed a number of concerns. Besides the fact, often noted by critics, that commonly used products could cause cancers in untypical test administrations, he referred to the development of a technology that was driving the level of detectable residues down toward one part per billion. These points were disturbing but did not make a dispositive case against the amendment. At least in the more general branch of the amendment, the problem of cancer-forcing through experiments was mediated by the statutory language "tests . . . appropriate for the evaluation of the safety of food additives." The unqualified language of the ingestion clause was stronger medicine. But it was certainly rational if one believed that there was no safe level for chemical carcinogens. Moreover, if that was the assumption, the technological point that detection methods were becoming more sensitive did not overcome the general case for the amendment, although it might change the risk-benefit calculations in many applications.

A different set of problems, in focus at the time, had arisen because of fallout from "publicity" about the "cancer scare." Congressman Dixon cited in particular an incident involving the confiscation of a carton of Florida celery—"properly" done because of pesticide contamination—which was followed by a 50 percent drop in the price of all Florida celery, including much that presumably was uncontaminated. The publicity, he said, was "greatly exaggerated" abroad as well as at home, and threatened to affect the U.S. export market. The Congressman's complaint thus suggested that an unwonted twist had occurred on the *in terrorem* effect of enforcement that singles out one case for punishment. The usual rationale for that kind of enforcement is its deterrence to the conduct of other potential wrongdoers. But making examples out of offenders in this way, the argument seemed to go, would adversely affect the economic relationships of even upstanding sellers. And although Representative Dixon did not say so, this in turn introduced a question of fairness that frequently runs near the surface in this discussion: Whether regulation of product hazards should entail compensation for innocent producers.

Another concern that Dixon did express was related to the boost in farm production—40 or 50 percent since World War II—that was said to be attributable to agricultural chemicals. These estimates lent force to a balancing argument based on total welfare: A really substantial increment to output, made possible by products carrying an uncertain long-term risk, might be worth the chance because of the benefits presently conferred on the economy generally—not merely as a matter of comfort and convenience, but of providing a decent existence. Congruent with that line of thought was the assertion that tight regulation of agricultural chemicals would drive research away from that area at a time when it was sorely needed. Relating dollars to disincentives, an official of a drug firm said that it required two to five years and from $750,000 to several millions to develop a new product, and declared that in the wake of the Delaney amendment, his company had stopped work "on items of this kind."[9] A most poignant example of the effects on research had to do with DDT—then not yet publicized as a villain. The fact that mosquitoes were beginning to become resistant to DDT underlined the need for more inquiry directed at developing substitutes,[10] and amplified the lament that the effect of the Delaney amendment was to establish barriers to innovative research. An obvious inference, which had to be faced by those who focused their fears on long-term risk, was that lives lost to mosquito-borne disease were lost more immediately, and more surely, than those possibly given up to cancers 10 or 20 years hence.

An editorial in the *Farm Journal* echoed the chorus of concern in the agricultural community. The "pesticide world," it said, "has been thrown into confusion." The FDA was not approving "any new food additive." HEW officials were scaring people with press conferences at which they raised the bugaboo of cancer in order to "emerge as the great defender of the people."[11] The focal point as a matter of legal policy was the *Farm Journal*'s complaint that all this was the result of a law that left "no room for scientific judgment."

The criticism of the Delaney amendment in 1960 was not merely a response to its presence in the food additives legislation. Its opponents now confronted a threat in another sector—the proposal that a similar clause be added to a bill requiring formal approval for color additives. A particular concern expressed by supporters of this bill, which provided for general safe-use regulation as well as embodying a Delaney clause on carcinogenicity, was the length of time it would have taken the FDA to comb through and test all of the color dyes then on the market. With then existing staff it was figured this would take 20 years, during which, as Delaney remarked, the public would be at risk of "daily exposure to dyes which have not been clearly proven to be safe."[12] The proponents of the new edition of the clause also offered other arguments, on rather specific problems. For example, added to the theme of the long-term risk and its uncertainty was an alarm about a potential special vulnerability of children, sounded in a statement by the president of the new Federation of Homemakers. Speaking particularly about the use of color dyes in lipsticks, she suggested there might be a problem in cumulative use of such products beginning at an age at which the cells are still dividing rapidly.[13]

Weaving around specific issues of this kind, it is the large theme of uncertainty about safe doses which appears and reappears in the history of the amendment. One of its principal vocalists, surprisingly, was Arthur Flemming, the Republican Secretary of Health, Education and Welfare. Quoting from a summary of research by Dr. G. Burroughs Mider, he said: "No one at this time can tell how much or how little of a carcinogen would be required to produce cancer in any human being, or how long it would take the cancer to develop."[14] From this premise of indeterminacy, Flemming developed an explicitly risk-averse position, one which blended a recognition of the inability of consumers to bargain on the question: "In the light of the rising number of cases of cancer, why should we take that risk? Why shouldn't the Government do everything possible to see to it that we do not involuntarily take that risk?"[15]

There was seeming irony in the Delaney clause's establishment of a counterpoint to the emphasis on judgment that the leading supporter of the color additive bill said characterized "modern concepts of consumer protection." Indeed, Congressman Oren Harris, speaking for the general safe-use approach of the bill, decried a situation in which, if a color were found to be toxic in laboratory animals at high doses, it could not be cleared for the market, "even though its actual level and manner of use may be completely safe."[16] The modern climate of opinion favored safety legislation providing for the use of judgment, both as a matter of consumer welfare and producer protection. How, then, could one support the Delaney amendment's apparently Neanderthal insistence on the prohibitory meat ax? Secretary Flemming supplied an answer with his insistence that "the [Delaney] clause allows the exercise of all that judgment that can safely be exercised on the basis of our present knowledge."[17] In this view, limitations on knowledge imposed limitations on judgment; until there was a "breakthrough" in cancer research, there simply was "no scientific basis on which judgment or discretion could be exercised in tolerating a small amount of a known carcinogenic color or food additive." This logic seemed to neglect the fact that all our dealings with uncertainty require judgment. However, Congressman Harris found himself able to cite Secretary Flemming's

remarks approvingly, while reporting that his committee had recommended a Delaney clause in a color-additive bill otherwise
based on the issuance of safe-use tolerances. The basic rationale
was "the uncertainty surrounding the determination of safe tolerances for carcinogens."

On the other side of the 1960 debates on the Delaney measure,
two lines of attack developed. One was essentially to gut the
amendment by giving the Secretary the power to determine from
expert evidence that under proposed conditions of use there was
"no reasonable basis to conclude" that an additive would present a
carcinogenic hazard. The other, focused on additives in animal
feed, was to permit sale of products in which no residue was
found in the edible portion of the carcass.[18]

Interestingly, one of the objections to the Delaney amendment
represents a somewhat curious reversal of Calabresi's thesis[19] that
there are some risks that will be consistently undervalued by consumers. This is the argument, which filters through the remarks
of some Congressional opponents of the amendment, that people
are so emotional about the threat of cancer that they are swayed to
an unnecessarily risk-averse position. As indicated by a Congressman's lament quoted above, the argument goes on to suggest
that legislators were pushed even further beyond an economically
rational solution because of a perception that a vote against Delaney would be counted as a vote for cancer. Although this view is
not to be dismissed lightly, I think that it fails to give adequate
weight to the very real physiological and psychological basis for the
fear of cancer. Risk aversion of this sort is a part of knowledgeable
consumer demand, sensitized to the severity of possible harm.
The Delaney clauses are arguably a proper political manifestation
of a rational attitude toward the risk of a dread disease.

When a law emerged from this debate, it contained the original Delaney language, but additionally it permitted a degree of
"scientific judgment": A manufacturer wishing to challenge the
agency's decision that a color additive was a carcinogen could ask
the Secretary to appoint an advisory committee of experts selected
by the National Academy of Sciences. This committee would
submit a report and recommendations, on the basis of which the
Secretary could take initial or modifying action.[20] As a Congressional proponent of this provision said, it did not modify the
absolute ban on carcinogens in the Delaney amendment; what it
did do was to "take into account the fact that men of science might

have divergent views on the same question," thus preventing "arbitrary action."[21]

Following the passage of this slightly compromised version, complaints about both the substance and administration of the law came from various sources. In 1961—three years after the Delaney amendment was tacked onto the food additive law, and the year after the color-additive legislation—one critic focused on the lack of research resources in the FDA. He asserted that there were "innumerable" consumer items that had never been "adequately tested" because of the lack of "quick, economical, and reliable methods."[22] Since it was the manufacturers' burden to conduct tests not only for carcinogenicity but for many other side effects of chemicals, this criticism apparently implicated the FDA's inability to review manufacturers' data generally. This did not, however, relieve the specific concerns of those who believed the amendment a wise addition to the food and drug laws.

On another front, the provision itself encountered sustained political opposition. By 1962, as Congress proceeded to consider a substantial revision of the process of FDA clearance of new drugs, producers of animal feeds were mounting an increasingly vigorous attack on the Delaney amendment. One source of their unhappiness was the rather whimsical effect of a grandfather clause in the original amendment for existing product uses. But the focus of their complaint was the claim that they were prohibited from selling products which the FDA would call safe for use as far as the feed animal was concerned and which left no residue in the animal's tissues.[23]

The pressure thus generated resulted in the passage of legislation modifying the original Delaney amendments to both the food and color additives laws. This 1962 provision, enacted with little congressional debate, cancelled the application of the Delaney clause to additives in animal feed that were found not to "adversely affect the animals for which such feed is intended," when no residue was found in the carcass after slaughter.[24] Objection came from Congresswoman Leonor Sullivan, who pointed out that a "no residue" standard would permit the sale of products in which future testing methods would reveal the presence of carcinogens that had been there all the time but had been undetectable.[25]

Given the modification on animal feed, however, it is clear that by 1962 Congress emphatically believed in the Delaney amendment as an instrument of public policy. Indeed, in 1967, Congress approved still another Delaney clause, in the animal drug amendments of that year.[26] This enactment was rather perfunctory, and effectively did not alter coverage already existing. It did include the exception passed in 1962 canceling the application of the Delaney rule to the use of animal feed if it could be shown that no residues appeared in the edible flesh of slaughtered animals. Generally, however, the 1967 version provides some evidence that the potential application of the clause did not outrage later legislators.

It is argued with some basis in the legislative record that the Delaney amendment—criticized as a "hobby-horse" of the Congressman whose name it carried—was a "lesser evil" accepted by HEW and the supporters of the food additives law in order to have a bill that would pass.[27] A proponent of this reading of history notes that Delaney's original proposal was even more stringent, barring products carcinogenic in any form of administration, and was softened after a response by Assistant Secretary Elliot Richardson and HEW's offer of a draft which proscribed only substances that caused cancer when "ingested."[28] A description of events slightly different in its shading than the "lesser evil" label may yield a more meaningful reflection of political reality: Taking into account that the broad bill was the principal focus of concern, and that Delaney had "no enthusiastic riders" for his amendment, it would characterize the matter as ventilated, considered, and, in the usual spirit of legislative process, compromised.

Whatever the most objective interpretation of the historical origins of the Delaney amendments, the advance of research technology has figured importantly in the general arguments over their wisdom. In particular, the increasing sensitivity of detection devices has thrown the problem of assessing additives into a new light. Scientists have now achieved the capacity of measuring one part of a substance in a billion, and the range of one in a trillion appears within reach.[29] Because of the very fact that these methods find substances where none were previously known to be present, they effectively expand the statutory class of "food additives." Most importantly, this technology enables detection of unintended additives as well as planned ones, a fact that could lead to characterizing some very ordinary products as contaminated. Thus it has been noted, for instance, that minute quantities of zinc compounds in galvanized cans will dissolve in milk.[30]

A parallel point on research problems implies the possibility of overreaction on carcinogenicity. Inferences that particular substances cause cancer may be unfounded for many reasons. For one thing, the substances used in testing may have been contaminated or may have undergone chemical changes. Illustratively, there is a case in which three batches of sesame oil induced no cancers in laboratory animals, but a fourth that had been on the shelf for fifteen years did. And in an instance of induced chemical change, sesame oil heated to 350° centigrade was found to be carcinogenic, although unheated sesame oil was not.

Changes not only in test materials but in conditions of administration may affect results: For example, some food dyes will produce cancer in animals if administered under the skin, but not when given by mouth. At the same time, significant problems arise from erroneous interpretations of data, particularly with reference to statistical inferences about the relation of administration of a chemical to frequency of tumors that occur spontaneously in test animals.[31]

These potential pitfalls[32] provide significant background for the continuing assaults on the Delaney amendment. Among the principal criticisms of the legislation are two facets of the argument that it allows no room for rational weighing of advantages and disadvantages. One of these complaints is that the statute does not permit scientists to offer their professional judgments. Another is that it prevents regulators from making cost-benefit analyses of a product that has been shown in some cases to produce cancer in experimental animals.

In assessing these arguments, it is useful to begin with an objective scientific definition of causation. In a valuable critical discussion of the Delaney amendment by Charles Blank,[33] we are enjoined to limit this definition to the terms of a "quantitative relationship between an independent variable (a 'cause') and its dependent variable ('the effect')."[34] With the overlay of meaning that this definition takes on for biologists, the "cause" of a disease is "any factor whose increasing magnitude is accompanied by increasing incidence or severity of the disease in the experimental population."[35] It is practically a truism that most untoward events have multiple "causes," and scientists speaking of the "cause" of a disease typically mean a single factor that is easiest to manipulate prophylactically.[36] This dispassionate kind of analysis provides lawyers with a method of looking at physical events that serves as a balance wheel against the less rigorous and somewhat metaphysical way in which causation receives its practical definition in the public and private law related to hazardous products and activities.

On the basis of this definitional approach to causation, it has been contended that it is irrational to make regulatory distinctions between weak carcinogens and toxic substances which have not been shown to cause cancer.[37] Blank, a biologist-lawyer, argues that acute poisons and carcinogens are so close in functional effect with reference to the question of safe dosage that there is "no more an absolutely safe dose for an acute poison than there is for a carcinogen."[38] He says that the real question is what the acceptable level of risk is, presumably for the average person, using the example of a one and one-half ounce shot of whiskey, which is safe for practically everyone but fatal to the ulcer patient.[39] Yet his selection of this illustration underlines an important problem—that of inadequate knowledge about what is safe for the average person. Putting aside the ethical questions involved in the exposure of "subaverage" individuals to particular risks, the case of the shot of whiskey is one in which there is information based on human experience. The case of even weak carcinogens is one filled with uncertainties arising out of animal data.

It should be pointed out that animal experiments do establish gradations in carcinogenic effect along a continuum of chemicals,[40] and that "within limits, any given incidence of cancer may be achieved by applying high concentrations of weak carcinogens or low concentrations of strong carcinogens."[41] The logical conclusion is that weak carcinogens at low levels will not cause cancer and should be permitted on the market. However, a major qualification to this logic is that indeed the basis for decision will invariably be one of animal data, and thus room for argument will remain about the existence or strength of carcinogenic effect for human beings. There is no avoiding the likelihood that a Delaney-type policy will exclude from commerce some animal carcinogens which do not in fact cause cancer in people. But the reason for doing this—even the reason for prohibiting sale or use of low doses of products that are animal carcinogens only at higher doses—is one of aversion to particularly dreadful risk. Indeed, those who share this aversion might argue that a vice of the

Delaney amendment is that its presence leads consumers to believe that the food on their tables is fully protected from carcinogens. This belief is erroneous; the clause does not, for example, embrace substances that naturally occur in foods, such as the potent carcinogen aflatoxin in peanuts.

Another important point concerns the meaning of legislative language. Specifically, it must be noted that the definition of carcinogens in the present Delaney clauses is not totally inflexible. The question of whether there was room for interpretation in this area lay in the background of Senatorial debate on the color-additives amendment. On that occasion the reporting committee chairman, Senator Hill, responded "I would say so" to a question by a concerned Senator Javits as to whether a "rule of reason" would be applied in agency interpretation of the amendment. This debate, in which Javits explicitly expressed his anxiety about the economic effects of the clause on producers, manifested the legislative tension over the subject in an almost humorous way. Praise of Delaney for his persistence and concern for the health of the public mingled in several exchanges with the argument that "application of the law," instead of "'go[ing] overboard,'" should "be fair."[42]

It is notable, with respect to the interpretation question, that a scientist-lawyer who has strongly criticized the Delaney amendment has himself showed that there are significantly different ways one could read the clause. These range from an interpretation that bans only the addition to food of chemicals that would "materially" affect the incidence of human cancer to a reading that proscribes any substance "that can be used in some particular experimental design to augment, if ever so slightly, the incidence of cancer in experimental animals."[43] It appears obvious that the considered passage of the amendment on two separate occasions, and its routine re-enactment a third time, indicated a desire to go beyond the first meaning. If the prohibition on substances that do "induce cancer" when ingested establishes a margin of safety with which many scientists quarrel, the trio of enactments confirms a Congressional commitment to a high degree of risk aversion. Moreover, the expression of an appropriateness criterion with respect to testing by other forms of administration—and the opportunity to request an advisory committee in the case of color additives—provide counterweights against the use of irresponsible experimental designs in that research. And if the balance in the ingestion clause is uneconomic in the short run, it no longer can be said to be hastily struck; nor, given the nature of the beast it seeks to contain, can it be condemned as irrational.

As we consider the broader potential consequences of the Delaney amendment, we cannot ignore the possibility that economic conditions could arise in which it might seriously fail its heralded purpose of life-saving. Illustratively, widespread and prolonged drought, causing drastic reductions in the food supply, would create a situation in which we would be disposed to use even proved carcinogens to squeeze out more food from depleted resources. A more currently realistic example, employed to show that reducing hypothetical cancer risk can cause increased overall danger to life, involves the use of nitrites as preservatives. Nitrites inhibit botulism, a fact which explains one approval of their use, in connection with preservation of Great Lakes chub.[44] But it is necessary even in that case to ask not only what the dollar contribution to the economy is—in the sense of making available food products that could not otherwise be distributed—but whether other substances are reasonable substitutes as food preservatives. It would also be important to know whether the enforcement of a higher standard of care in present methods of transportation and storage could significantly prevent botulism. The fact that there is a high probability of carcinogenic effect associated with nitrites— clearly a basis for banning them as a color additive—ordinarily would provide strong reasons for Delaney-type regulation of them as preservatives. Although the FDA has taken the position that a technical statutory exemption for prior use permitted nitrites to escape the application of the clause, a question arose in 1977 about the validity of this interpretation. Speaking more in policy terms, if one considers the matter as an original question of whether it would be wise to apply the Delaney clause to nitrites as preservatives, one must conclude that the problem is a difficult one, presenting the need to weigh a clear present risk against a long-term one that is uncertain but judged to be of high probability. Yet it should be stressed in this regard that a principal practical justification for the amendment lies in the very breadth of its signal to producers and regulators across the entire range of food categories; the provision carries with it the implicit theory that along that spectrum taken as a whole, it protects against more risks than it generates. It is true that if the food supply included a significantly larger number of actual risks, or if it was quite

shrunken, the Delaney solution would properly incur public dis-
favor. As matters stand, however, it represents a reasonable political reaction to uncertain danger.

An important controversy about trade-offs in personal health
arose in 1977 with the FDA's announcement that it would ban
general additive use of the artificial sweetener saccharin, which
presumably was an aid in controlling obesity-connected diseases.
The FDA action was based on the detection of bladder cancers by
Canadian scientists in male rats whose parents had been fed very
high doses of saccharin. As might be expected, arguments by
opponents of this Delaney application centered on the size of the
experimental dosages and their implications for human consumption. One claim was that human beings would have to drink 800
cans of diet soda a day over a lifetime to consume as much saccharin proportionally as the laboratory rats.[45] Viewing the case of
saccharin in isolation, one is tempted to say that to require warnings on containers of products to which it had been added would
in itself be a sufficient resolution of the problem.[46] Yet, as we have
already seen, the multiplicity of products and cautionary notices is
so great that new warnings may tend to get swallowed up. Moreover, to limit regulation to warnings tends to obscure the fact that
children constitute a major client group of products containing
saccharin. The principal reason for the outcry about saccharin
probably lay in its established place on the market. Few would
lobby so passionately were it a new item.

To place the product on prescription, as some suggested,
would produce an odd ring, in view of its established presence in
commerce. Such a regulation might be rationalized on the basis
that it would require serious thought by two persons—doctor and
patient—and if prescriptions were permitted to be long-term, this
would relieve some of the sting of paternalism. But it would carry
irreducible costs in the process of writing prescriptions, and quite
possibly in the establishment of an underground market. Presumably it was for these reasons, among others, that while the FDA
confirmed its intention to ban the product as a manufacturer-
added item in foods and beverages as well as in cosmetics and
animal feed, Commissioner Kennedy said the agency was considering approval for sale as "a single-ingredient drug without prescription for diabetics and others who may need it for medical
purposes."[47] Such a step might not slow the flood of saccharin to a
trickle, but with a warning label, it could effect significant reduc-

tion in use. And if it had a certain smell of finessing the statute, with the inclusion of a general food-additive ban it arguably would strike a reasonable balance.

The FDA found itself preempted on these proposed strategies, however, when Congress passed the Saccharin Study and Labeling Act.[48] This legislation created an exception to the Delaney clause, while at the same time requiring conspicuous warnings in consumer labeling. I have already indicated my reservations about this kind of approach, and I adhere to these reservations, although I do not find the saccharin law by itself an unacceptable resolution of that particular problem. Yet I think the saccharin legislation is instructive generally, for the effort at selective abrogation of the Delaney principle allows us to focus on a still-developing and powerful rationale for the clause—its role as a brake on environmental overloading of carcinogens. The Delaney amendment does cut broadly, but citizens who have an ax to grind—for saccharin, cyclamates, nitrites, or whatever—might well ask how many exceptions of this sort they would vote to make on an ad hoc basis. I would suspect that the answer is that Congress will not create many new legislative replicas of the Saccharin Act applicable to other products. The Delaney amendment is a translation into law of our reluctance to allow uncontrolled numbers of potentially dangerous products into the only life we have. There is no denying the apparent inconsistency of a government policy which bans some uses of saccharin but freely permits the sale of cigarettes.[49] But in a world of such product pluralism, there will always be jagged edges on the boundary of regulatory law with respect to the differential deadliness of any products we choose to compare. Perfect symmetry is not attainable across product lines. What we seek, sometimes stumblingly, is the highest sensible level of general public protection in a time when economic and political necessity force us to tolerate some dietary and environmental carcinogens. In taking this position, I do not assert that it would be unreasonable to enact a rule which would simply require officials to weigh risks and benefits. I merely wish to emphasize that in an uncertain world where more than one regulatory solution is reasonable, the Delaney formula represents a rational political choice.

The conclusion of a Johns Hopkins research team that "neither saccharin nor cyclamate in physiologic doses is carcinogenic in man,"[50] published more than a year after the FDA's announcement of its intended saccharin ban, provides important data on a crucial factual question concerning that particular product, but does not change the policy prescription. Indeed, the ability to conduct this investigation—a retrospective study of a group of 519 persons who had bladder cancer and another group of 519 who never had cancer—suggests that over time, the application of a Delaney rule augmented by further research will produce safety during an interim of uncertainty and a welcome security for consumers in those cases where the disease hypothesis is disproved. Moreover, the statement of the chief Hopkins investigator that he did not "believe my study or any other single study should be regarded as definitive regarding important issues of human health"[51] underlines the difficulty of the issues and the necessity for research, and implies the need for a rule that cuts broadly at the outset.

We have noted some criticism of the Delaney amendment that goes beyond its lack of a balancing test and its potential economic effect to the way the political process spawned it. Most troubling in this regard is the assertion that this legislation is the product of emotion. One critic implicitly derogates the broad public policy choice represented by the statute, as well as attacking as "advocacy" the views of scientist supporters of the amendment while contrasting his own, technically rigorous analysis.[52] Yet legislation properly reflects a certain amount of emotion even on subjects with quantitative aspects. And courts accept emotional bases in laws with some rational foundation, proceeding to condemn them only when they offend well-established constitutional prohibitions, for example those designed to protect rights of personal liberty and political expression. Moreover, even if one views rigor and rationality as cognate, and sees the Delaney amendment as founded partly on emotion, it is difficult to argue that it is an irrational state of mind which has sustained a law of this kind through three enactments over a ten-year period. In this regard one may ask why the problem of heart disease and cholesterol has not produced a latter-day James Delaney advocating a 1970s counterpart to the cancer clause. The answer may well lie in a realization that the public does in fact know its own mind, and has used a rational calculus to devise a sliding scale of regulation proportional to the terrors it perceives in threats to health and safety.

Even if the risk averseness of the original Delaney amendment was in part an aversion to political risk, the idea has become enough of a fixed star so that a Republican Secretary of Health, Education and Welfare of the seventies could emphatically oppose legislation to allow residues in marketed food of animal carcinogens which were concluded not to be cancer-causing in human beings. Secretary Weinberger, replying to a Congressional inquiry, said simply that his department lacked the "scientific information necessary to establish no-effect levels for carcinogenic substances in animals in general and in man in particular." Studies in progress might provide that information, he said, but until it was shown that animal data could be extrapolated "with confidence" to human beings, scientific ignorance as well as the "lack of public consensus" for changing the law weighed against a modification. Indeed, he declared, even amendment or repeal of the Delaney clauses would have "no effect" on the department's policies, because in the existing state of knowledge, the general safety provisions of the legislation would not permit "detectable residues of carcinogenic animal drugs in human food." In line with a point made above, however, Secretary Weinberger did hypothesize one possibility that might require a balancing test; this would be the case in which the need for expanded food production made it necessary to employ an "alternative accommodation between benefit and risk."[53] Thus, while confirming the existence of a risk-averse government perspective on potential long-term hazards, he made clear that this assumed a present general level of affluence, a state of affairs in which Delaney-type regulation is not a cause of starvation. Certainly legislation aimed at preserving lives in the future becomes possible only in proportion to an absence of definable threat to present ones.

Several other considerations are worth mentioning with respect to the wisdom of the Delaney amendment. Covering a variety of subjects, and partly overlapping the discussion above, they concern advertising, consumer expectations, and the relationship of legal and scientific judgment. After briefly reviewing these matters, this chapter will conclude with an appeal to history.

As I have argued elsewhere should be the case with civil liability for product dangers,[54] it is important for public regulation to proceed from a broad representational perspective. As an example of a case in which a representational analysis aids our view of the problem, let us consider a Congresswoman's reasonable assertion that the consumer who purchases artifically colored foods or cosmetics "takes it for granted" that the coloring dyes are safe.[55] What must be emphasized is that this assumption arises in large part from a background of advertising that contains no hint that the dyes might present a safety problem. It is in this sense that the basis for regulation of products with uncertain risks is in significant measure representational. It is true that if one takes this view of the problem, a theoretical possibility exists that sellers could negate the basis for regulation by voluntary disclosure of risk potential. However, given the natural reluctance of sellers to talk about risk, especially to be the first to do so,[56] this will not often happen.

Though a representational analysis generally presumes a market in which consumer choice is sovereign, I do suggest that in some cases it will be necessary and proper to make legislative decisions about the desirability of certain kinds of products, judgments significantly tied in with considerations of safety. Legislators confront a complex set of factors here, with a chicken-and-the-egg kind of problem arising in the feedback between consumer "desires" and advertising. Consumers may "want" their oranges to be orange instead of greenish, and their lemon cokes to be yellow instead of white, but these wants are related in large measure to merchandising. Recognizing this reality, it is appropriate for Congress to make the judgment that purely extrinsic changes in the appearance of products, such as those achieved by color additives, command a lower social priority than defense against potential long-term risks.

Interestingly, our central concern about uncertainty—an important rationalization of the Delaney amendment—is also a significant element in arguments raised by its opponents, as well as by advocates of a flexible interpretation of the clause. An expert panel reporting to the White House on the Delaney color additives amendment spoke of the need for "discretion" in the interpretation of the definition of "carcinogen," stressing that "from the very nature of such research . . . definitive answers useful in extrapolation to man may not be expected for many years to come."[57] This ignorance about carcinogenicity is used as ammunition by those who would substitute a balancing test in order to maintain production that is dependent on suspect compounds. However, we must reiterate the significance of this factor to proponents of the relatively rigid Delaney formula. It is true that at least under one branch of the Delaney amendment, the language

ness] for evaluation" now provides leeway for sci-
But the uncertainty feature of the problem has
iding legislative judgment which sets regulatory
use that are different than those that would exist
it, and presumably the amendment will result in some
prohibitions on marketing that would not otherwise be imposed.
Given the interpretative flexibility inherent in the statutory language, it would appear that the Delaney clause is likely to effect
more lifesaving than we would get if it were repealed; and this is
precisely because of what scientists do not know.

Illustrative of the tensions between law and science in this area
is the charge that some scientists' support for the Delaney
amendment was "lack[ing in] scientific rigor." Offered as an
example of the lack of sophistication of the arguments favoring
the amendment is one researcher's declaration before the House
Commerce Committee that he doubted that ordinary substances
like salt and sugar could cause cancer. A critic scorns this statement as apparently embodying the belief that "carcinogens are an
exceptional and restricted class of substances."[58] In a sense, however, this alleged technical misconception may serve to emphasize
the value of the Delaney amendment, given the goals that underlie regulation in this area. One must concede the theoretical possibility that the unqualified breadth of the clause could support a
ban of some common household item found to cause malignancies in cancer-sensitive rats at extraordinarily high dosages.
Arguably the step from saccharin to sugar is not an impossible
leap. However, even if this should occur, Congressional reaction
on the saccharin question[59] provides a solution. Allowing for that
single exception fashioned in a period of two decades, the general
case for the Delaney clause still stands on grounds of ignorance
about carcinogenesis, general long-term uncertainty, and concern
about synergistic effects as well as about isolated consequences of
single chemicals. Because of these considerations, it seems desirable to keep the general Delaney principle, leaving Congress at
liberty to make exceptions for individual products whose utility is
thought to be especially high.

On balance, the amendment does indeed compensate for its
theoretical potential for overregulation. One of its saving graces
lies in the way it avoids the evils associated not only with our lack
of knowledge about carcinogenicity, but also with the constant
incentives on producers to take a chance on other people's safety.

It is true that if one views scientists as on the make, "rigoro
enforcement of the policy" may invite "contrived experimenta
tion."[60] However, along with the room for interpretation that
does exist in the Delaney clause, we may rely on the traditions of
scientific argument, as well as the balance wheel of politics, for
defense against the irresponsibility of contrivance.[61] A matter of
concern at least as great is the possibility of overexperimentation
on an unknowing public, as symbolized by the fact that even with
the Delaney clause, cattle feeders continued to use DES beyond
the stipulated withdrawal period. In accounting for such tendencies, the legislation strikes a reasonable balance between crediting
unproved suspicions of hazard and providing the necessary
checks on avarice.

Finally, we should consider a classic case for application of the
Delaney amendment, one that is instructive with respect to cer-
titude and uncertainty. It involves the pesticide aramite. When
Congressman Delaney used aramite as an example of the need for
his original proposal, the product originally had been recommended for a nonresidue regulation, but then received a tolerance of one part per million when the FDA reversed itself and
followed an advisory committee's recommendation. However, at
the same time it promulgated this tolerance, the agency recommended another two-year study of the product, and finally took
action to ban it.[62] The ground for this prohibition, as Congressman Delaney described it, was that the chemical was "even
more harmful that at first supposed."[63]

Not only in the area of additives covered by the Delaney
amendments, but in such cases as oral contraceptives, study often
has shown that initial assurances of safety were unwarranted.
With respect to some products, like aramite, the damaging data
have come from laboratory work. In other situations, the injurious potential of a product has been discovered only by market
experimentation; the story of the Pill provides a continuing, and
chilling, mystery. The scientific history of carcinogens in particular does not confirm the judgment that in the passage and administration of the Delaney clauses "something went wrong."[64] Indeed, in many instances the amendment's relatively uncompromising approach may provide as much refinement as we wish
to afford when it is we who are the guinea pigs. The next chapter,
dealing principally with a known animal carcinogen, offers more
support for this view.

6 DES: Magic Wand and Terrible Sword

ABSTRACTIONS OF LAW AND POLICY weave in and out of any analysis of the regulation of long-term, uncertain hazards. But useful discussion of the problem requires consideration of particular products and processes. The remarkable substances called estrogens have stimulated a significant amount of regulatory controversy recently and have provided some important lessons. We have seen the essential role that estrogens play in the chemistry of oral contraceptives. And it is a versatile synthetic estrogen that puts a number of the problems we have been discussing into especially sharp focus, because its range of possible uses makes it a center of concern both in the area covered by the Delaney amendment and also under the laws dealing with prescription drugs.

The subject of these disputes is the hormone diethylstilbesterol (DES), whose almost magical range of biochemical effects allows it to be used both to choke off life and to promote growth. It is interesting to compare the problem of DES with that of the Pill. In the nationwide furor over oral contraceptives, the depth and amount of contention stemmed not only from their widespread use, but from the direct daily encounter that use entails. By comparison, the bulk of DES usage took place outside the view of consumers, and the battle over that product occupied less of the spotlight. However, on occasion DES also cropped into the view of the general public, and in terrifying ways.

Unfortunately, the kind of growth that DES promotes sometimes includes the wild and uncontrolled variety called cancer. This was known at least as long ago as 1947, when government approval was first given to a new drug application for use of DES in poultry production. It may seem astonishing that 29 years later the FDA was still trying to ban use of the substance as a growth stimulant in cattle and sheep. The story of that effort gives a lesson in the realities of regulation. The poultry chapter in particular illustrates the amount of time and resources sometimes required to remove from commerce dangerous products that are already marketed.

163

When the synthetic estrogen was first approved for use in fowl, it was thought that it would leave no significant residue in edible tissue. It was on this assumption that a new drug application was received in 1957 for a DES formulation called Stilboserts. The product consisted of pellets implanted in the loose skin just below the head of caponettes, designed for slow release into the system of the animals in the weeks before marketing, with the aim of fattening and tenderizing them. The application became conditionally effective in 1958 and fully effective in March 1959. But even as the drug was making its way to the animal feed market, a group of FDA scientists was developing a bio-assay method to detect residues of estrogen in poultry. Utilizing this method, and calculating on the basis of the 12 and 15 milligram doses used in Stilboserts, an agency scientist estimated that 12 milligrams would leave a residue of 20 to 50 parts per billion in the liver, or 9 to 20 micrograms per pound, and that 15 milligrams would leave 25 to 50 parts per billion, or 10 to 20 micrograms per pound.

Thus it was that Stilboserts had a legally clean bill of health for only a few months. In December 1959 the Secretary of Health, Education and Welfare concluded after a study of the use of DES in poultry that the drug presented a potential cancer hazard to the public. Then the FDA, after an administrative proceeding, decided to suspend new drug applications for that usage.

The legal situation which faced the hearing examiner in this proceeding—and subsequently the reviewing court—presented some interesting technical wrinkles. Congress had recently passed the original Delaney amendment in the food additives legislation of 1958, with that clause's commercial death knell for food additives shown to cause cancer in animals. However, possibly believing that it could not apply this law to a product being manufactured before its passage, the FDA elected to attack DES use in caponettes through the then applicable statute dealing with new drug applications—the law under which the use originally had been approved. That legislation provided that applications could be suspended if it were shown that a drug was "unsafe" on the basis of "clinical experience, tests by new methods, or tests by methods not deemed reasonably applicable when such application became effective." The manufacturer of Stilboserts argued that the suspension of approval of his application was not based on evidence from tests or clinical experience after the application became effective. Indeed, he said, the FDA had at one point withheld its approval in order to study the same tests which it later used to support suspension. He contended that since at the time his application was approved, the amount of DES residue in caponette tissues was thought to be insignificant, the suspension represented an attempt at "improper retrospective application" of the Delaney clause.

However, the hearing examiner was unimpressed by the petitioner's position on the safety issue, because he held the product "unsafe" within the meaning of the provision on new drug applications; and a reviewing court was persuaded neither by the manufacturer's arguments on safety nor his contention that the agency was illegally twisting statutes together. The appeals court in this case, *Bell* v. *Goddard*,[1] placed detailed emphasis on the fact that DES and other estrogens had been shown to cause cancers in many parts of animals' bodies—including the breasts, endometrium, uterine cervix, pituitary, testes, ovaries, adrenals, and kidneys—as well as leukemia in mice, rats, rabbits, hamsters, and dogs. It pointed out that "chronic estrogenic stimulation" of the uterus, "whether due to excessive ovarian production or abnormalities of the reproductive cycle, results in increased cancer of the endometrium." It also referred to the "histologically remarkable similarity between cancers of the endometrium in humans and animals." Moreover, it noted that both men and women had been shown to develop cancer of the breast under estrogen therapy, that the estrogens normally secreted by the ovaries and adrenals in women had been shown to sustain breast cancer, and that removal of those organs resulted in observable clinical improvements of these cancers.

For the court as well as the FDA Commissioner, the central meaning of all of this lay in the judgment of experts "that DES is a carcinogen to man." Of related significance were research showing that prolonged exposure to small amounts of carcinogens was more dangerous than single or short-term exposures to the same or larger quantities, and the conclusion that there was "no known threshold or safe level for DES, either as a cause or stimulator of cancer."

The court was unmoved by the manufacturer's argument that the FDA's area of maneuver on a suspension was restricted to "wholly new tests of a drug arising after the effective date of the application." The court specifically noted that in the case of Stilboserts, "an extensive re-evaluation, which drew together clinical experience in a manner not previously attempted and which perhaps brought its full impact to the attention of the experts for the first time, provided the basis for the Commissioner's findings." To disallow new applications of existing information, said the court, "would do violence to the paramount interest in protecting the public from unsafe drugs."

This reading of the statutory evidence requirements provided background for the specific concerns about DES that swayed the court. At issue was the meaning of "unsafe" in the context of the uncertainty about whether small amounts of DES in food would cause human cancer, an uncertainty heightened by the long time it took for the development of chemically caused carcinomas. The maker of Stilboserts pointed out that if caponette production were spread over the American population, there would be sales of only one bird a year for every third family in the country, which would involve a per capita exposure on the average of less than one microgram a year. On the basis of a safety margin of 100 to 1, he argued, this would make the exposure of DES in the diet per person a maximum of 100 micrograms—which he characterized as "an inconsequential, nonharmful residue." The petitioner also noted that estrogen occurred in many natural foods and indeed was produced naturally in the human body, and that excess estrogen was normally detoxified and conjugated in the liver.

But none of these arguments, given the combination of proved hazard and long-term uncertainty, was sufficient to convince the court that DES should stay on the market in a form in which it found its way onto people's dinner plates, even in such tiny amounts. It summarized its concern crisply: "The answer to the petitioner's contentions in great part is that DES is a carcinogen." It was "definitely a cause of cancer in animals, at least an inciter of incipient cancer in man, and possibly a cause of cancer in man."[2]

The uncertainty was two-edged. From the producer's point of view it was notable that it had not been proved that DES caused cancer in man, let alone in what quantities. Yet this very lack of knowledge weighed against allowing the product to remain on the market, especially since it might take many years—as the court said, "as much as the greater part of a life span"—for a carcinogen to cause a detectable cancer.

Since the consumption of caponettes was not evenly spread over the population, the court rejected the attempt to use average per capita consumption as a measuring rod. And the court did not find persuasive the argument based on natural occurrence of estrogen in some foods. Here it grew judgmental. This, it said,

> does not warrant the intake of DES by a deliberate means of exposure through the implantation of such drug in a chicken so as to make it tastier and to save feed costs. If estrogens are contained naturally in certain items of diet, there is no justification for adding more by an artificial method.[3]

This statement of the "ought" of the law obviously drew on testimony of witnesses described as "experts in cancer research," who declared that their clinical experience indicated that to the extent practicable, no quantity of DES should be added to the diet.

One noteworthy aspect of *Bell* v. *Goddard,* manifest in the passage just quoted, is the court's active concern with the artificiality of products and processes. There seems to be an implicit premise that nature may sort out her own hazards, but that the food and drug laws allow regulators to be extremely choosy about the works of man. It is not clear just how much weight the court gives the artificiality factor as distinguished, insofar as it can be, from the known carcinogenic effects of DES. Carcinogenicity per se was the court's central concern in a case in which the statutory focus was clearly on safety, to the apparent exclusion of the positive effects of DES in achieving a "premium product" by making the animals more tender and flavorful as well as by improving the ratio of feed to weight gain. However, it seems significant that the court disapprovingly articulated the fact that the product had been introduced into the food supply by the supplier's willful act.

The court's opposition to continued use of the implants seems based on a calculus that includes a fundamental aversion to risks established by expert testimony as significant possibilities. We have noted how a similar aversion, perhaps even a more pronounced one, lies at the root of the Delaney amendment itself. In light of the embodiment of this attitude in statutes and the existence of judicial sympathy for it, as we view events following the 1966 rendition of judgment in *Bell* v. *Goddard,* it may seem remarkable that DES was to remain on the market in various forms into the seventies. This was the case, however, and indeed further reported judicial assessment of its dangers had to wait until 1974. A description of the hormone's continuing resistance to regulation follows.

Following the Stilboserts case, attention came to focus on the use of DES in cattle and sheep. The concerns that had generated *Bell* v. *Goddard* did not prove as compelling to the FDA with respect to cattle feed. In 1970, it continued previous approval of that use of the drug by sanctioning a supplemental NDA for 5 to 20 milligrams per head per day.[4] It must be noted that the incentives for use of the product, and for pushing its use to the limits of the time when residues would appear in slaughtered animals, were substantial. Even in 1960 a pharmaceutical official, testifying on the Delaney clause in the food additives legislation and its proposed use in the color additives bill, referred to an estimate that DES had saved Iowa farmers $15 million in one year.[5] More recently and more specifically, it has been estimated that the use of DES to fatten a 500-pound steer up to 1,050 pounds will save 511 pounds of feed and 31 days of feeding time.[6] It was therefore understandable that despite the Delaney amendment's ban on the use of carcinogens that left residues detectable by approved methods, inspections continued to show DES in amounts as high as 36.9 parts per billion in sheep, and 15.4 p.p.b. in cattle. Moreover, nine states were represented by the first 10 animals found with DES contamination in 1971; therefore, whatever its incidence, the phenomenon was not geographically isolated. One aspect of the problem thus lay in the difference between law on the books and law as enforced, and it was accented by the fact that even an announced step-up in meat inspection for DES residues would cover only one hundredth of one percent of federally inspected cattle.

Another part of the problem inhered in the remaining technological constraints on finding residues. By 1971, tests for DES had achieved a theoretical detection limit of 2 p.p.b., but in practice had discovered only residues of 3.7 p.p.b. This combination of obstacles to inspection and detection moved some senators that year to introduce a bill prohibiting the use of DES as a growth stimulant for livestock.[7] Uncertainty factors mingled with regulatory discretion in the FDA's initial determination in 1972 to allow the continued implantation of DES in animals' ears while banning its use in feed. Condemning the permissive aspect of this decision, Senator Ribicoff pointed not only to the possibility of undetected traces generally, but to the fact that the Agriculture Department proposed to test for residues in beef cattle using a sample of only eight animals.[8]

Then, in April 1973, the FDA decided to withdraw approval for the implants also. It was this action that triggered the second major public litigation[9] on prohibitory regulation of DES. As has happened more than once in this area, the agency's new effort was founded on a technological advance. Slaughtered animals had not exhibited DES residues under the method of detecting residues in carcasses approved since 1962, which was called the "mouse-uterine" test, at least when the chemical was withdrawn from feed 48 hours before slaughter. However, using a method of gas-liquid chromotography (GLC), Department of Agriculture specialists had found small amounts of the hormone in beef livers in 1971, leading to the agency's issuance in 1972 of a notice of public hearing on the subject.

There were essentially three avenues of approach which the agency could have used in its attempt to remove DES from animal feed. The FDA did not at first elect to employ the Delaney clause with its specific anticancer provision, possibly because of uncertainty as to the character of the residues. Nor did it try to utilize the provision in the new animal drug application (NADA) statutes that allows withdrawal of an imminent hazard to health. Instead, with the Commissioner emphasizing that there was "no reason to believe that the use of DES presented a public health hazard,"[10] the agency invoked the summary judgment provisions of its regulations under the NADA law. Under these regulations, the agency was allowed to decide, after "due notice and opportunity for hearing," that there was no "genuine and substantial issue of fact" which precluded withdrawal of the approval of the application.

The FDA's position was that the makers of the implant had not raised sufficient material issues of fact to oppose its summary holding which withdrew approval. However, it was necessary for the FDA to show at least a lack of evidence that the product was safe in order to prevail under the NADA statutes, despite its disavowal that there was a finding of hazard to the public health and its emphasis that it was acting only for what it described as "regulatory" reasons. In this context, it was on grounds of administrative law rooted in notions of "basic fairness" that a reviewing court found that the agency had given insufficient notice to the manufacturers—including reference to specific data—of the basis for its intended summary decision that the product was not safe for use.

On this challenge by DES producers to the withdrawal of approval for their NADAs, the narrow issue was one concerning the agency's legal right to refuse an evidentiary hearing. However, the court of appeals opinion in *Hess & Clark* v. *FDA*[11] also raises broader questions concerning the regulation of potentially dangerous chemicals, particularly those alleged to have carcinogenic residues.

On the technical question, Judge Leventhal's opinion for the court found that the FDA's refusal of a hearing under its summary judgment procedure was not merited because the agency had not given the manufacturers an opportunity to respond to information available to it. The Commissioner had finally moved to withdraw approval for the implants on the basis of yet a third method of detection—radioactive tracing—and did this on April 27, 1973, after receiving the test results only on April 16. Since the generalized notifications that the agency gave the manufacturers during 1972 did not disclose this method, this seemed a fair point.

Beyond this judgment on administrative fairness, Judge Leventhal went on to raise some interesting questions about the substantive content of the FDA's obligations under the NADA statute. The court effectively rejected the FDA's contention that upon its introduction of evidence that the drug was unsafe, it became incumbent upon the manufacturers to demonstrate safety through test results in order to avoid summary judgment. The court stated the first issue as one of whether the FDA had adduced "new evidence"—the statutory requirement—sufficient to reimpose on the manufacturer the burden to demonstrate safety it had carried when the application originally was approved. Judge Leventhal concluded that without making a positive showing of safety, the manufacturers had produced enough evidence to raise doubts about the agency's initial showing that the product was unsafe.[12]

Some of the safety issues on which the FDA failed to sustain its summary judgment burden were rather technical scientific ones, demonstrating the room for controversy that exists at the molecular level. One factual question tied into these issues was whether the residues the Department of Agriculture had found were a substance called "DES conjugate" rather than free DES. On this point, the court held that documentary submissions by the manufacturer were sufficient to raise material issues of fact requiring an agency hearing. This holding presented a further obstacle to the agency: The manufacturers had offered expert evidence that DES conjugate was safe, so if the residues were DES conjugate rather than free DES, the safety question would itself present still another issue of material fact. And that was not the end of the parade of factual questions. Adding yet another area of dispute was the court's finding that a question had been raised about the relationship of detected residues to the tests themselves, entailing the startling implication that "the residues are caused by the test."[13]

Even if the residues were shown to be free DES, there was a direct joining of a further issue. This was the question of whether small amounts of that chemical were safe—a matter on which one of the manufacturers had submitted affirmative data. At this point the FDA's euphemistic use of a "regulatory" label was unmasked completely to reveal a positive charge of lack of safety, and the agency faced pointblank the difficulties of using the NADA statute rather than the Delaney clause. Judge Leventhal further suggested that a showing that larger amounts of DES than those found in the residues would be carcinogenic was not enough by itself to ban the product without a hearing under the NADA provisions. As he pointed out, the FDA itself "routinely allows sale in limited quantities of drugs that would be lethal in substantial amounts,"[14] and indeed a manufacturer's brief quoted testimony by an FDA official to the effect that pregnant women would encounter no hazard in consuming liver with 2 parts per billion of DES.

Inherent in the question of whether traces of free DES could cause harm was the issue of whether the benefits the hormone conferred would outweigh any danger it did pose. The court linked a reference to the relativity of drug safety to the notation that there were intermediate regulatory possibilities, such as a ban limited to the sale of liver, which was the only food in which residues had been detected.[15]

Finally, decrying the FDA's apparent efforts to impose what it called a "paternalistic sagacity," and emphasizing that an eventual finding of imminent hazard to the public health would be grounds for banning the implants, the court concluded that the questions about the presence and safety of DES demanded more evidence. Under traditional principles of administrative justice, the decision was one of high quality. However, in addition to the issues on which the case was remanded to the FDA, significant questions of general policy remained unaddressed in the background. One was whether the marketing of a substance shown by some experimental literature to be hazardous should in effect be permitted as a right during a period in which new evidence is generating increased suspicion. A related, specific issue of remedies was whether in conditions of uncertainty, a threshold showing of suspicion that a product will cause serious physical harm presents a case for temporary prohibitory regulation. The question also arose of at what point the concerns presented by physical hazards of this kind will be judged to break the mold of a rigid cost-benefit welfare formula, because of the agony that they can inflict on victims and their families and friends. The viewpoint inherent in these questions is close to the surface of Congressional consciousness in various forms of safety legislation. Those considerations related to uncertainty and serious physical injury, together with the usual lack of information in consumers about risks of biochemical hazards, suggest that the vector of regulation should be drawn rather strongly against even potential dangers of this kind.

The suggestion is not a facile one and does not ignore that difficulty of the matter. Problems of both evidence and politics were reflected in the Commissioner's decision to use the NADA statute rather than the Delaney clause, as well as in his efforts to show the product unsafe while at the same time he declared that it gave no evidence of a "public health hazard" and allowed the continued slaughter and marketing of cattle in which DES already had been implanted. One can fully recognize the depth of these problems while emphasizing the strains of public concern about uncertainty and individual suffering that lie beyond the complexity of this particular litigation; and one may yet argue that a combination of legislation and regulation could rationally and wisely be used to shift the burdens further against market experimentation.

Shortly after its orders were vacated in the implants case, the FDA undertook to revoke approval for the previously used methods of detecting residues and to require holders of NADAs for DES to offer a "suitable method" of detection, as well as to present data showing that no residues would occur in edible tissue when the product was used according to the labeling.[16] The agency was emphatic that it was "essential" that suitable detection methods be developed "with a greater sensitivity than is presently available." It also propounded a requirement that manufacturers show that "proposed changes in conditions of use" would be "reasonably certain to be followed in practice"—a provision evidently responsive to the reality that regulation of dangerous chemicals often must maintain a split focus on the manufacturer and the user. The manufacturer may adopt the ingenuous position that he is only a seller, while the user may expectably employ the product in a way that leaves potentially harmful residues that are practically impossible to track down.

Behind the agency's persistence were layers of unknowns. One potential problem of DES biochemistry was the possibility of long-term consequences arising from scientifically undetectable phenomena. With respect to the use of the hormone in animal feed, the regulatory focus had been on residues of the product in carcasses. But French researchers had found cattle fed on the meat of animals fed with DES that became infertile, despite the apparent absence of residues in the beasts whose flesh was used.[17] Whether this was attributable to residues that could not be detected in the present state of technology or subtle changes in the tissues of animals that no longer exhibited any residues at all, it was precisely the kind of result that signaled caution in the use of artificial additives.

This mysterious correlation was illustrative of the kinds of problems that DES shared with many other products and processes. And even more arcane dangers lurked in other uses of the remarkable hormone, quite apart from its employment as an additive to animal feed. Specifically, public concern was aroused about the alleged consequences of a DES product intentionally formulated for direct use in human beings—specifically to prevent miscarriages. Although the potential exposure was relatively limited, both the precision and elongation of linkage made the matter especially disturbing. Originating back in the 1940s, the case provided grim commentary on the long latency period of chemically caused cancer, and the defenseless posture of its victims. Involved was an irony spanning two generations: mothers who were administered DES in order to prevent miscarriage bore daughters who themselves developed cancer about twenty years later.

This discovery, first reported in 1968, led the FDA in 1971 to caution doctors against the use of the drug on pregnant women and to require warnings to that effect on DES labels. By 1975, more than 200 young women whose mothers had taken DES while pregnant had developed an especially vicious form of vaginal cancer. Testimony to a Senate subcommittee reported an incidence of this cancer as high as 4 cases per 1,000, a figure which seemed alarming in view of the fact that DES had been administered to perhaps 1 million pregnant women over a 30-year period. Moreover, it appeared that 90 percent of the daughters of such women had a lesion labeled vaginal adenosis, which was described as "apparently benign but perhaps pre-cancerous."[18]

In historical perspective of these events, it is especially interesting to read a 1960 statement about DES by a pharmaceutical official, prepared for a Congressional committee and offered in opposition to the Delaney amendment. The executive, Dr. Thomas P. Carney of Eli Lilly and Co., referred to "many publications of outstanding authorities in the field of endocrinology" which had "demonstrated that stilbestrol is safe as administered to human beings." He specifically mentioned articles in the *Western Journal of Surgery* and the *Journal of the American Medical Association* which he characterized as concluding that there was "no danger of cancer production from estrogen treatment." He also said that no cancers had been reported in the millions of cattle and sheep to which DES had been fed, and that in most strains of test animals scientists had not been able to produce cancers with the hormone. Most animal studies in which cancer had been caused, he asserted, used "mice specially bred to develop spontaneous cancers."[19]

These confident remarks about safety in human beings lost credibility not only with the appearance of the vaginal cancers but with another report of intergenerational problems. In 1975, the Health Research Group claimed that the sons of women who had taken DES while pregnant ran increased risks of reproductive difficulties. Animal tests had demonstrated high rates of sterility in male mice, and an controlled, retrospective study of young men whose mothers had ingested DES in a 1952 experiment showed that 24 percent had reproductive tract abnormalities, as compared with 3 percent in the control group.[20]

Even as the data on the consequences in male children became public, a large number of DES daughters were initiating private claims for their afflictions. Following a lawsuit in Detroit on behalf of 74 victims of cancer or precancerous lesions, alleging causation from ingestion of the hormone by their mothers during pregnancy,[21] a group of Long Island women sought $100 million in compensatory damages as part of a class action which asked $1 billion in punitive damages. This group also demanded that the 19 drug firm defendants set up a half billion dollar fund for examination and treatment of women claiming injuries attributable to the hormone.[22] Still another class action carried the assault to the Gothic towers of the University of Chicago, whose Lying-In Hospital allegedly had used DES in an experiment in which those taking the hormone claimed they had been told they were being given vitamin pills.[23]

In a sense these litigations simply made the need for public regulation even more evident. The difficulty in leaving the matter to the market, supplemented only by the common law, lay not only in the lack of knowledge of the patients at the time the drug was given, but in their inability to marshal information that would help to fix responsibility when the carcinogenic effects of DES began to manifest themselves. In illustration of the problem, one attorney who was handling a number of DES cases found a total of 29 manufacturers who had made the drug[24]—and the trial judge in one action by multiple plaintiffs dismissed the suits of all those who could not identify the makers of the particular products they had been given.[25]

To be sure, developing news on DES and vaginal cancers indicated that uncertainty prevailed in both directions on statistical charts. While many of the episodes described in this book have involved hazards that appear increasingly worse with time, an important sounder of alarums on this use of DES reported that perhaps the early statistics were unduly pessimistic. Dr. Arthur Herbst, chairman of the Department of Obstetrics and Gynecology at the beleaguered University of Chicago, who had been concerned for some years about the effects of DES exposure *in utero,* reported that the risk of vaginal cancers was on the order of 1 in 1,000, and perhaps even smaller.[26] However, accompanying this change in the profile of a particular uncertainty were other, less encouraging data. In the same talk, Dr. Herbst told the American College of Obstetricians and Gynecologists that more frequent side effects in DES offspring included kidney and urinary abnormalities as well as the vaginal adenosis, and mentioned his apprehension that other forms of cancer might result from other hormones taken during pregnancy. Herbst's maintenance of a registry on DES-exposed women provided continuing testimony to this concern.

We already have spoken of the problem of calculating the social costs of products that present long-term hazards. In assessing government intervention in various forms of DES marketing, we should note that the use of the hormone to prevent miscarriage presents an unusually poignant example of the difficulty of making standard determinations of risks and benefits. Putting aside such quantifiable items as wage loss, medical bills, and funeral expenses, in one balance will appear the terror and the pain of cancer for the daughters of the DES patients, while in the other are the undoubted gains associated with the survival as embryos of hundreds of thousands of wanted children, assuming that the chemical did in fact achieve this.[27] The question of how to weigh such factors has frustrated courts for decades.

Undoubtedly, dollar pricing of these costs and gains on some utility models would yield a net benefit from the use of DES,[28] assuming that the adenosis phenomenon remains benign. Yet this sort of calculation has not been characteristic of current regulation nor of the social consensus it apparently represents. The thrust of that consensus and those laws has generally been in a different direction, seeming to place a premium on protection of lives against illness and injury—perhaps well above conventional measures of utility. At the very least, we may say that the trade-off between dollar calculations and deaths needs more analysis in application to concrete cases by lawyers, economists, and philosophers. But even with an unreformed efficiency calculus, a significant part of this facet of the DES problem lies in the uncertainty about whether the adenosis statistics will continue to be benign. For if half or even a tenth of these conditions should develop into malignancies, any social calculation would show a net loss, and a policy of allowing sale until harm is indisputably proved would appear unwise indeed. The fact that DES had not been approved for this use for several years reflects this judgment.

The capacity of DES to generate problems of law and policy was not yet exhausted. The literally fatal attraction of the versatile drug was creating still another area of concern at the same time the tragic statistics on vaginal cancers found their way into the medical press, and then more generally published sources. Versatility was indeed a keynote. Quite in contrast with the hormone's advertised use as a preserver of conceptions, by the early 1970s it was coming into vogue as a "morning-after" contraceptive—particularly on college campuses. It should be noted that on this count there was little disagreement as to its effectiveness. The FDA's Advisory Committee on Obstetrics and Gynecology had unanimously concluded that DES worked as a postcoital contraceptive when administered at high dosages twice daily for 5 days, beginning within 72 hours of intercourse.

The advisory committee was generally sanguine about side effects on patients of this short-term use, although one might find troubling echoes of recent events in its specific statement that "a carcinogenic potential from this dosage has not been proven." A lay person might have been permitted to wonder how much comfort this conclusion offered in light of the medical testimony in *Bell* v. *Goddard* recommending against the use of any DES in the diet. Moreover, whatever the facts about the carcinogenic properties of the morning-after pill, the committee did express concern about the "possibility of a harmful effect on the fetus either from a pregnancy existing at the time of treatment from a previous exposure or resulting from a patient failure during treatment." Even though "an action of this kind on the fetus is not known to exist," the committee cautiously suggested that conventionally induced abortions be "seriously considered." Indeed, its general conclusion was that the morning-after usage should be "considered as an emergency treatment."[29]

After an initial proposal in 1973, it took two years for the FDA to issue a definitive regulation on patient package labeling for DES as a postcoital oral contraceptive. The agency was persuaded by comments on its proposal that it should be more definite about the risk of vaginal cancer in female offspring, and thus changed the word "may" to the word "will," so that the patient labeling said "the child will have an increased risk of developing cancer of the vagina or cervix later in life." The agency also attempted to accent this point by placing it in a new, separate paragraph. Moreover, it added to the patient insert a statement, also included in physician labeling, that it was not definitely known whether the drug would cause other abnormalities.

When it published this final regulation, the FDA remained unconvinced that a short course of treatment with DES would expose patients themselves to an increased risk of cancer, but it could not say that such a risk definitely did not exist. Therefore it required a paragraph citing tests conducted in animals, which showed that estrogens given for long periods had increased the frequency of cancer.

The required patient labeling as promulgated was quite emphatic that the morning-after pill was only to be used to "prevent pregnancy in an emergency, for example, after a rape." After this statement, which appeared in the first paragraph, the document repeated in the next paragraph that the treatment was "for emergencies only and should not be used repeatedly." And three paragraphs later, it said that it is "sensible and prudent to avoid the high dose of estrogen used in this treatment unless absolutely necessary," and that this was "why this method of contraception is recommended for emergency use only and should not be used repeatedly." The patient labeling also referred to various side effects, the most serious being blood clotting, which was described as being "rare but . . . at times . . . fatal." The regulation also mentioned specific contraindications.[30]

In the same month it issued this regulation, in February 1975, the agency's concern with the "morning-after" use of DES led it to add a prohibitory statement to all labeling for DES tablets except those specially packaged and accompanied by a patient leaflet. This statement, which was required to be in block capitals, declared "THIS DRUG PRODUCT SHOULD NOT BE USED AS A POSTCOITAL CONTRACEPTIVE," and had to appear before the description of the drug in the physician's package insert. The regulation also required the same statement to appear prominently and conspicuously on container and carton labels.[31] This was as direct and blunt a method of communication as any in the literature of products hazards. But its appearance came several years after the hormone's first use as a morning-after pill. It is a telling point that to this writing, no manufacturer has been bold enough to ask that DES be approved for this purpose.[32]

The regulatory mills ground on, but slowly. By July 1975, the reports of vaginal adenosis in DES daughters moved the FDA to require that physician labeling include information on that subject in addition to the warning previously required about vaginal carcinoma. The adenosis statement noted occurrence of that condition in 30 to 90 per cent of postpubertal girls and young women whose mothers had taken DES in pregnancy, and recommended "periodic examination of such patients," although it said it was "unknown"[33] what this statistic meant with respect to the possible development of carcinoma.

A confluence of concerns over the various uses of DES occurred in September 1975 on the Senate floor, where a vote was taken on a bill to ban the chemical as a growth stimulant for cattle and to assure restrictions on its use as a morning-after pill. Spirited debate on animal use featured claims by cattle-state senators that prohibition of DES as a growth stimulant would cost consumers up to $35 a year per capita. These arguments were bolstered, perhaps revealingly, by the demand of Senator Carl Curtis of Nebraska to "show me one peson who has died of cancer in 20 years as a result of eating beef fed with DES." From the standpoint of those who desired regulation, the query proved too much: no such showing could practically be made because of the difficulty of tracing such causal linkages and the associated uncertainty about the chemical's carcinogenic action in people. Moreover, if one was disposed to credit the apprehension about the possible effects of the hormone, it was relevant that though there had been a falling-off of DES levels in meat after the original rise in concern, by 1975 residues had returned to their highest levels. And if no one could show Senator Curtis "one person," there were reputable experts who feared hazards to many. Specifically, the director of the National Cancer Institute declared that women in the first three months of pregnancy should not eat beef liver because of the possible teratogenic effects of the drug. With this background, Senators Edward Kennedy and Gary Hart tacked on an amendment requiring that the ban on DES as a stimulant for animal growth should remain until there was an affirmative government determination that this use was not harmful to human beings.

The portion of the bill dealing with contraceptive use went the FDA one better. It would have required a warning on prescription containers that "this drug may cause cancer," and a statement that it "may not be used as a contraceptive after sexual intercourse except in cases of rape or incest or a comparable medical emergency." Even more extraordinarily, it required the patient or her guardian to affirm in writing that she had been given a full description of the medicine's hazards, including cancer, by the prescribing doctor—and that this statement be submitted to the Department of HEW so it could keep surveillance on over-prescription.[34] The Senate's passage of the bill by a 61–29 vote at least appeared to manifest agreement with its committee's statement that "until the full extent of DES carcinogenicity in human beings is known, the American people must have the benefit of [the] doubt." That, of course, is an application of the major thesis of this book.

With the bill mired in the House—it did not emerge alive—the FDA issued a new proposal in January 1976 to revoke approval of all NADAs for the use of DES as an animal growth stimulant. The agency adduced statistics showing that traces of the chemical had been found in the livers of 36 animals out of 4,371 tested since 1974.[35] But a regulation on cattle feed, published on March 15, 1976, made clear that the case against DES had not yet carried the day. It allowed continued uses of the drug, by itself and in combination with other chemicals, for fattening of sheep and beef cattle. The principal restrictions were that it was to be withdrawn seven days before slaughter and was not to be fed to breeding or dairy animals; additionally, some parts of the regulation imposed prohibitions on use in livestock under certain weights.[36] Despite this continued permission, one might conjecture that the bad press the product was getting would at least marginally reduce uses that tended to produce residues. Perhaps it did, although surveys taken over this period continued to show that regulation was not totally effective, for traces of DES were still turning up in some beef livers.[37]

The story of DES regulation contains many of the principal elements of the problem of law, science, and policy which this book addresses. Before summarizing its lessons, it is useful to describe another product history which crosses several conceptual boundaries we have discussed. This product, tradenamed Depo-Provera, is a contraceptive, and it has caused cancer in animals. However, for various reasons, some of which may be inferred from the nature of the consumer group at which it is directed, it has not engaged public attention in the same way as DES. It presents a strong case for allowing limited marketing for the same reason that a powerful argument is made against it: the relatively low mental capacities of the proposed users. In this regard, it provides an interesting comparison to the commerce in DES—in both the formulations that impinge on the general public and those directed at small, defined classes of persons—that has been the subject of recent controversy. For the unfortunate clients of Depo-Provera are in a sense surrogates for all of us, as ignorant as we are about the vital processes on which the products of our modern chemical revolution do their often mysterious work.

Depo-Provera—technically, medroxyprogesterone acetate— was a drug designed for women whose mental faculties were such that they could not be relied on to take contraceptive pills daily. It was to be introduced into the body by injection rather than by oral self-administration, and its great advantage was that its contraceptive effect lasted for at least three months. The issues I shall discuss concerning this product were similar to others analyzed here with respect to uncertainty and market experimentation, but it will be seen that one dimension, involving the element of "consent," was unusual.

The FDA's record on the drug is fairly characterized as a zig-zag one. This description is offered not so much as a criticism of the agency as to underline the difficulties of the issues enmeshed in long-term uncertainties and of the problems posed as new data trickle in, raising warning signals at first only dimly visible.

Some signals had appeared by 1973, when the FDA proposed to approve the drug "for a limited and well-defined patient population."[38] The perceived need for contraception in this group of women was great, at least in the view of the experts with whom the agency's officials consulted. It was on this basis that the FDA believed that the benefits to be derived from the drug would outweigh its risks. But among those risks, as one commentator put it, was that the drug seemed to work "just a little *too* well."[39] Not only did it prevent conception for three months, but, in the FDA's own words, it was shown that "the regimen can cause prolonged and possibly even permanent infertility." Moreover, in addition to "many of the less significant adverse reactions" associated with the Pill, high doses of Depo-Provera had been shown to cause breast cancer in female beagles and lower dosages had been associated with the development of benign breast nodules in the dogs. Although the FDA said that "the significance of the findings in beagles to humans . . . is not known," it noted that versions of the Pill which produced similar results in beagles "have been withdrawn from the market in light of the availability of other oral contraceptives which did not cause tumors in animals."

Despite these rather forbidding reports, the FDA concluded that it could achieve a favorable risk-benefit ratio in the target population with certain "cautionary measures." An agency proposal on the subject included restrictions on distribution, such as a requirement that would focus responsibility on physicians by forcing them personally to sign order blanks to be sent directly to the manufacturer. Two measures related directly to patients. One was an "informational leaflet" in the drug package, designed to explain to the patient or her parents or guardians what the risks were. The proposal specified that if the patient could not understand the information, the guardian must be given the package insert and must consent for the patient before the drug could be injected. The second of these features was to be a "more detailed brochure as a part of the drug package" which would be given to patients or guardians "to be read for additional information."[40]

The Commissioner's responses to the comments this proposal engendered were instructive. In a regulation originally published in September 1974,[41] he was agreeable to a suggestion that the information in the proposed brochure should be presented "in a less harsh and punitive manner." He announced that the patient leaflet had been reworded for more simplicity, and that study was continuing on the "adequacy" of both the leaflet and the brochure. Not entirely convincing was his rejection of arguments to the effect that the "informed consent" procedures did not give the patient enough "lead time" to review risks and benefits. Critics on this point had reasonably questioned what gains could be had from giving the patient the detailed brochure after the drug had already been administered. The Commissioner's response was that the physician was the focal point of the "informed consent" issue, and should make sure that the patient or her guardian had read and understood the patient leaflet. As to the detailed brochure, he said that it was designed to provide a "better understanding of the drug" so that the patient could decide whether to stay on it in the future. Since presumably injections of Depo-Provera constituted elective rather than emergency treatment— except in the sense that, for example, the parent of a retarded daughter would want an effective method of contraception as quickly as possible—this seems an unusual admixture of paternalism and personal choice. Moreover, there resided some doubt as to the agency's legal ability to require physicians to do any of the specific things the regulation prescribed.

Quite as much at the heart of the matter were the comments received concerning the "potential risks and lack of sufficient data with respect to these risks." The Commissioner here noted his previous ban on Pill versions containing a combination of the Depo-Provera chemical and ethinyl estradiol because of their tumor-causing effect in dogs. But he emphasized that by contrast with the daily Pill, there was no "suitable substitute" for Depo-Provera injectables. His view was that for the "limited and well-defined patient population" involved, and given the benefits it would confer in that group, the drug was relatively safe. This rationalization creates a rather peculiar situation, in which safety regulation takes on an unusually affirmative tone. Typically the only result of FDA regulation is to place limits on patient exposure; notably in this case, although in form the regulation is a limiting one, it effectively has another edge as well, of being virtually prescriptive in the "limited population."

This aspect of the Depo-Provera case further engages our concern about the significance of "informed consent" in this context. The problem is one with obvious ramifications across the field of medical treatment for those of limited capacity. When the FDA points out that its Depo-Provera regulation represents the first time it attempted to require informed consent for the administration of a new drug, one is not entirely convinced that the agency has exalted freedom of choice, because one wonders how meaningful the choice is. The Commissioner took note that the target group was "envisioned" as "minor and institutionalized women . . . , the poor, and welfare recipients," and said that this matter was of "particular concern." He declared that use of the drug would be closely monitored, that he did not expect abuse, and that he would respond to it if it occurred. Detached from the facts of what information the proposal offered at which points, this has an abstract, superficial persuasiveness. But given that most women who started a program of Depo-Provera would do so before the fullest data had been given to their guardians, the practical effect of the regulation was to promote a pharmaceutical *fait accompli*.

I shall not plumb the issues raised by allowing consent by surrogates, although they are troubling. If one grants that a retarded patient has an objective personal interest apart from that of her parent, for example, one must confront the possibility that the incentives of the parent will sometimes drive him or her to choose a course of treatment that diverges from that interest. One need only imagine, and could easily sympathize with, the intense desire to avoid conception that might color the views of many parents and guardians. What is important is the existence and strength of that motivation. Further in this connection it is fair to note the sources of promotion for Depo-Provera: Much of the support for its use came from population-control professionals, including the Center for Population Research in the National Institutes of Health and the International Planned Parenthood Federation. The commitment of these groups is one of the heart as well as of the mind, as evidenced by the emotional character of a speech in which a director of International Planned Parenthood said, "I have seen Depo-Provera used in the long houses of Sarawak . . . a community two generations removed from head hunting. . . . I have seen it used in the villages of northern Thailand."[42] One cannot discount the impetus to use the drug that this passion generates. But assuming for a moment a perfect identity of interest among not only patients and their families but public health officials, hospital administrators, and private groups interested in population control, one returns ultimately—as did the Commissioner—to the question of risk.

In this case a most serious issue involved the danger of carcinoma *in situ* of the cervix. This risk had been reported by National Cancer Institute studies in 1971 to be several times higher for users of Depo-Provera than for the general population. The surfacing of that information provides a sobering lesson in the dependence of regulation on the vagaries of discovery and communication of discomfiting evidence: An FDA official told a Congressional subcommittee that when the subcommittee staff brought these data to the agency's attention, it was "literally within a few days" of approving the drug for contraceptive use, where it previously had been cleared only as a palliative for womb cancer.[43]

In spite of this history, the Commissioner's defense on the question of carcinoma *in situ* took the offensive when he offered his rationalizations for "limited population" use of the drug. The Commissioner's argument stressed the long-term nature of carcinogenicity as an indicator that the drug was not culpable. He pointed out that of 24 cases of carcinoma *in situ* in Depo-Provera users, 12 were reported in the first year of use of the drug, and 20 within the first two years—facts at variance with a hypothesis of Depo-Provera causality. Given that "without exception, the documented examples of chemical carcinogenesis in man have all occurred after a lag time of 3 years or longer," and usually more than ten years, he concluded that "such early tumors cannot be considered as drug-related." There was nothing in the history of animal testing of Depo-Provera, said the Commissioner, that suggested it would be unique with respect to the lag time for cancer formation. Moreover, he was prepared to advance alternative reasons why the incidence of carcinoma *in situ* might be higher in the population in which Depo-Provera had been used. For one thing, women in a contraceptive trial would probably have more pelvic examinations and Pap smears than the population generally. For another, many of these women had used the oral Pill. Also, the test population was one which normally had a higher risk of cervical carcinoma than the rest of the population, a fact attributed cryptically to "socioeconomic factors" and number of pregnancies.[44]

All of this had a certain scientific logic, and seemed dispassionate enough. Again, there was logic in the hinted inference that Depo-Provera would not cause cervical carcinoma *in situ* in women because its only cancer-causing activity established by animal experiment had been in the breasts of beagles, not the cervix. However, one of the alternative explanations for the carcinoma *in situ* data in Depo-Provera patients created disturbing fallout over a much wider area: as noted above, the Commissioner had pointed out that most women who were test subjects for the injectable drug had also used the Pill—and in this connection he referred to the "long-standing concern that all steroidal contraceptives, especially estrogens, may increase the incidence of genital cancer." This, he said, was the "larger problem" of which Depo-Provera presented only a segment. What was significant was the very fact that this broader subject was identified as a problem over which he declared that there was "appropriate concern." With the Commissioner having said this, it was interesting that his conclusion—that there was no evidence to alter his approval of Depo-Provera for a "limited and well-defined patient population"[45]—necessarily subsumed a judgment that market experimentation with a known animal carcinogen might proceed. But providing a notable counterpoint was the fact, referred to three times in the document accompanying his Depo-Provera order, that there was continuing concern about the uncertainties attached to chemical contraception generally.

Just before the final release of this document, Congressman L.

H. Fountain of North Carolina, gadfly of the FDA in his role as chairman of the House Intergovernmental Relations Subcommittee, wrote a long letter disapproving the agency's decision to the Secretary of Health, Education and Welfare. Citing various reports and studies about the cancer rate associated with Depo-Provera—including research reported by FDA workers—Fountain criticized the omission of cancer risks in the FDA-approved patient leaflet. He also quoted an internal memorandum from the director of the agency's Office of Scientific Evaluation calling for "additional studies" on the drug, as well as a memorandum written by an agency medical officer who referred to implications of a "serious public health hazard" from use of Depo-Provera in the approved population.[46] Within two weeks, Congressman Fountain's letter had achieved the desired effect. On October 22, 1974, although protesting that it had originally acted only after careful consideration, the agency drew back. The Commissioner decided to delay decision on the new drug application for Depo-Provera pending "further public consideration," because of his stated belief that it was, as he put it, "essential to public confidence in the safety of its drug supply that it be clear that benefit-risk issues have been resolved to the fullest extent possible."[47]

To report this history is not overweeningly to judge that the forces of oppressed and information-deprived consumers have won a clearcut victory. Against the suffering from possible hundreds or thousands of cancers one must weigh the toll, both physical and emotional, that would be produced by more thousands of unwanted offspring born to mothers who could no more formulate a responsible choice to have children than they could be relied upon to take the Pill daily. The joinder of problems of long-term uncertainty and market experimentation to traditional issues of risk-balancing makes such cases difficult. Yet the outcome achieved through Congressional pressure seems on the whole the best one. Taken together, Congressman Fountain's letter and the scrambling agency response roughly represent the degree of risk averseness that I believe guardians of public health and safety—both legislative and administrative—should and often do bring to their official judgment on these issues.

The lessons of Depo-Provera emphasize a general need to reduce the imposition on the public, and numerous subpublics, of risks that they do not understand, in situations in which consent is practically meaningless. While we cannot ignore the perceived necessity for use of hazardous products, such as the proposed limited use of Depo-Provera, those who experiment on all of us must face increasingly heavy burdens as the novelty and complexity of their goods increase. The case of this injectible contraceptive simply accentuates our concern about experimentation because of the more than usually focused impression it conveys that human beings are being used as objects. With the lessons of Depo-Provera in mind, we may now venture a more comprehensive view of the problem of carcinogenicity in things ingested by human beings, with specific attention to the case of DES and further reference to the Delaney amendment as a benchmark for regulation.

A very thorny part of the task of doing justice in public regulation of safety lies in the politically evolved differentiations concerning a great variety of risks. To illustrate the problem we may compare the statistically certain number of fatalities from automobiles each year with what remains only a suspicion of future suffering and death from the use of DES in animal feed. With this background, it was proper as well as pungent for an opponent of the Delaney amendment to ask rhetorically whether Congress would vote to ban automobiles.[48] However, there are numerous reasons why Congress would not stop the assembly lines of Detroit while seriously considering a prohibition on the use of DES. One is the fixed position of cars in our national life. Here we encounter the way that politics defines categories of relative luxury and necessity. To ban DES and leave automobiles on the market would simply signal a social judgment that to add a few extra pennies per pound to meat prices, driving some families down to the next cheapest cut or even forcing a curtailment of their consumption of beef or lamb, would not cause as significant an inconvenience as stopping automobile traffic. It should be noted that a prohibition of DES use in animal feed is not a ban on meat; a closer analogy is that of the requirement of certain safety features on cars.

In making this comparison, we must remember the grounds for supporting a ban on DES, reasons associated with the uncertainty and the long-term character of its potential risk. These factors present a significant contrast with most of the accident problems posed by automotive design, which are relatively well-known and statistically definable. To resolve the paradox of why we might incline to more stringent regulation of the product whose risks are unproved in the present, we must look to the fear—a reasonable enough one from the vantage point of

Congress—that DES could produce a truly terrible cancer epidemic many years hence, dwarfing annual automobile fatalities. It would not have been arbitrary for Congress to decide that it was sufficiently risk-averse to that possibility that it would take no chances on DES use in animal feed.

A ban on this usage might be accomplished under a general risk-balancing standard, but I think it is useful at this point to rehearse the possible application of the relatively broad-bladed approach represented by the Delaney amendment to the regulation of product hazards. Initially, it should be said that in the area which it covers, the Delaney amendment represents a more rational way of solving problems than might appear on first view of its deliberate eschewal of risk-balancing. In this regard we may refer to the statistical argument that events which raise risks only slightly are not cause for governmental concern—a point persuasive in isolation but one which misses the genuine political appeal of the legislation. Consider, for example, the fact that an event which increases the risk of death by 0.02 per cent would raise the death rate by only 29 30-year-olds out of every 100 million who would not otherwise have died.[49] In an impersonal statistical sense, this may seem too trivial a problem to justify governmental intervention. Although one could argue that any rise in deaths without counterbalancing savings in lives is enough reason to regulate, that might not be enough to make the case, given the costs of regulation itself. However, a large part of the problem to which the Delaney amendment addresses itself is that risk-balancers will extrapolate their data wrongly, allowing on the market a product that produces a carcinogenic catastrophe. Presumably the amendment does not concern itself so much with 29 in 100 million as with the possibility that the toll will be in the hundreds of thousands or even millions.

Moreover, though it is useful in analyzing any potentially hazardous activity to seek to quantify the added risk, this is only one of several problems. We also must ask: what is the nature of the risk in terms of the human suffering it may cause? What is the particular social benefit conferred by the challenged conduct? How great is the uncertainty that the risk will be transformed into the reality of injuries, and over what period of time? The Delaney legislation reflects valuations on certain risks and benefits that cannot easily be quantified, dollar against dollar. It also represents a judgment that we prefer not to take chances with possibly irrevocable processes that sometimes can be measured only over a decade or more.

It is true that defenders of the Delaney approach must themselves reckon with uncertainties. For example, it has been said that there is "no guarantee that all substances are not in some circumstances carcinogens." This theoretically could apply even to "normal nutrients, since anything which enhances the rate of cell division may be expected to increase the time rate of cancer occurrence."[50] But here a rule of reason reveals itself in the infrastructure of policy behind the legislation. If it were shown that irresponsible experimentation and eccentric administration of the law were combining to prohibit the marketing of "normal nutrients," this would be cause for concern and doubtless would bring legislative revision. Yet the case of DES—to which we might naturally look for the manifestation of signs of official abuse—has not provided an example of the feared arbitrariness. DES has remained a growth stimulant for cattle despite passage by the Senate of a bill to ban that use. (Too, the powerful hormone has stayed on the prescription drug market[51]—where admittedly the clause does not apply—although with each year that passes it is becoming more evident that the returns were not complete on treatments long since past. To the established linkage of vaginal cancer in the daughters of mothers who had taken DES and the early reports of reproductive tract abnormalities in sons has been added another study which found increased rates of urogenital problems in sons.[52]) Moreover, when one refers to actual bans on products in specific Delaney territory, no examples appear of officials on the rampage. And clearly one could not condemn the FDA's attempted saccharin ban in 1977, which utilized the Delaney clause as an alternate ground of decision, as administrative whimsey. Though highly controversial, it was a statutorily justified and considered decision.

Viewed as a matter of practical administration, the clause becomes simply a rough-and-ready guide to regulation. It does vary the approach, based explicitly on reasonableness and risk-balancing, which otherwise sets the basic vector of many public health and safety statutes, including many safety-related provisions of the Food, Drug and Cosmetic Act. However, despite the seeming lack of discretion conferred by the provision, the meaning that has worked out for it in practice is one sensibly related to the potential evil addressed by Congress. One can support a Delaney approach while believing that there is "no guarantee" against practically everything causing cancer in people. The clause does not operate without a scientifically respectable showing of causation in at least animals. And it may be fair to say that the effective premise of the law is only that government should be able to act when there is no guarantee that a substance that is an animal carcinogen will not cause cancer in people.

The Delaney amendment is a risk-averse statute, embodying respect for the caution of scientists regarding uncertainty, as well as concern for the physical integrity of potential victims. History since 1958 has not shown the social judgment it represents to be irrational, although Congressional modification of it in the Saccharin Study and Labeling Law of 1977 has refined its transcription of public opinion. Yet even though I contend here for a generally risk-averse approach, I do not suggest that the Delaney idea should be legislatively cloned for application to all problems involving uncertainty and long-term risks. I do think it at least a defensible solution to the specific problem of food additives and the risk of cancer. And given the complexity of new products and the continuing lag in our knowledge about their effects on the human body, it provides a useful outer milepost for conceptual analysis by those who regulate a wide variety of dangerous products and processes.

7 Asbestos Discharges: A Shadow in the Lake

THE RESERVE MINING COMPANY made plans in 1947 to extract low-grade iron ore, known as taconite, from a mine in the great Mesabi Range of Minnesota. Desiring to process the ore on the shores of Lake Superior, it sought and received from the state of Minnesota a permit to allow it to discharge wastes into the lake. By 1955, it was shipping the ore to a "beneficiating" plant at Silver Bay, Minnesota. At this facility there took place a process designed to produce pellets of high iron-ore content: machines crushed the taconite, magnets pulled out the iron, and the remaining "tailings" were flushed as a slurry of about 1.5 per cent solids into the clear, cold waters. The slurry itself acted as a current which carried most of the suspended particles to the bottom of the lake.[1]

The efforts of the federal government, three states, and various environmental groups to stop this practice spanned several years of negotiation and litigation, beginning in 1969. The controversy, carried on for four years over the issue of water pollution alone, expanded in 1973 to include the problem of emissions into the air from the Silver Bay plant. The history of this legal battle is instructive on the difficulties faced by both producers and vulnerable citizens in dealing with uncertain possibilities of serious injury from the fall-out of industrial processes. It is a chapter in the catalogue of slumbering hazards in our stage of technological development that is worth study for itself, but also as a comparison to the problem of side effects from products intended directly for human use.

In considering the Reserve Mining case as an instance of the problem of uncertainty and long-term hazards, I first summarize the facts, insofar as the judicial process was able to develop them, and the attendant definitional issues. After describing the judicial reaction to the air emissions and the discharges into the water in terms of the substantive law involved, I discuss the legal questions that faced federal trial and appellate courts in their efforts to construct a remedy.

The first tribunal whose performance is chronicled here is the federal district court in Minnesota which heard the witnesses, including its own experts, and issued a far-reaching order against the company which was the subject of much dispute. The reviewing court was the Court of Appeals for the Eighth Circuit, which substantially modified that order. Indicative of the strength of the passions in the case was the fact that at one point in the litigation, the Eighth Circuit removed the district judge from the case because in its view he had "shed the robe of judge and assumed the mantle of the advocate."[2] As I narrate this judicial story within an industrial saga, I shall analyze the factual and legal issues in the case initially from the standpoint of the district court, interweaving the judgments of the court of appeals both where it approved and rejected the views of the district judge. After this examination of judicial responses, I shall comment on the Reserve Mining case as a paradigm of the more general problem treated in this book.

Some threshold issues confronting the court in the Reserve case concerned the definition of terms. These definitional problems, reflecting the scientific uncertainty that pervaded the case, all related to the character of the minerals that Reserve was extracting from the Mesabi Range. The third most abundant material in the iron formation of the East Mesabi was a silicate called cummingtonite-grunerite.[3] This designation included a group of minerals called amphiboles, which were quite abundant in the formation; they constituted at least 31 percent of the first step of concentrating and pelletizing the material from the mine. The district court defined amphiboles as a group of minerals with "essentially alike crystal structures" that had a silicate chain and generally contained three groups of certain metal ions. The first question of scientific definition with a legal entanglement was whether these amphiboles were "identical to" or "similar to" amosite asbestos.

Those only vaguely familiar with the arguments over the cancer-causing propensities of asbestos may be surprised to learn that the term is a commercial one without independent significance as a mineralogical definition. It is a word that describes a group of hydrated silicates that separate when processed into flexible fibers comprised of fibrils. About half a dozen different products, including chrysotile and amosite, have commercial use under the name "asbestos."[4] Amosite—a trade name derived from the name of a mine in South Africa which also was without technical significance in mineralogy—signifies a "range of mineral compositions with a range of bulk chemistry" rather than a "specific mineral composition."[5]

The importance of precision of terminology related to the fact that amosite asbestos is known to be a human carcinogen. Reserve produced expert witnesses who claimed that the gross morphology—the physical structure—of the Mesabi cummingtonite-grunerite and South African amosite were different.[6] However, the district court said that even these differences, which had to do with the microscopic features of refractive index and angle of extinction, manifested themselves only in groups, not in single crystals. Several witnesses were in fact unable to distinguish the morphology of the minerals, and there was testimony from both sides to the effect that the crystallography and chemistry as well as the morphology of the substances were indistinguishable.

Specifically on the disputed issue, the district judge said that amosite fibers and fibers in the Reserve discharge could not be distinguished. He based this finding on examination of electron microscope photographs and a presentation of infrared spectroscopy.[7] It should be noted, however, that the court's usages in its comparison of amosite and the Reserve tailings did some switching between "identical" and "similar." Perhaps most neutrally scientific in tone was the district judge's statement that of the particles of cummingtonite-grunerite found in the tailings, "a percentage were chemically within the amosite range." He concluded that the Reserve discharges contained "fibers within the cummingtonite-grunerite range of fibrous amphiboles and within this number there are fibers that have the identical morphology, crystallography and chemistry as amosite asbestos."[8] This conclusion was laconically accepted by the court of appeals, which described it as holding that the Reserve discharges were "substantially identical and in some instances identical" to amosite.[9]

It is useful to examine the court's response to this issue with reference to the broad framework of scientific inquiry discussed in the first chapter. We have noted that the objects of scientific investigation are things that investigators never see directly. The phenomena with which scientists do deal are therefore artifacts of the underlying reality they explore. Highlighting the uncertainty about the "facts" of the case is the court's need to judge on the basis of these artifacts, structuring its decision on what in the final legal analysis could practically be understood only as a quantitative relationship of causation. Operating with these constraints, the court may be said to have used morphological similarity as an index to what might be called conceptual similarity. This characterization helps us to see that in this litigation the vital question becomes what the artifact represents in terms of the law—what the chemical entity is as a concept with legal significance. This, in traditional legal terminology, may be called fact-finding. But it may be better understood in terms of concept—a concept that the judge derives from evidence including the best scientific representations of the thing itself, such as crystallographic images.

Assuming that the Reserve discharges could be equated with asbestos, other primarily factual questions came to the fore. An important one related to the air emissions was characterized by the court of appeals as involving the "level of exposure": how many fibers spewed out by the plant were present in given units of air? One would have thought that it was possible to have a fairly precise finding on this point, relatively unencumbered by what might be termed the artifactitious element. But it seemed that it was impossible to know even this present "fact" with anything approaching certainty.

Dr. Arnold Brown, testifying as the court's expert, opined that as a general matter, the level of fibers in both air and water was not readily susceptible of measurement.[10] How unsusceptible it was appeared from the varying estimates of several witnesses who testified on fiber counts. Dr. William Nicholson of the Mount Sinai School of Medicine testified that he found concentrations ranging from 400,000 amphibole fibers per cubic meter of air at a point south-southwest of the pellet storage area to 140 million fibers per cubic meter in a sample taken at the top of a Reserve smokestack. Experts for Reserve, converting their measurements to equivalents with the Nicholson data, said the figures ranged from about 6,000 fibers per cubic meter to 81,000, in the report of one witness, and to a maximum of 320,000 in the count of another. The court took its own air samples, but the district judge said apologetically that he had not given the sampling program long enough to run because of the pressure of time. Specifically, there was insufficient opportunity to minimize the possibility of chance occurrences, because of precipitation on or before two of the four days when these samples were taken. With this admittedly unreliable basis for measurement, the court's experts reported concentrations that ranged from 1,620 fibers per cubic meter to 145,200.[11]

The court also directed criticism at the experts for the plaintiffs and for Reserve. It said the "major deficiency" in Dr. Nicholson's findings was that they were "worst case" data, obtained right under the smoke plume; and it criticized the counting method used by Reserve's experts—a technique that in the case of one photomicrograph produced a count of just one fiber where arguably there were five.[12] Further confounding the issue, it appeared that scientific statistics on fiber counts have what to lay persons would seem a large margin of error. In the Reserve case, with what was characterized as a "relatively imprecise state of counting techniques," this margin was estimated at ninefold, so that a test count of .0626 fibers per cubic centimeter could represent an actual count of from 0.5634 to 0.0069 fibers.[13]

With all this conflict and uncertainty, the district judge came to a conclusion that one might have derived without such intensive investigation. Given reports of fibers per cubic meter ranging between 1,620 and 140 million—and that any count could err by a factor of ten—he found that there undeniably was a "significant burden of amphibole fibers from Reserve's discharge in the air of Silver Bay."[14] On review, the court of appeals declared the count a "scientifically perilous undertaking," but judged that the excess of fibers in Silver Bay air as compared with St. Paul as a control city was "statistically significant" and could not be disregarded.[15]

An interesting subissue with respect to the air discharges had to do with the length of the fibers, most of which were "short fibers" of less than five microns in length. This issue, like the fiber-count problem reflective of the room for scientific argument throughout the litigation, was a significant one. The question of practical medical concern was related to the propensity of the asbestos group of minerals to cause mesothelioma, a very invasive membranous tumor usually associated with the lungs and the abdominal cavity. Mesothelioma, it may be noted, is a prime example of the fact that deadly substances may do their work through a variety of contacts: a substantial number of cases—up to one half in a South African study—have been discovered in persons who live near rather than work in asbestos plants. Moreover, many occurrences of this particularly cruel cancer have been found in people whose only known contact with the substance was that they lived in households of asbestos workers.[16] Quite as unnerving are reports of excess mesothelioma among occupational groups that did not deal directly with asbestos but worked near shipyard insulation workers who did.[17]

Exemplifying the complexity of the fiber-length question were conflicts, both direct and tangential, among the experts. A former Rochester medical professor asserted that there was a "cut-off" length below which mesothelioma could not be induced by injection into the pleural cavities of animals. The head of the Institute of Occupational Medicine in Edinburgh reported an experimental correlation between reduced tumor production in test animals and the shortening of fibers. Yet another witness for Reserve conceded that it was not settled what the effects were of the "milling" process usually necessary to produce short fibers, thus admitting the possibility that the plaintiffs were right when they argued that milling changed the original character of the fibers.

This set the stage for the redoubtable Dr. Irving Selikoff, an asbestos and occupational diseases expert from Mount Sinai School of Medicine. Dr. Selikoff described a study in which two groups of rats were exposed to fibers of chrysotile—a form of asbestos—of varying length. In one group all but 1 percent of the fibers were 3 microns or less, and in the other, 5 percent were longer than 5 microns. The rate of development of mesothelioma was the same for both groups—40 percent—although it took longer for tumors to occur in the group exposed to the shorter fibers.[18]

There was even some testimony indicating that perhaps the danger from shorter fibers was greater. This came from a witness who reported that most fibers discovered at the center of the lungs of a group of asbestos manufacturing workers, and nearly all of the fibers found at the periphery—where pleural mesotheliomas occur—were shorter than five microns.[19] An explanation advanced for findings that incriminated short fibers more than long ones was that being shorter and thinner, they penetrated most deeply into the lungs.

Piled upon the conflicts in evidence were various attacks on experimental method. For example, the principal court-appointed expert, Dr. Brown, declared that the investigators, presumably on both sides, did not use electron microscopy to "size" the fibers properly. As a result, he said, it was not known whether experimental animals were exposed to only short or only long fibers.[20] Reserve in its turn claimed that the methodology of the plaintiffs' studies did not isolate small fibers sufficiently. And a broader criticism advanced by plaintiffs' witnesses, specifically related to the problem of long-term risks, referred to the rule of thumb that the latency period for malignancies is about twenty years. These witnesses were critical of worker studies for not tracking employees for a long enough time, and suggested that follow-up research might show excess cancer deaths after twenty-five years even in groups with relatively low exposure to asbestos.[21]

A further complication was a legal one, growing out of the fact that the Secretary of Labor had required the counting only of fibers more than five microns in length for purposes of determining occupational exposure to asbestos.[22] Reserve, of course, argued that this should be dispositive that the shorter fibers were safe. However, Dr. Brown, despite his criticism of the experimental methodology on fiber length, declared that "fibers less than five microns are just as dangerous as those over five microns."[23] And a report of the National Academy of Sciences had said that there was "No body of knowledge that permits the assigning of relative risk factors to fibers in the electron microscope range compared with fibers in the light microscope range."[24] Thus there was significant expert opinion indicating that the risk was the same, or that at best there was no way to determine if it differed, among various lengths of fiber. Moreover, Dr. Selikoff and another physician, both of whom had participated in the formulation of the Labor Department asbestos standard, said that the five micron figure was primarily a concession to technological limitations in laboratories which did not have the equipment to count smaller lengths.[25] After considering all this testimony, the district court decided that short fibers could not be shown to have a lower relative risk than long fibers—a conclusion cited with apparent approval by the court of appeals.[26]

The problem of the air emissions became even more perplexing when the courts addressed the question of what effects Reserve's discharges in particular were likely to have on the public. It was known that amosite asbestos caused mesothelioma in human beings in occupational settings. But there were multiple tiers of uncertainty in this case, not only because of the difficulty of determining exposure levels for the Reserve emissions—and therefore of comparing levels in asbestos mines or mills—but because only a part of the emissions were identical to amosite. Particularly frustrating in this regard was the lack of knowledge as to whether the carcinogenic properties of amosite were characteristic of the other fibers coming from Reserve's stacks. On this point, the court of appeals referred to testimony that particular forms of asbestos occupied a wide range of carcinogenicity, with crocidolite thought to be the worst offender and there being considerable doubt expressed as to whether tremolite caused cancer at all.[27] On balance, the court of appeals thought the district court correct in its reliance on an NAS report which emphasized the lack of knowledge of the differences between asbestos forms and concluded that no type of the mineral could be "regarded as free from hazard." But it also referred to the "further uncertainty" imported into the situation by the discharge of fibers "dissimilar from amosite."[28]

A model for the tentative character of the appellate court's assessment of this risk—and for its inclination to a generalized risk-averseness—appeared in the testimony of the court-appointed witness Dr. Brown. The court of appeals characterized his view as holding the evidence "insufficient to make a scientific probability statement as to whether adverse health consequences would in fact ensue," but also described him as having "a public health concern over the continued long-term emission of fibers into the air." Dr. Brown found himself "unable to predict" that the number of fibers in the air of Silver Bay would bring cancer to the community. Yet he also said that the presence of a "known, human carcinogen" was "cause for concern," and asserted that if there were "means of removing that human carcinogen from the environment, that should then be done." He declared that until the safe level of asbestos was known, he could not, "as a physician, consider with equanimity the fact" of human exposure.[29]

When issues of causation confront us with uncertainties and wide-ranging statistical estimates like those in Reserve Mining, the practical decision often will turn on this sort of general assessment. In my view, such expressions of concern by dispassionate, qualified scientists present at least a prima facie case for governmental action.

Responding to such statements, the courts in Reserve Mining seemed at least implicitly to follow a principle of risk-averseness which applies to situations where there is conflicting evidence on the scientific artifacts, where responsible testimony indicates that there is a risk factor, and where what is at issue is a judgment on the quantum of risk. It should be emphasized that this case not only drew into question the effects of what might be called different models of the same product, but involved disagreement about whether what was being measured was one model or another. Certainly when there is controversy relating to the production of scientific knowledge, it seems desirable that regulation should be biased toward avoiding risk in complex situations, and that courts should err on the side of caution in making judgments on the basis of heavily contested expert interpretations.

Despite the prospect of diminution in productive activity, intervention is justified when the predicted danger is one that would fall fortuitously and severely on groups of persons unable practically to provide protection for themselves. The very dearth of definitive knowledge on the subject, the relative lack of choice in the target population, and the gravity of the potential consequences all argue for legislative regulation, or in its absence, positive judicial response. The possibility that such actions may inflict disproportionate economic hardship on the target population itself presents a special problem that requires further analysis. I shall not explore this problem in detail here. For the moment, we may say that when the judgment is that it is intolerable to permit the hazardous conduct to continue, the solution may lie in direct compensation payments from a combination of sources. A Reserve situation would present a classic case for legislative cushioning from the general revenues, at least if one assumes ignorance of the hazard in the population when the process began and while it continued.

In addition to the problems presented by the air emissions, an additional set of uncertainties existed concerning the effects of Reserve's discharge into Lake Superior. First, as the court of appeals expressed it, there was a question of whether the ingestion of fibers from water would create "any danger whatsoever." To answer this question, the district court undertook to have a comparative study made of tissues from the bodies of long-time Duluth residents who had died, and tissues of Houston cadavers. Commenting before the completion of this study, Dr. Selikoff predicted "We should find some fibers there," although he said, "We're looking for needles in a haystack." If asbestos fibers were not found "in appreciable quantities," he asserted, he would "risk a professional opinion that there is no danger, at least up to this point, to the population no matter what our samples show or water samples." The conclusion of Dr. Pooley, a court-appointed expert who explained the results of this study, was that the "needles" were not there—that "residents of Duluth have not been found to have asbestiform fibers in their tissues when compared

with Houston."[30] Yet despite this finding—and Dr. Selikoff's prospective statement that it would signal a practically risk-free situation to him—the district judge evidently wanted to save the city
from even the shadow of evil. Citing an argument that fibers
might have been overlooked because the tissue specimens were
only a minute area of the body, he ruled the study was not conclusive on whether the water discharges presented a hazard. The
court of appeals agreed, although it said the negative findings had
to be given "some weight" with respect to probabilities of harm.

The court of appeals believed that the uncertainty about the
existence of a danger in the water discharges weighed heavily
against a finding of emergency or "imminent hazard to health,"
thus militating against the immediate abatement ordered by the
district court.[31] Yet the appellate court left open the question of
whether there was enough danger to justify "abatement on less
immediate terms." There was some evidence, at varying levels of
scientific abstraction, that might support a less severe remedy.
Concerning the question of whether ingested asbestos fibers could
penetrate the mucosa of the gastrointestinal tract, there was a
direct conflict, with investigators reporting opposing results from
studies of animal tissues. On the basis of at least two studies showing that fibers had crossed tissue walls, Dr. Brown was characterized
as concluding that there was "some support" for the view that this
could happen. One might wish for more as a basis for judicial de-
cree. By analogy, it may be observed that allowing the testimony
of one expert to constitute "substantial evidence" in an administrative law setting can be vexatious. But given the stakes in personal
safety involved in a case like Reserve Mining, a court should be entitled to credit the conclusions of one or two scientists as a basis for
extrapolation to judgments about risk.

Beyond the evidence from animals was the fact of a rise in
the rate of gastrointestinal cancer among workers exposed to asbestos dust. This increase was "substantially lower" than those of
mesothelioma and lung cancer rates associated with inhalation,
and there were various alternative explanations for it—as Dr.
Selikoff himself noted. Selikoff did opine that ingestion of particles, which presumably were coughed up and then swallowed, was
the "probable" cause of the excess in gastrointestinal malignancies, and the court of appeals concluded that the ingestion
theory rested on a "tenable medical hypothesis." Bulwarking this
was the statement by the court expert, Dr. Brown, that the evi-

dence was "probably good enough" to conclude that it was "likely" to expect "an increased incidence of cancer of the gastrointestinal tract in occupationally exposed people."[32] But with testimony thus burdened with qualifications, the court would go no further than to say that the occupational studies supported "the proposition that the ingestion of asbestos fibers can result in harm to health." Clearly, the case is shadowed by the prospect that the rather provisional conclusions of scientists may lead to considerable economic dislocation. Yet there is a reason that courts will give weight to the "probablies," "likelies," and "cans" in this kind of situation; it appears in the darkness of the shadow of the hazard itself.

A further question concerning the lake water was whether the level of exposure was hazardous to those who drank it. The court of appeals' treatment of the expert testimony, and its conclusions, reflected the fact that no one really knew the answer to this question. Studies of the amount of asbestos fibers that would be swallowed by Duluth residents in their drinking water were quite diverse in both design and findings. Dr. Nicholson, whose testimony was persuasive to the trial judge, concluded that residents would ingest about two-thirds of the amount of asbestos fibers in 18 years that an asbestos worker would swallow in 4 years. However, his assumption of fiber concentration of 25 million per liter was twice what the court had found as the mean concentration of all amphiboles. And a Reserve expert, Dr. Gross, declared that it would take 60 years of ingestion at several hundred million fibers per liter to reach levels comparable with those of persons occupationally exposed.

The court of appeals found Nicholson's testimony "evidentially weak," but said that with other evidence it supported the conclusion that there was "some risk to health" from asbestos ingestion, although to "an undetermined degree." Should assessments so loaded with qualifications, so tentative, form a basis for governmental action? It is here that the judgment of science reaches its limits, and one must resort to the qualitatively different sort of judgment that law embodies. An interesting analogue, particularly relevant from the standpoint of this analysis, appears in Dr. Brown's distinction between the "scientific" and the "medical." As a scientist, he said, he found that the trial raised "many questions," generating a hypothesis that one would like to pursue "in the abstract scientific sense of an interesting intellectual question for which there is suggestive evidence." Yet in response to the trial judge's request that he put on his "medical hat," Dr. Brown's perspective changed. Apparently viewing the problem as a matter of public health protection, he concluded that "the fibers should not be present in the drinking water of the people of the North Shore."[33] This prescription was not cut-and-dried, for even in this part of Dr. Brown's testimony there was the implication of economic balancing: "As a medical person," he said, "I think that I have to err, if err I do, on the side of what is best for the greatest number." This rough statement of principle implied the question of how such a utilitarian judgment should be made under conditions of uncertainty. It also raised the difficult problem inherent in the intervening union's claim that the ill health that could result from prolonged unemployment caused by the shutdown of the Reserve plant might be "more certain than the harm from drinking Lake Superior water or breathing Silver Bay air."[34]

With this background of threatened immediate economic effects and scientific uncertainty about the long term, the court of appeals turned to an analysis in terms of "concepts of potential harm." It drew on the then recent panel decision in the EPA's litigation with Ethyl Corporation[35] to characterize two approaches to the problem, one fixed on "probabilities and consequences," the other on "risk and harm." Focusing on a "probabilities analysis," it was unwilling to say that the "probability of harm" in the Lake Superior discharges was "more likely than not." Moreover, the "level of probability" did not convert readily "into a prediction of consequences": From the record of the case, one could not forecast an increase in cancer rates attributable either to the water in the lake or the air breathed by community residents. Even so, the court declared that "the public's exposure to asbestos fibers in air and water creates some health risk," and that "such a contaminant should be removed."[36] This conclusion about risk, it must be emphasized, rested on a chain of hypotheses about how many fibers there were, whether they could cross tissue barriers, and how much danger of disease this would bring to those who inhaled or ingested them. The court, viewing the conflicting evidence on these questions in the context of a variety of statutes, appears to have adopted a generally risk-averse perspective on potential long-term hazards of a scientifically complex nature. The wellsprings of this approach are not entirely clear. They may lie partly in a special horror of cancer in the public mind; evidently they also arise from the mixture of professional intuition and concern for individual bodily integrity that is reflected in the testimony of Dr. Brown with his "medical hat." Such testimony takes on a complex, partly normative character in this context, blending as it does elements of quantitative analysis and a generalized desire to avoid the causation of disease.

Judges, like any people, indulge in "oughts" and "shoulds," but the payoff in litigation always appears in the remedy. Approaching that question after hearing the contradictory and uncertain evidence that I have summarized, the district court found its patience with Reserve exhausted. Originally it ordered an immediate stoppage to the discharge.[37] Then, considering the matter after a cooling off period of 70 days imposed by the court of appeals, District Judge Lord reiterated his finding that there was a "health threat" and emphasized what he called the court's role in "an equity suit brought by various sovereigns for the protection of the health and safety of these citizens." In this legal setting, he said, even in the absence of specific legislation, a court "must give great weight to the protection of the citizens."[38] Having originally asserted that Reserve was in a position to end the discharge without ruination, and having described its work force as "hostages" to the firm's desire to maintain its profitability,[39] he reiterated his view that the discharge should cease.[40]

The court of appeals took a lower-key approach to the problem—one more explicitly concerned with weighing Reserve's present dollar contributions against the long-term uncertainties. It focused critically on the district judge's employment of the word "substantially" to describe the endangerment created by the emissions and discharges,[41] attacking the failure of that usage to respond to the need for an assessment in terms of "probabilities or consequences." As to the water, the court of appeals concluded that the probabilities of injury "must be deemed low"; there was no showing of past health harm, but only a "medical theory" implicating ingestion "as a causative factor" in increased occupational incidence of gastrointestinal cancer. With respect to risk in the air emissions, there was "a higher degree of proof," founded in correlations between inhalation of asbestos dust and disease. Yet even in that case, the court said, there was no measurement "in terms of predictability"; the judgment "must be made without direct proof."

The tension that this state of the evidence created for the court appeared in its subsequent statement that "the hazard in both the air and water can be measured in only the most general terms as a concern for the public health resting upon a reasonable medical theory." The tentative tone of this characterization reflected the difficulty in making the legal connection between evidence which signals but does not confirm a danger and the perspective on risk that society is evolving about hazards of this kind.

Without doubt an impelling force in the appeals court's decision on the remedy—one which generally may be described as risk-averse although it does not lean as strongly in that direction as the trial judge's mandate—is manifested in its simple statement that "Serious consequences could result if the hypothesis on which [the medical theory] is based should ultimately prove true."[42] This fear was real enough that despite the "coulds" and "ifs," the court thought itself "not powerless to act." Although it refused to affirm the district court's order of an immediate shutdown, it could not "ignore the potential for harm in Reserve's discharges." Therefore, it declared that the water discharges must stop and the air emissions must be reduced "below a medically significant level," but left the time to be negotiated between the State of Minnesota and Reserve subject to further judicial supervision.[43]

One should not minimize the differences between the district judge and the court of appeals as a matter of either technical analysis or jurisprudential approach. The appeals court's decision is one that effectively permits significantly more leeway for risky conduct. But what does seem noteworthy is the confluence of the view in both opinions that something should be done, with at least some alacrity, about a process whose hazards were still a matter of "hypothesis," and which over and over again were emphasized to be a matter of "uncertainty." This seems confirmation of a general principle of risk aversion, assuredly in part a creature of the air and water pollution laws of the last decade but partly growing from an independent concern of courts for preservation of public safety, which informs judicial decisions in cases of uncertainty about long-term risks.

The district judge refused to accept what he described as the argument that the discharge should be permitted until it could be shown that it "has actually resulted in death to a statistically significant number of people." His premise that "the sanctity of human life is of too great value to this Court to permit such a thing"[44] may seem unrefined alongside the court of appeals' balancing of the discomforts that an immediate shutdown would bring to the persons if affected. Yet an insistence on that "sanctity," if a less passionate one, seems significantly to inform the appeals court's less severe formulation of a remedy. An implicit message is that when a definable possibility arises that terrible consequences will fall with unequal weight on a group of helpless citizens, their physical integrity becomes a factor valued beyond simple dollar calculations. The opinions of the Reserve courts embody a recognition that present American society requires that valuation, and that courts are semi-independent guarantors that it be made. This is not to ignore the importance of the benefits of present production to the very group that is threatened. What happens as these conflicts develop is that the court becomes a mediator. On the one hand it recognizes our commitment to productivity joined with our understanding that all life poses radical uncertainty; on the other, it captures our averseness to even uncertain risks of the most fearsome harms as well as our ideas of justice in allocating the physical costs of technology.

Viewing the court of appeals' reference to "danger to public health"[45] in its starkest connotations, it may seem too compromising that conduct so described should be allowed to continue even for a week. But there is common sense as well as legal sense in the decision. By its declaration that there is a risk requiring judicial intervention, the court makes clear that its basic approach favors public protection against even uncertain hazards. At the same time its tailoring of the remedy represents the degree of risk averseness it derives from the relevant statutes, absorbs from general attitudes, and finds responsive to the facts of a difficult case. Taking a somewhat resigned perspective on the previously established existence of the risk, it responds to the tensions created by conflicting interests that rend residents in the same community, at once maintaining the role of the judiciary as legislative interpreter as well as independent preserver of public health and safety. Inculcated in this approach is the idea that all law is a balance.[46] Yet even in its recognition of competing interests, the decision teaches that in a "day of synthetic living," the basic line of the balance has shifted toward risk aversion because of the very artificiality of the processes that fuel that life-style.

Supporting and complementing the judicial response to the specific facts of the Reserve case, the statutory language applicable to the water discharges reflects a legislative aversion to possible as well as probable risk. Especially clear in this regard is the wording of the Minnesota water-quality legislation, which defines "pollution" as contamination rendering water "impure so as to be actually or potentially harmful or detrimental or injurious to public health, safety or welfare."[47] Relatively opaque is the requirement in the Federal Water Pollution Control Act that to be actionable, pollution must be "endangering the health, or welfare of persons."[48] But given a Congressionally declared purpose of enhancing water resources and establishing "a national policy for the prevention, control and abatement of water pollution," the court of appeals found the term "endangering" to connote a "lesser risk of harm" than the phraseology of "imminent and substantial endangerment" in another clause of the statute allowing emergency suits for immediate injunctions. It viewed this use of "endangering" as "precautionary or preventive," an interpretation which permitted it to consider "evidence of potential harm as well as actual harm." Given a "reasonable medical concern over the public health," arising from "an acceptable but unproved medical theory" as to carcinogenicity, the court found that the "endangering" standard had been met.[49] This seems a proper reading of a broad legislative concern about risk in a situation which in responsible medical opinion offers grounds for apprehension. The initial judicial filtering of the legislative message yields the rough substantive judgment that those who utilize modern technology should be prevented from taking chances with other people's lives. The court's decision that Reserve should be "given a reasonable time to stop discharging its wastes" into the lake[50] simply represents a more precise application of that judgment on the specific facts.

Matching and even going beyond the Minnesota water-quality law in making possibilities of harm actionable are that state's air-quality regulations, which were held to be violated in the Reserve case. Among other infractions, the courts found violations of "primary" standards, which were defined by the regulations to include levels of air pollutants above which, "on the basis of present knowledge, health hazards or impairment may be produced." The tentative character of the "may" is further stretched by a definition of health hazards that includes "production, aggravation or possible production of disease."[51] From the nature of the proof in the Reserve case one might infer that the application of the regulations to the air emissions was based on the "possible" terminology. It should also be noted that the Minnesota regulation's definition of "secondary" standards speaks of "levels which are desirable to protect the public welfare from any known or anticipated adverse effects," including "annoyance and nuisance of person."[52] Although presumably a court would read a balancing test into the nuisance language, on its face it is quite elastic as to the level of discomfort. It is true, interestingly, that the language of "anticipated adverse effects" in the secondary standards is arguably not as capacious as that of the primary standards definition. However, it could certainly be interpreted to include a possibility of harm of a kind judged sufficient to create a danger to the public welfare. The general point is that the wording of these regulations encourages administrative risk aversion, perhaps even to a degree beyond the position I have advanced here.

One must be cautious about generalized interpretations of statutory language of "danger" and "hazard," since these terms arise from specialized legislative backgrounds. Often courts will be bound by specific legislative history indicating Congressional choices of particular meanings. With this qualification, it is useful here to refer to Judge Wright's opinion for the court in the hotly contested contemporaneous case of *Ethyl Corp.* v. *EPA*,[53] which is the most sensitive general judicial treatment to date of language of this kind. Writing with reference to regulations that progressively reduce lead content in gasoline, he dealt with a statutory clause that allowed control or prohibition of the manufacture of fuels or fuel additives that "will endanger the public health or welfare." In a sense, Judge Wright's response went beyond the necessities of the case, for though this phraseology presented the agency with a somewhat more difficult legal task than that posed by the statutes and regulations in Reserve, the administrator in Ethyl had hurdled that barrier in finding specifically that lead in auto emissions would endanger the public health.[54] Yet it was in appropriate recognition of the realities of this kind of litigation that Judge Wright offered, as he did, an interpretation of the statutory language that permitted broad elbow room for agencies and judges. The court would not demand "rigorous step-by-step proof of cause and effect," he said, "[w]here a statute is precautionary in nature, the evidence difficult to come by, uncertain, or conflicting because it is on the frontiers of scientific knowledge, the regulations designed to protect the public health, and the decision that of an expert administrator."[55]

He emphasized that he intended no suggestion that the agency could act "on hunches or wild guesses." But if the administrator "rationally justified" his conclusions, Judge Wright would permit him to "apply his expertise" to draw them "from suspected, but not completely substantiated, relationships among facts, from theoretical projections from imperfect data, from probative preliminary data not yet certifiable as 'fact,' and the like."[56] Such a conclusion—"a risk assessment"—could fulfill the "will endanger" language if only it was "rational." It is a formula that lacks the precision of gauges and dials. But in a situation where "we must deal with the terminology of law, not science,"[57] in which words are "better than logarithms" for purposes of judicial adjustment of competing interests, it is persuasively articulated.

The subsequent history of the Reserve case emphasized the need for courts and agencies to give fullest implementation to the risk-aversion inherent in the kinds of statutes and regulations at issue in that litigation. These events pointed up in particular the built-in bargaining margin that a prospective injunction involves when it is made subject to negotiation. The initial measure of that margin in the Reserve case was sixteen months: The court of appeals having directed in April 1975 that Reserve and the State of Minnesota should have a "reasonable time" to agree on an on-land disposal site, it was not until August 1976 that the district court concluded that failure to reach agreement—the parties were 13 miles apart in their proposals—required a halt to the discharges within one year.[58] The court of appeals affirmed this order, and also the imposition of $837,500 in fines.[59]

Still there was more to come, in the form of a complication of federalism. The court of appeals in its brief opinion left open the possibility of resolving the on-land dumping question "by agreement or through litigation in state court." Responding to this invitation, Reserve persuaded a panel of state district judges to require issuance of a permit allowing it to dump the tailings at the point it preferred—Milepost 7—rather than the Milepost 20 contended for by the state's pollution control agency and its department of natural resources. Reserve's advantage in fighting a holding action was evident at that point from the fact that once a site was fixed, it would take two years to construct proper disposal facilities. Thus the combination of a conditional injunction and a state avenue of litigation provided plenty of room for maneuver. The company then capped its defense when the Minnesota Supreme Court unanimously affirmed the state district court's Milepost 7 decision,[60] which included a disposal permit limited to five years and specified the use of the "best available technology." The state decided not to appeal to the United States Supreme Court. The judicial process of two systems had thus eventually yielded a result that reduced risk though it did not avoid it entirely. As a generality, this had a satisfactory sound. Its specific outcome would have to abide efforts at compliance—and further measurements.

The story as it continued up to the proof stage of this book reflected Reserve's determination to push its legal rights to the limit, and an apparent wearing out of the patience of the Minnesota Supreme Court. Having extracted from the Minnesota agencies the Milepost 7 permit ordered by the state trial court and affirmed by the state supreme court, Reserve next pressed its suit with objections to several conditions in the permit. In this newest round, the company convinced the state trial court that fiber levels for both air and water must be approved by the Pollution Control Agency unless they were "in excess of a medically significant level." The Minnesota Supreme Court rejected this standard, however, emphasizing its finding in its earlier decision that "medically significant" levels of fibers in the air could not "be determined with scientific or medical precision," and that there was "no evidence of what level of water pollution is medically significant." Noting that the federal appeals court had said that controls "may be deemed adequate" if they reduced the fiber count to the level "ordinarily found in the ambient air of a control city such as St. Paul," it declared that "neither the PCA, the mining companies, nor the state courts, are at liberty to modify or set aside that standard." It also held that the agency could apply a "non-degradation standard" for the water "until and unless a medically significant level is in the future determined with scientific precision." Finally, commenting tartly that "protracted litigation of this kind" did not serve "the interests of clients nor the administration of justice," the court declared it was "the responsibility of Reserve, an industry important to the people of Minnesota, and of PCA, an agency charged with protecting the environment, to make mutual conces-

sions and exercise restraint to reach an accord and end this controversy."[61]

I should now like to add to this analysis of the law applied in
the Reserve case some more general observations about its meaning in the broader background of national concern with potential
hazards posed by scientific and technological progress.

It is important to note that the general principles of regulation
governing this sort of activity are formulated in an extremely
abstract way. Illustratively, while granting a stay of Judge Lord's
order of an immediate shutdown of Reserve, and quoting Chief
Justice Burger's declaration that "the world must go on and new
environmental legislation must be carefully meshed with more
traditional patterns of federal regulation," the Eighth Circuit gave
voice to the principle that "foremost consideration must be given
to any demonstrable danger to the public health."[62] There is
many a slip between standards so broad and applications in specific cases, as the continuing saga of the Reserve litigation demonstrates. Yet even such articulations do provide some index to a
social consensus.

A parallel point about the use of language is that the terminology of danger moves, eluding interpretation, in and out of specific statutory phraseology, bumped and twisted one way and
another by courts. The district court in its original decision to shut
down Reserve made a finding that the "discharge . . . substantially
endangers the health of those exposed."[63] This characterization
did not find favor with the court of appeals, which said that the
evidence was "insufficient to support the kind of demonstrable
danger to the public health" that would justify an immediate closing of the plant. Its parallel characterization of the question of
whether any relief should be granted was whether there was "any
risk to the public health," and if so, whether it was "legally cogniz-
able."[64] This variation in usage is only illustrative of the difficulty
of establishing scientific referents for the "danger" nouns and
verbs and their associated adjectives of gravity and severity. Given
the complexity of the environment to which these terms are addressed, this is to be expected. But although there is a range of
acceptable verbal formulations of the problem, Judge Wright's
language in the Ethyl case, quoted above,[65] probably supplies the
best general interpretation of statutory "endangerment" concepts.

The demand for accurate testing poses problems for the law in
territory where the seeming precision of science fades into the

need for judgment. The difficulties involved should not surprise those familiar with the scientific enterprise generally. We have noted that even what appear to be "hard" data have behind them a certain craftsmanship, as distinguished from a simple reading of instruments. Indeed, science does not produce "perfect" data, but only an agreement to measure to standards derived from direct investigative experience as well as from the continuous process of learning from teachers and colleagues.[66] Thus while science preserves those elements of craft discipline that will continue to generate reasonably reliable data, it becomes necessary for law to facilitate resolution of disagreements on reliability itself, as well as on the significance of agreed-on experimental results. The judicial process in the Reserve litigation yielded mixed results in this regard. The difficulties in the case lay not in a dearth of data and opinion, but in the problems of judgment both as to what was found and what it meant. The use of a court-appointed expert was helpful in this regard. The haste with which some of the court's own testing was conducted was a negative feature of the case. More generally, the development of a jurisprudence relating to the problem of scientific uncertainty and physical hazard— begun by such cases as Reserve and Ethyl—should insure that future decisions of this kind are at least better wrought, if not easier.

An important issue, which is related to testing and is also symptomatic of the legal problems of dealing with cancer in particular and complex risks in general, concerns the significance of the results of animal experimentation for human beings. Showings that substances cause cancer in animals traditionally have been used to justify regulation; the 1977 ban on saccharin as an additive provides a controversial instance. An interesting issue on the other side of the coin appears in the holding of the court of appeals in the Reserve case that negative animal testing could not be dispositive for people on the question of fiber ingestion. This, it said, was because animal cancer susceptibility was not "as a general matter ... directly equivalent of human experience."[67] The ruling puts makers and users of substances in a position where they must bow to findings of carcinogenicity in animals, but cannot escape by showing that there is no such evidence. Abstractly, this sounds unjust, but in at least some applications it is a defensible working rule, as in cases in which animal evidence casts suspicion on some forms of human contact with the product. For example, under the principles of risk aversion developed here, it

would seem appropriate to take severely restrictive or even prohibitory action against the water discharges in the Reserve case even
if there were no evidence of gastrointestinal penetration from
ingestion, so long as there were incriminating animal data on
inhalation. Strong evidence of this kind would be sufficient to
render legally suspect the discharges that would be ingested, at
least to the point of placing a burden on the producer to demonstrate safety through further tests. Although I recognize that this
position is open to the criticism that it ignores a well-established
scientific distinction between modes of product contact, I think it
is justified. When one route of administration is shown to be
harmful to the tissues of creatures used as experimental surrogates, in conditions of uncertainty this should be enough to require the proponent to show with a high degree of assurance that
other sets of surrogate tissues are not vulnerable to similar effects.

   We would not want to encourage the judicial chasing of
shadows. But the nature of the uncertainty involved in situations
like Reserve has shown courts that often they cannot make findings of "fact" of the traditional sort.[68] The court of appeals recognized this when it noted that many of the issues before it did not
involve " 'historical' facts subject to the ordinary means of judicial
resolution." It said explicitly that "the finder of fact must accept
certain areas of uncertainty" and that its findings could go no
further than trying to "assess or characterize the strengths and
weaknesses of the opposing arguments."[69] It may be added that
the very disjunction in the use of "assess or characterize" underlines the necessity for courts to define their judgmental approach
to risks of physical hazard.

   The need to define the vector of judgment is quite evident
with respect to questions like that of the significance of animal
data for people. A problem equally illustrative of that need arises
when a court must deal with conclusions that while a substance
has not been proved hazardous, it has also not been shown that it
is not harmful. Providing an example is Judge Lord's statement
about a statistically small excess of deaths in Duluth from rectal
cancer. In the face of his own expert's statement that there was
"no evidence" that a small number of excess cancer deaths in
Duluth was attributable to drinking Superior water,[70] he declared
that it could not be said that the increase was "not due to ingestion
by these persons of asbestos from Reserve's taconite waste." What
can be said for a conclusion of inability to prove a causation nega-

tive is that it may be used to support regulation under a generally risk-averse approach when it is associated with persuasive theory or findings that affirmatively indicate the possibility of long-term risks. This is the most that can be said. Yet while the argument may be used rather ingenuously, it should be stressed that it is precisely the element of present indeterminacy that gives it weight in an area where we are counseled by history and medical opinion, and a common sense educated by both, to avoid risks whose contours remain ill-defined. The problem of asbestos-caused cancer is a paradigm of long-term uncertainty. The trial judge's insistence that one could not conclude that the Reserve discharges were not carcinogenic reflects the fact that it generally takes two decades or more for these effects to show up.[71]

The issue is both delicate and difficult. A valuable attempt at resolution, incorporating an effort to define more generally the judicial role in such cases, appears in the court of appeals decisions of 1974 and 1975—the first granting a stay of Judge Lord's order to close the plant, and the second ordering an abatement over a period to be negotiated. With respect to the plea for an immediate shutdown, the court of appeals thought there had been no showing of a "demonstrable health hazard." It thus found that Judge Lord had "tipped the balance in favor of attempting to protect against the unknown," and had taken a position that "resolve[d] all doubts in favor of health safety," which it characterized as representing "a legislative policy judgment, not a judicial one."[72] Yet despite its emphasis on the conjectural nature of the district court's findings, the court of appeals later ordered conditional abatement because of the "potential for harm in Reserve's discharges," saying that this "impart[ed] a degree of urgency" to the case that was generally lacking in suits for "ecological pollution."[73] The decisions emphasize that the substantive law surrounding long-term risks is in significant part a function of the remedy. It is a truism, implicit in the first decision by the appellate court, that while legislatures set broad courses of policy, fashioning remedies is a judicial specialty. In this traditional framework, the court of appeals' eventual choice of remedy indicates a belief that judges have an independent responsibility to communities which are only potentially threatened by hypothesized by undefinable risks.

Recent history supports this kind of judicial approach. In cases involving varied products and processes, changes in medical intuition concerning the hazards of substances illustrate the desirability of a risk-averse perspective on matters concerning which there is respectable opinion that potential danger exists. An instructive profile appears in the views of an expert who served as a consultant to a large asbestos user, and then as a witness for Reserve Mining. This witness, Dr. George Wright, had told occupational safety and health hearings in 1972 that he thought that amosite fibers of the kind discharged by Reserve, as well as the asbestos fiber crocidolite, required stricter control than chrysotile—the primary material used in asbestos manufacture. In the Reserve trial, Dr. Wright said that he now thought amosite and chrysotile were equally dangerous.[74] This is simply exemplary of the fact that time and again the development of new data—or of new perspectives—changes scientists' judgments. It is for that reason that the legal system must permit, and perhaps should encourage, vigorous administrative and judicial response when experts first sound alarms of possible danger.

To be sure, one must guard against overreacting. Distinguishing the responsible forecast of a fearsome risk from the rank speculation of publicity seekers poses a difficult problem for judges. However, judicious use of court-appointed experts and of the adversary process itself can help to insure that risk aversion does not become destructive timidity. There surely are costs associated with prohibitions and restrictions, but they can be held to a minimum by proper attention to the credentials of experts on both sides, and to the history of similar product profiles as well as of analogous certitudes.

A particularly significant lesson in public response to long-term risks appears in certain facts concerning the taconite processing at Silver Bay as it related to the chronology of the litigation. Not only did this activity continue for at least fourteen years until it was initially challenged, but the water discharge aspect of the case—eventually found to be the more benign—was the only focus of grievance for well over a year, until the plaintiffs began to argue the air-pollution question. This underlines not only the lack of public awareness that may attend the conduct of such enterprises, but the difficulty of getting at the nub of the problem once they become controversial.

One of the most telling arguments for severe limitation, and sometimes prohibition, of the use of substances that carry even potential long-term risks is advanced by physicians as a matter of medical opinion rather than scientific fact. Identifying his view as one of advocacy, Dr. Selikoff declared that "to the extent feasible . . . carcinogenic substances should not be added to the environmental burden in which we live." In a more personalized way, the court's expert witness, Dr. Brown, referred to "some sort of compulsion to protect ourselves against known agents that produce cancer until we know what the safe levels are," which he associated with being "a physician, who would rather see well people than sick people."[75] This "compulsion," I submit, represents a consensus, partly rational and partly intuitive. And even as intuition, it is not uneducated; for it embodies precisely the same kind of judgment that we expect from our personal physicians, judgment which most patients will follow even if they suspect that it is offered out of an excess of caution.

In suggesting that we should be extremely wary of suspect scientific novelties, I do not ignore the general proposition, sanctioned by both science and law in various degrees in different contexts, that there are many substances that may be harmful if encountered in large quantities, but for which there are safe levels at the ordinary, low level of human exposure. There is one extraordinary legislative judgment that may be said generally to oppose this view as an operational basis for policy, and it has been enacted on three separate occasions: the Delaney amendment. However, the notion of safe use has prevailed more generally with respect to substances that may cause a wide range of disease or injury.

A safe-use standard is in fact implicit in the Eighth Circuit's decision staying the injunction to shut down Reserve Mining. But although that court granted the stay, being unconvinced about the existence of a demonstrable health hazard, some of the testimony to which it referred has a double edge: In pointing up how hard it was for those challenging an activity to show what is unsafe, it underlined the difficulty of demonstrating it was safe. The appeals court said that to show the kind of health threat requisite to uphold the injunction, it would have to be proved that the circumstances of exposure were "at least comparable to those in occupational settings" where disease had occurred, or that occupational studies had established "principles of asbestos-disease pathology" that could be predictively applied in altered circumstances. Having noted the relatively low levels of asbestos fibers in the air over Silver Bay as compared with occupational settings, the court said that prediction of "the likelihood of disease at lower levels of exposure" required a rather precise determination of those levels. And this was only a threshold to the crucial inquiry—"it must be determined whether the level of exposure is safe or unsafe."[76] Yet to put these questions was only to emphasize the uncertainty of the ground on which decision must rest. Despite the fact that the court's own expert hypothesized that there was in fact a dose-response relationship for asbestos and cancer, the case contains the ingredients of the classic bout of law with unknown risks—and for the reason that inspired the broad brush stroke of the Delaney amendment: the same witness said that he had not "the foggiest idea . . . as to what that level might be." And though agreeing "as a generalization" to the proposition that there would be levels of asbestos exposure "that will not be associated with any detectable risk," he reiterated that he did "not know what that level is."[77]

The problem as it initially develops lies in the lack of knowledge about causation in the population generally. Dr. Brown's dubiety on this point appears and reappears in the various renditions of the case. His view was reflected in the appeals court's own uncertainty, for example in its statement in the decision staying the injunction that "it is not known what level of exposure is safe or unsafe."[78] It crops out again in the decision provisionally abating the discharges where the court quotes Brown's refusal to "draw firm conclusions," which he said he could do only "if I knew what a safe level was in the air, if I knew what a safe level was in the water." He asserted that "that information is not available to me, and I submit . . . it's not available to anyone else."[79]

But the determination of safety is not simply a matter of compiling "information" in the sense of gathering and averaging data from the relevant community, although as the Reserve litigation shows, that is difficult enough. Even when there is "information . . . developed in a scientific way," to use the standard articulated by Dr. Brown, the recurring, vexatious question is what is meant by "safe." Given differential sensitivities among people to exposures to particular substances, that definition could range from an absolutist conception that we must not permit carcinogenicity in any foreseeable use of a product to a standard that permits trade-offs of production for the lives of especially sensitive citizens.

We do eschew risks as the numbers of vulnerable persons get larger. The problem becomes more difficult as sensitivity moves toward idiosyncrasy. In theory, a proper response might be to require physical tests to determine sensitivity, when that is feasible, along with the advance provision of compensation. But as a practical matter, given the expense of testing, the general uncertainty concerning such effects and the difficulty of precisely defining idiosyncrasy in terms of certain levels of exposure, the preferable alternative often will be not to take the chance. This assures protection to persons over the entire range of sensitivity, while avoiding the explicit political choice of defining particular percentages of people as idiosyncratic and therefore condemned to sacrifice, and the associated ethical problems of using a few citizens as buffers or distant early warning systems for the rest of the population. Surely, where it is possible to generate and communicate pertinent information about risk, it is desirable to encourage bargaining and choice—for example, a forewarned resident of Silver Bay could choose to move or elect to stay and take compensatory payments if and when he became afflicted. This would allow for the continuance of production where halting it to avoid the risk of disease will bring life-threatening economic deprivation. In any event, however, it is essential that we maintain our focus on the moral problem beyond the task of data collection, with a continuing awareness that courts as well as legislatures must sometimes make choices between the lives of a few and comforts for many.

8 DNA Regulation: Law To Tame the Genie

ON AUGUST 2, 1939, ALBERT EINSTEIN wrote a letter to President Roosevelt. Brief from the standpoint of its portents, it said in part:

> Some recent work by E. Fermi and L. Szilard, which has been communicated to me in manuscript, leads me to expect that the element uranium may be turned into a new and important source of energy in the immediate future. . . .
>
> In the course of the last four months it has been made probable . . . that it may become possible to set up nuclear chain reactions in a large mass of uranium, by which vast amounts of power and large quantities of new radium-like elements would be generated. . . .
>
> This new phenomenon would also lead to the construction of bombs, and it is conceivable—though much less certain—that extremely powerful bombs of a new type may thus be constructed. . . .[1]

This letter, though it described possibilities known to a number of sophisticated scientists, was not publicized. The American people did not know about the potential of nuclear power until August 6, 1945, when the first atomic bomb was dropped on Hiroshima.

A letter with something of the same laconic tone appeared in *Science* magazine on July 26, 1974.[2] Somewhat more scientifically descriptive, it included the following passages:

> Recent advances in techniques for the isolation and rejoining of segments of DNA now permit construction of biologically active recombinant DNA molecules in vitro. . . . There is serious concern that some of these artificial recombinant DNA molecules could prove biologically hazardous.

There are a number of noteworthy points of comparison between these documents. They were similar in announcing scientific developments which carried great hazardous potential and in their understated style. However, in the case of nuclear power,

218

the letter implied approval of a predicted destructive use, at least in a foreseeable military context, whereas with the DNA recombinants, the problem for the letter signers was one of unwanted as well as unpredictable side effects.

Perhaps the most striking difference lay in the manner of announcing the message. In contrast to the secrecy surrounding the Einstein letter, the communication to *Science* was open. In fact it was not the first public document on the subject, but its appearance represented the swelling of a tide of concern among scientists themselves.

The date of publication of the *Science* letter also underlined the incredible pace of change in molecular biology, one matching the speed of development in the atomic-energy field after 1939. Among the savants of the revolution in molecular research was Marshall Nirenberg, who in 1967 had warned that the acquisition of techniques for manipulating genes would precede society's ability to formulate goals for that work.[3] By 1972, a scientific paper had described a DNA recombinant technique used by the authors,[4] and the British journal *Nature* published a brief, critical commentary on the possible dangers of this kind of research.[5]

American researchers really began to "go public" on the subject in September 1973, when a letter to *Science* representing "a number of scientists" communicated their "deep concern" that "hybrid molecules may prove hazardous to laboratory workers and to the public."[6] The profile of potential risk identified in their letter was a familiar one to readers who have followed our story of other products and processes: "Although no hazard has yet been established, prudence suggests that the potential hazard be seriously considered." Subsequent to this came the previously quoted *Science* letter of 1974. Signed by Paul Berg of Stanford, an author of the original 1972 paper, and several others, it restated the problem generally and recommended that investigators voluntarily abstain from two specified categories of experiments.

The principal problem specifically addressed here arises from the fear of the destructive biochemical potential that might inhere in the unpredictable power of the gene. The drama in this extraordinary world of science fiction become reality—as will appear presently, researchers now thought seriously of stitching together pieces of life from toads and from bacteria—is a story of science confronting regulatory attempts that is well worth study in itself. It is also an episode that is especially interesting in a general sense to those concerned with uncertain perils associated with scientific and technological advance. In a pivotal historical document on the subject, the 1976 HEW guidelines on recombinant research, the director of NIH declared in his introduction that the field is one that illustrates "the potential impact of basic science on society as a whole." Indeed, a unique aspect of this chapter in regulation is that it involves direct control of basic research. The difficulty of the problem of policy-making is directly proportionate to the scientific excitement being generated by the remarkable development of the field. A characteristic feature of this area of "extremely technical and complex experiments"—and one particularly relevant to the present book—is the fact that even active molecular biologists with "means of keeping informed" may "fail to keep abreast of the newest developments."[7]

DNA—dioxyribonucleic acid—has been described as "the material that determines the hereditary characteristics of all known cells."[8] Even a layman must sense that to force changes in this material might entail grave consequences. What were these experimental techniques, and why was their use so attractive to the accomplished scientists who both wanted to use them and found their potential for harm so great that they at least temporarily drew back? Carrying the argument that some of these procedures should cease to a symposium in Minneapolis in June 1974, Richard Roblin of the Harvard Medical School mentioned several experimental achievements and possibilities and also spoke of their potential for long-term hazards.[9] Descriptively, the most fundamental point was that it was possible to combine into new molecules fragments of DNA from sources as different as toads and bacterial plasmids, i.e., DNA molecules in some bacteria that exist apart from the chromosomes and replicate on their own. The necessary technology depended on the finding of enzymes which could break down DNA strands at specific sites and couple the broken fragments in new combinations. Discovery of these enzymes made it possible to insert foreign genes into viruses or plasmids, which could be used as "vectors" to introduce the foreign genes into bacteria or into the cells of plants or animals in test tubes. Genes transplanted in this way would "impart their hereditary properties to new hosts."[10] Experimenters had introduced a recombinant molecule into a bacterium called Escherichia coli (E. coli), which resides in the human intestinal tract and is often used in genetic research. It had been shown that this recombinant molecule would replicate itself during the bacterial growth cycle. Roblin said that these techniques offered "a generally applicable approach to the isolation, amplification, and ultimately the large-scale production of discrete, gene-sized DNA sequences from essentially any organism of interest, from fruit flies to man."[11]

He described the plans of several named experimenters to introduce genes from entities as diverse as fruit flies, sea urchins, and a protozoan named Euglena into E. coli. He referred to the "considerable interest" in producing recombinant DNA with animal virus and plasmid DNA, and inserting this new product into E. coli. Even more specifically, he spoke of a particular virus which transformed mouse and hamster cells into cancer cells as a "likely candidate for such experiments." Roblin suggested that E. coli strains which replicated a recombinant of this virus, designated SV40, "could be used as factories" to produce SV40 DNA for use in nucleic acid hybridization experiments. This possibility alone, he said, provided a "powerful" incentive to make the recombinant. But there were other reasons to proceed with this work, not the least of which was that it held promise in research on the possible causal relationship between the virus herpes simplex and human cancers. Still other possible fruits of this kind of investigation might include employment of E. coli as a "factory" for the production of insulin and antibiotics, and the transfer of genes which achieve nitrogen fixation to microbes which live near the roots of corn and wheat, thus reducing the need for chemical fertilizer.

Others were prophesying uses of gene technology that spanned the range of human pleasures and sufferings. Vast remedial possibilities are implicit in the assertion that there is a "genetic basis" for "most diseases"—from schizophrenia to diabetes to cancer and certain forms of heart disease—with up to one-quarter of all diseases being thought to be "predominantly" genetic in origin.[12] One logical response to such hereditary factors with important legal implications is genetic screening. Strong policy arguments support proposals that testing for certain characteristics be made mandatory for eugenic purposes; the welfare burdens imposed by the birth of defective children present concerns that reach beyond immediate families.[13] Yet serious constitutional issues would attend such legislation. Exerting a strong pull in the other direction are the interests of both freedom of choice and privacy of prospective parents. This sort of issue is only illustrative of the legal and ethical complexities surrounding the recombinant techniques. Battalions of horribles have been paraded as examples of the possible consequences of genetic manipulation—for instance, the ability to breed ruling elites and masses of obedient slaves.[14]

Yet threatening to outstrip these fundamentally social and political issues in immediacy of impact was the unpredictable potential for hazard borne by the creation of new genetic products. In his symposium talk at Minneapolis, Dr. Roblin raised several possibilities of harmful fallout, including the "widespread dissemination" of new strains of bacteria. Apprehensive about the possible effects if such biological products were to colonize the human intestinal tract, he asked, without answering the question, whether these consequences might include additional risk of "cancer or other . . . diseases." Moreover, even if the strains originally selected as hosts, such as E. coli, proved to be harmless after receiving the recombinant product, could this begin a process of communicating genetic information to other species which would produce hazardous consequences? E. coli was in fact a transfer vehicle, and what would happen if it transferred a recombinant plasmid with special antibiotic resistance to a pathogenic bacterium?

Other disturbing questions grew out of the apparently benign proposal to utilize recombinants to produce insulin. If an E. coli strain carrying the recombinant product were to get into people's intestines, could this upset human regulation of insulin production? And, Roblin asked, might not that event "lead to new manmade disease"?

These were simply illustrations of the uncertainties that bedeviled scientists who had been working on these exciting investigations. But the uncertainty cut two ways, and in a fashion that makes the problem of gene recombination a specially fascinating one. By contrast with the more typical problem in which society derives a certain short-term benefit but worries about uncertain long-term risks, in this case one had to speculate on gains as well as losses. At the same time, continuing the conceptual parallelism of uncertainties, the predicted gains might be as dramatic as the possible hazards could be disastrous. Thus, as Roblin noted, to restrict research in this new technology "could doom future cancer patients and the undernourished."[15]

The possible opportunities forgone were doubtless painfully

obvious to the signers of the 1974 letter to *Science,* headed by Berg
and including the Nobel Prize-winning discoverer of the DNA
structure, James D. Watson, as well as Roblin. Yet, as I have indicated, the seriousness of the possible consequences of some of this
research led them to recommend a voluntary moratorium on two
classes of experiments. One of these was the making of bacterial
plasmids that could produce increased antibiotic resistance in bacteria that did not have it—or the construction of plasmids that
themselves achieved novel combinations of resistance. The other
was the linkage of DNAs from oncogenic (that is, cancer-causing)
viruses or other animal viruses to "autonomously replicating DNA
elements," including bacterial plasmids or other viral DNAs.

The Berg letter also called for special caution by scientists who
were planning to link animal DNA fragments to bacterial DNA or
DNA of the antibody agents called bacteriophage, because "many
types of animal cell DNAs contain sequences common to RNA
tumor viruses." Although the letter did not seek complete absten-
tion from these experiments, it warned that they "should not be
undertaken lightly" because "joining of any foreign DNA to a
DNA replication system" would produce recombinants "whose
biological properties cannot be predicted with certainty."[16]

An especially interesting aspect of this manifestation of professional concern was the letter's declaration that it was "based on
judgments of potential rather than demonstrated risk," since there
were "few available experimental data" on the hazards of these
molecules. Many branches on the decision tree were shrouded,
and one could only hypothesize the form that the hazard might
take. In this posture, the case posed rather directly the question
of how society should respond to the expressed anxieties of scientists based on professional intuition of possible catastrophe.

Such a situation seemed to demand something beyond individual, voluntary restraint, and the Berg letter did ask for more
positive action. Reflecting the lack of data and the general difficulty of the problem was its request for appointment of an advisory committee which would oversee an experimental program to
evaluate the hazards of the recombinants. The letter also said that
such a committee should develop procedures to minimize the
spread of the new molecules and formulate guidelines for
researchers—a suggestion almost immediately taken up when
NIH appointed its Recombinant DNA Advisory Committee in
October 1974.

A further suggestion in the letter was for "an international meeting of involved scientists from all over the world," to convene early the next year. This inspiration carried through to the convocation of the remarkable conference at Asilomar, California, in February 1975. Although shadowed by the prospect of regulation, the meeting was noteworthy both for its voluntary nature and its sober response to a question of social importance.

The report of this conference[17] represented a response to perceived possibilities of risk. Emphatic in its contention that "containment" of the new biological agents must be an "essential consideration" in experimental designs, it declared that the effectiveness of containment should be matched "as closely as possible" to "the estimated risk." The report undertook to classify types of experiments by the kinds of risks involved, and to describe rather precisely the procedures which should be utilized with respect to each one. These involved two kinds of containment—one biological, utilizing the properties of specific molecules as safeguards against the propagation of dangerous agents, the other using physical methods ranging from the design of buildings to the specification of air-cleansing processes.

Illustrative of what the conferees regarded as a "minimal risk" experiment was one involving prokaryotic agents—organisms such as bacteria with poorly formed nuclei—that were known to exchange genetic information naturally. For such experiments, the Asilomar report recommended the physical procedures normally employed in clinical microbiological laboratories. These include the use of at least cotton-plugged pipettes and preferably mechanical pipetting devices, as well as prohibitions on drinking, eating, or smoking in the laboratory. By comparison, the conferees rated as "low" risk the propagation of recombinant molecules from DNAs of species that ordinarily did not exchange genetic information, thus generating "novel biotypes," but in a way that apparently had little chance of creating serious side effects such as increases in pathogenicity or antibiotic resistance. Reflecting some increase in hazard, this category required, among other things, a prohibition of pipetting by mouth and the use of biological safety cabinets.

By still further contrast, the Asilomar report called for the use of "moderate"- or "high"-risk containment for experiments that either involved pathogens or "genetic determinants that may increase the pathogenicity of the recipient species." The elements of "moderate" risk-containment, as defined, included precautions such as the use of gloves in the handling of infectious materials, as well as a requirement that transfer operations be carried out in biological safety cabinets, such as laminar flow hoods. As the virulence of the organisms increased, one would have to step up to a "high"-risk category of procedures, the description of which conveyed a futuristic image: isolation of the research area by air locks, the use of treatment systems by which the laboratory could inactivate contaminating agents that might otherwise be discharged in exhaust and solid wastes, and a requirement that all personnel take showers when leaving the facility.

With respect to experiments involving animal viruses, the report focused on the use of biological barriers, which were to be complemented by moderate-risk physical containment. Specifically, it declared that vector-host systems used with DNA from warm-blooded animals must have "demonstrably restricted growth capabilities outside the laboratory." This emphasis was aligned with the report's statement of general principles on the use of biological barriers, which it limited to "fastidious bacterial hosts" that could not survive in natural environments, and nontransmissible vectors that could only grow in specified hosts. The report underlined the necessity for rigorous testing of the "barrier" quality of hosts and vectors.

The conferees found "most difficult to assess" the risks of joining random fragments of DNA from eukaryotes—that is, higher organisms with well-formed nuclei—to prokaryotic DNA vectors, and the propagation of the resulting recombinants in prokaryotic hosts. The report asserts that "a priori," DNA from warm-blooded vertebrates is more likely to contain certain chromosomal gene complements called cryptic viral genomes, which are potential human pathogens, than would DNA from other eukaroytes. Based on this assumption, the recommendation for procedures of this kind combined both physical and biological containment in the same way as the one applicable to animal virus experiments: they should be conducted only with vector-host systems whose capabilities for growth outside the laboratory have been shown to be restricted, and in a moderate-risk facility.

Manifesting the uncertainty of the experts themselves about this research was the report's statement that "nothing" was known about "the potential infectivity in higher organisms of phages or bacteria containing segments of eukaroytic DNA"; moreover, "very little" was known about "the infectivity of the DNA molecules themselves." Yet there was evidence of genetic transformation of bacteria in animals, which suggested that "recombinant DNA molecules can retain their biological potency in the environment."

Most soberly, the report said that there were some experiments that should not be carried out at all because their dangers were so serious. This category of present horrors included the cloning of recombinant DNAs derived from "highly pathogenic" organisms—for which a classification system by relative degree of hazard had already been established. A prohibitory recommendation also went to DNA containing toxin genes. And quite importantly from the conferees' viewpoint, there should be no "large-scale experiments"—those involving more than 10 liters of culture—which used recombinant DNAs "able to make products potentially harmful to man, animals or plants." This reference to large-scale usage is repeated in the report as a subject of concern; and it is interesting that the quoted language used to describe the proscribed category is as broad as the abstractions in the general language of any safety legislation.

The Asilomar meeting is an important benchmark. Especially significant was the voluntary aspect of the conference. Convoked at the instance of individual researchers, it produced a report urging scientific brethren to use its proposals "as a guide" until "national bodies" could implement codes of practices. As a historical demarcation line of this research, the report brings home the awesome nature of its combination of uncertainty with the potential of truly dreadful possibilities. This amalgam makes the case of gene recombination a metaphor grown large for the general problem of controlling the dangerous products and processes which are the fruits of modern science. In the locution used here, it is an especially apt symbol, for the "product" of this kind of experimentation is itself a "process"—that of life itself.

The uncertainties of the research remained in the forefront of concern as the government began to respond to the evident need for officially sanctioned standards. The lack of knowledge about long-term consequences was manifest in the comments received by NIH on its Recombinant Advisory Committee's July 1975 proposal of draft guidelines, which were attacked by a "majority" of critics who thought them too lax, as well as by a number who considered them too strict.[18]

In particular, there was substantial controversy on the question of whether nature has already "tested the probabilities of harmful recombination." The more sanguine investigators, noting that prokaryotes such as human intestinal bacteria exchange DNA with their eukaryotic host, contended that the fact that altered prokaryotes cannot be detected shows that the ability of such recombinants to survive is "sharply limited." But those who called for more restrictions posited that harm could stem from the alteration of hosts if they developed competitive advantages which fostered their survival "in some niche within the ecosystem." The argument that hosts might be altered in "unpredictable and undesirable" ways thus ran head-on into the contention that the necessary tests already had been conducted in nature's own laboratory. The Director of NIH exposed the profound uncertainty about this issue in a crisp sentence: "The fact is that we do not know which of the above-stated propositions is correct."[19]

It was also well to keep in mind, while focusing on possible dangers, that there were unknowns on the positive side. In addition to the affirmative spinoffs predicted to come from the research, it might confer enormous benefits that could not be precisely forecast. For example, a font of knowledge about genetic diseases might be awaiting investigators.[20] Yet it was primarily the uncertainty about potential hazards that informed the issuance of full-dress guidelines in June 1976,[21] 16 months after the Asilomar conference. Along with the ensuing debate focused on these guidelines, the bureaucracy generated yet more paper on the problem, including recommendations from an interagency committee that the guidelines standards—applied in terms only to research funded by NIH—be legislatively extended to all recombinant DNA research, private as well as public. In September 1977, the NIH director issued a proposed revision of the 1976 guidelines,[22] one which was the subject of debate at this writing as a part of the larger controversy and attendant Congressional backing and filling over the question of what legislation, if any, should be enacted to deal with the question.[23] The story is thus one that seems likely to continue for some time. I shall focus here on the 1976 guidelines, which are a central document in this history, analyzing them not only for their historical interest in a fast-moving chain of events, but for the general instruction they provide with reference to the broad subject of this book. They shed light on a range of experimental forms with varying potential for market control or governmental surveillance; in particular, they indicate that when basic research becomes a candidate for regulation, considerable leeway necessarily must be left for the exercise of professional responsibility. I should add, in this connection, that my employment here of the term "regulation" to refer to the guidelines is a rather loose usage that implies an enforcement authority that may not in fact have existed at the time. From their initial promulgation in 1976, serious issues existed as to the legal effect of the guidelines, specifically with respect to the question of whether they could properly be termed "regulations"; indeed, in early 1978, a proposal was formally made to promulgate them in an explicitly binding way under that heading.[24]

The policy content of the guidelines is closely related to the scientific environment which they concern. They deal with both physical and biological containment, and they also prohibit certain kinds of experiments entirely. After discussing each of these categories, I shall mention some applications to specific cases.

The guidelines set up four classes of physical containment levels. These categories approximated those which already had been proposed at the Asilomar conference, as well as the classifications used by the Center for Disease Control. As a baseline, the document referred to "good microbiological practices" as embodying the "first principle of containment." It then proceeded to define the P1 level, labeled "minimal," which included such standards as the requirement that work surfaces be decontaminated daily and after spills of recombinant materials. Parallel to the lowest Asilomar classification, the P1 formulation permitted pipetting by mouth, but expressed a preference for mechanical devices. The P2 or "low" level embodied a significant disclosure feature, which was that only persons who had been advised of the potential biohazard could enter the laboratory. This guideline required the use of laboratory gowns, coats, or uniforms. It also mandated biological safety cabinets and/or other physical containment equipment to minimize the hazard from procedures that produced a "considerable aerosol," such as the use of blenders.

The P3 level, labeled "moderate," reflected a considerable increase in perceived risks. Laboratories meeting these specifications must be separated from areas which are open to the general public by controlled access corridors, airlocks, locker rooms, or other double-door facilities not available for general public use. Equally indicative of the level of hazard of P3 experimentation was the requirement that before materials were removed from biological safety cabinets they had to be sterilized or transferred to nonbreakable sealed containers which would then be removed through a decontaminating unit, such as a chemical tank. Among other provisions, the guidelines required directional airflow within the controlled laboratory area and special treatment of exhaust air before it was recirculated, as well as biological safety cabinets for all aerosols. The P3 rules also demanded the posting of the universal biohazard sign on all laboratory doors. They even spelled out the kind of laboratory clothing that could and could not be used—for example, front-buttoned laboratory coats were held unsuitable—and they declared that street outerwear should not be kept in the laboratory.

P4 safeguards—the category for "high" risks—were designed to contain the most dangerous permissible research. These experiments would involve micro-organisms characterized as "extremely hazardous to man" or capable of causing "serious epidemic disease." At this level, among other precautions, there must be airlocks through which supplies and materials could be brought safely into the facility. Heightening the reader's sense of futuristic dread, the guideline required that P4 facilities be constructed of monolithic walls, floors, and ceilings in which airducts, electrical conduits, and utility pipes were sealed to assure the isolation of the work area. Moreover, experiments at this level must utilize the safest kind of biological safety cabinet—a Class III cabinet. This is a "closed front ventilated cabinet of gas-type construction," fitted with arm-length rubber gloves and operated under a negative pressure of at least 0.5 inches water gauge. Class III cabinets must have their supply air either filtered through a high-efficiency particulate filter or incinerated before being discharged to the outside environment. In addition to these stringent controls on the air itself, the document set out specific decontamination procedures for all materials to be removed from P4 laboratories. And along with requirements related to building and device design, the guidelines focused on the worker as a potential carrier of hazard. Not only was clothing prescribed—at the P4 level one must wear a complete set of laboratory clothing, discarding it into hampers before exit—but also workers must shower before leaving the facility.[25]

The other containment guidelines, utilizing three levels of biological barriers, are themselves remarkable to the nonscientist who examines them. Even if practitioners regard the process of recombining biological agents as still in a primitive state of development, one point that comes clear to the layman is the sophistication of the art. For example, the guidelines matter-of-factly referred to a number of "vectors"—plasmids and bacteriophage—as established experimental vehicles.

The most worrisome point conveyed by the biological containment standards concerned a familiar theme: the lack of definitive knowledge concerning the effects of the experimental agents. An illustration appeared in the agency's decision to name the intestinal bacterium E. coli K-12 as the host-vector system of choice. The guidelines referred to anxiety over the "potential dangers" which "are compounded by using an organism as intimately connected with man as is E. coli." Their efforts to quiet apprehensions reflected the difficulty of establishing a balancing process for unknowns.

The document described three different kinds of E. coli K-12 host-vectors, of which the first, labeled EK-1, was "estimated" to provide a "moderate" level of containment. In discussing the EK-1 host-vectors, the guidelines found some comfort in the fact that experimentally used E. coli K-12 does not "usually" colonize human bowels. But this result might vary with the intestinal flora in given individuals. And "viable" E. coli K-12 had been found in human feces, which signaled that "transductional and conjugational transfer" from E. coli K-12 to resident bacteria in feces had "to be considered" as a possibility. The upshot of this was that investigators should proceed "cautiously" with E. coli; and the guidelines suggested a commitment of "serious efforts" toward developing alternative host-vector systems.[26]

In this connection, the NIH director's introduction did say that E. coli K-12 had been the subject of "more intense investigation than any other single organism," an experience record that led him to believe that it would be a safer host-vector system than other proposed microorganisms. The general level of risk in the research was evident in the fact that while encouraging the development of alternative systems, he noted that each would involve the same questions about risks from recombination applicable to E. coli.[27]

Besides articulating general cautions, and a stated commitment to a search for substitutes, the guidelines spoke specifically about the possibility that plasmid vectors would be disseminated by accidental ingestion. Their comments and strictures on this point illustrated both the ignorance of experts about the consequences of this research and the need for precision about who was being protected from what. The document said that the probabilities of such dissemination were "low" if only standard microbiological practices were followed, and especially if researchers avoided mouth pipetting.[28] It is unclear why this practice, which was grudgingly permitted under minimal (P1) containment but prohibited at the P2 level, should be allowed at all. It would seem that when there is ground for residual concern about such a practice, it should be banned, unless there is a strong cost justification and risks are inconsequential. These are questions of fact, to be resolved in particular circumstances. A more general point is that when regulation is called for, hortatory declarations are of little use. Providing a contrast was the statement, in the same paragraph, that people who had received antibiotic therapy within seven days "must not" work with recombinants from any E. coli K-12 host-vector system. Less stringent was the statement that people whose stomach or bowel had been surgically removed "should avoid such work."[29] When one views these provisions together, one cannot help but be struck by an aspect of them common to this sort of regulation—the uncertainty they reflect about what is really necessary. And it is noteworthy that although these guidelines presumably were designed primarily for the protection of the public rather than laboratory workers, the sense of the permissive clauses is one of allowing workers to choose the level of risk.

Feeling their way into realms of greater potential danger, the guidelines further specified EK-2 and EK-3 host-vectors. Both of these provided "high" levels of biological containment, with EK-3 having the added advantage of confirmation by testing in humans as well as animals.[30] The stringency of EK-2 containment alone was such that the director declared that more experience was needed to know whether this would in effect bar "some lines of important research."[31] The rigor of the standards was manifest in the limitation that no more than 1 in 10^8 host cells should be able to perpetuate the vector or a cloned DNA fragment under conditions designed to represent the natural environment. Moreover, approval of a special NIH committee was required for use of EK-2 and EK-3 vectors. Providing a counterpoint to these specific precautions, the necessarily informal aspect of scientific endeavor and the dissemination of scientific knowledge was evident in the exhortation to investigators to report "as rapidly as possible" data they acquired about proposed EK-2 systems, and to make safer cloning systems available to others. This language of encouragement rather than prescription illustrates the reliance that even tight systems of control must place on individual responsibility, as well as indicating NIH's own uncertainty about its enforcement authority.

The reference to EK-3 systems was entirely prospective, as they were yet to be fashioned. The director in his introduction referred to the "general" language dealing with this kind of containment and "the concerns for a more completely defined system of testing."[32] Indeed, even EK-2 safeguards were in the "first stage of development," with only the first such system having been certified contemporaneously with the release of the guidelines.[33] Thus, at the time the guidelines were published, regulation formally permissive at higher levels of risk bordered on the prohibitive for lack of a well-developed set of the biological tools held necessary to conduct this kind of research.

An interesting illustration of the uncertainty generally surrounding the subject of DNA recombination appeared in the guidelines text relating to bacteriophage variants which bear the symbol λ. Bacteriophage can escape from the laboratory, it was pointed out, either as mature infectious phage particles or in bacteria host cells. Scientists had to rely on estimates of the probability that λ could survive in and infect human beings. The fact that this probability was assessed to be "small"—because of the biochemical characteristics of λ and researchers' inability to detect infective λ in human feces—did not change its nature as an estimate. Further reflective of the provisional character of knowledge in the area was the statement that λ-sensitive E. coli strains "seem to be rare," followed immediately by the cautionary notation that since a "significant fraction" of E. coli carried nuclear components called lambdoid prophages, "this route of escape should be considered."[34] Thus the seeming precision of this fundamentally scientific document tended to give way to a tentative and predictive tone when judgment was required. This should not be surprising, given the fact that their work so often requires scientists to use judgment and intuition. The point that merits emphasis is that this responsibly restrained character of scientific assessment accords here with the needs of the social system for policy decision.

It is striking to the lay observer, who might expect that the vagaries of biological agents would render them more chancy containment vehicles than physical barriers, to find the guidelines adding that while the "estimates" for containment achieved by specified host-vectors are "not exact," they are "at least as accurate as those for physical containment." This positively worded comparison was itself revealing, given the uncertainties about biological containment. It was generally symbolic of the contingent nature of knowledge that the guidelines reflected about both dissemination and colonization, as well as about the comparative advantages of biological barriers and physical ones.

The guidelines identified five kinds of experiment which should not be undertaken. These ranged from the cloning of recombinant DNAs from the most dangerous three classes of pathogenic organisms to the deliberate formation of recombinant DNAs which contain genes for the biosynthesis of potent toxins, such as snake venoms. Also prohibited was transfer of drug resistance traits to microorganisms that were not known to acquire them naturally if this "could" compromise the use of a drug in human or veterinary medicine or agriculture.[35] The guidelines conceded that it was arguable that some of these recombinants "could be adequately contained at this time." What underlay the prohibition was a recognition that it was possible that containment might fail. Referring to this possibility, the guidelines said that the possible dangers that "may ensue" would be of such a magnitude that it seemed the "wisest policy" at least to defer such experiments until there was "more information to accurately assess that danger and to allow the construction of more effective biological barriers."[36] It is worthy of note that the guidelines made explicit that the prohibition on using DNA derived from pathogenic organisms included experiments with cells known to be infected with these organisms. Moreover, the final document extended the prohibitions to include clones from moderate-risk oncogenic viruses as defined by the National Cancer Institute, and cells known to be infected with them.[37]

On the whole it appeared that comments by the more risk-averse scientists had prevailed on the prohibited classifications, for the guidelines said that these rules are "more stringent than those initially recommended."[38] The specific reference in the final document to possible failure of containment manifested this cautious attitude, which also showed itself in such provisions as the one on drug-resistance traits, for example, in the use of the word "could" as the standard for prohibition in that clause. We may generally conclude that in this system of controls, with its matching of safety procedures to predictable risks, aversion to risk increases markedly with increases in the combined magnitude of the levels of potential hazard and unpredictability.

It should be added that despite urgings in that direction, the draftsmen were reluctant to extend the class of prohibited experiments to include all procedures that would result in resistance to any antibiotic, regardless of medical or agricultural use. They emphasized that there is another side to the story, inherent in the facts that antibiotic resistance occurs naturally among bacteria, and that resistance is a "valuable marker in the study of microbial genetics in general, and recombinants in particular."[39] To secure these benefits, the guidelines as promulgated undertook to remove an apparent ambiguity in the draft, which arose from a general prohibition coupled with statements that appeared to allow experiments that would extend the range of resistance of E. coli to drugs. The NIH director explained that because E. coli acquires resistance naturally, it had been decided that "the prohibition directed against increasing resistance does not apply." The relative redundancy and predictability of the risk provided a comparison to the classes of prohibited experiments, in which the problem lay in a horror of fearful unknowns.

With respect to permitted experiments, the guidelines set forth an elaborate classification system for procedures using particular kinds of recombinant DNAs. The document generally required higher containment levels for experiments involving the insertion of eukaryotic DNA into prokaryotes. The director described these risks as "having quite uncertain probabilities."[40] One possible hazard he mentioned was the production of a "rogue" bacterium—for example one that could produce insulin—which would be beneficial if it could be contained, but "a nuisance or possibly dangerous if capable of surviving in nature." Moreover, there was a "more concrete reason" for requiring higher levels of containment as eukaryote hosts became similar to man; this was the possibility that viruses which were capable of propagating in human tissue could contaminate DNA, replicate in prokaryote hosts, and infect the researcher.

In the case of high-risk experiments using eukaryotic host-vectors in animals, the guidelines were rather specific about the properties a DNA molecule must have, requiring investigators to possess such information as the location in it of origination and termination sites of DNA synthesis.[41] They effectively permitted the use of only two viral DNAs for this purpose—polyoma and SV40, the latter, as we have previously noted, an agent with considerable potential as a "factory" for nucleic acid hybridization experiments.

The case of SV40 strikingly exemplifies the nature, both known and unknown, of the more dangerous agents used in this research. The guidelines emphasized that as compared with polyoma, SV40 was less desirable because of its production of antibodies in laboratory personnel and its association with human illness, including neurological disease and malignancies. Although this monkey virus had not been definitely pinned down as the culprit of any disease in man, the director said there was "an intensive search" in progress for evidence that it might cause cancer or otherwise be pathogenic. It was known that SV40 could be grown in human cells and that on "very rare" occasions it had been isolated from human beings. However, although expressing appreciation for the concerns of those who urged a complete ban on the use of the virus, the director said that available knowledge provided "sufficient sophistication" to ensure its safe handling at the P4 containment level.[42] An added constraint was that SV40 research must be done with genomes that were "defective"—that is, their propagation must depend on the presence of a complementing "helper" genome. Where the guidelines bent on containment levels to permit the use of P3 facilities for SV40, they stated extremely rigorous conditions. One of these, reminiscent of the animal feed proviso to the Delaney amendment, required that it be shown that "*no* infectious virus particles are being produced."[43]

Besides these limitations on research with the highest degree of risk deemed tolerable, the guidelines imposed containment requirements of varying rigor on all other permitted experiments. They often specified combinations of physical containment levels and biological barriers. For example, with respect to experiments involving animal viruses and E. coli K-12 hosts, the guidelines required that P3 plus EK-1 or P2 plus EK-2 must be used. Of particular interest from a legal standpoint was the allowance of P1 plus EK-1 for experiments with cloned DNA recombinants which had been "rigorously characterized" and for which there was "sufficient" evidence that they were "free of harmful genes." A footnote to this provision admitted that the terms "characterized" and "free of harmful genes" were "unavoidably vague." But what is most significant, despite the necessarily abstract character of the language, is the way this articulation of a combination of standards draws together the judgmental aspects of law and science in conditions where desired knowledge is lacking. Symbolic of the kind of law being evolved is the major safeguard: the requirement of NIH approval for the adoption of containment conditions lower than those used to clone the DNA. The guidelines conditioned this approval on the production of persuasive data relating to a group of factors. One, relatively understandable to laymen, was "the absence of potentially harmful genes." Another was a technically elaborated reference to "the relation between the recovered and desired segment," requiring particular kinds of laboratory analysis. Finally, there must be data concerning "maintenance of the biological properties of the vector."[44]

In sum, this system of regulation, cut from the stuff of life itself, involves constraints blending fairly specific mechanical requirements and biological properties, and backed up by a normative review which carries with it the ultimate clout of funding. The detailed nature of the guidelines and the requirements of combinations of protective elements seem comforting. Still disturbing is the remaining possibility for human error—one pictures as possible weak links the latent defect in the air lock or the worker who takes a hurried shower. It is true that if one assumes frequent and searching site visits by the controllers of funds and a high degree of researchers' concern for reputation as well as their own personal health, the incentives for safety are substantial. Even so, one is left with some lingering, if vague discomfort about the danger and uncertainty. Moreover, while a subject so technical requires specific regulation rather than general injunctions to do good, the detailed nature of the guidelines together with the rocketing pace of change almost insure that a seemingly comprehensive document will suffer from gaps in coverage.

An illustrative problem, and a practical resolution of it that structures research procedures to combat apprehensions of danger, concerns the potential infectivity of SV40. The guidelines had judged this virus to be a relatively undesirable vehicle from a risk standpoint—far less desirable in that regard than the alternative agent polyoma—but they did permit its use because of its extraordinary potential as a tool of cancer research and as a "factory" for needed pharmaceuticals. The qualified allowance of P3 conditions for work with SV40 provides a paradigm for regulators confronted with research which flirts with possible catastrophe in its efforts to relieve individual suffering. The trade-off for the experimenter who wants to descend the precaution ladder from the highest achievable safety system that is P4 is that he must compensate with a zero tolerance in the creation of harmful products. The requirement of this degree of risk-aversion seems appropriate when diminutions are permitted in the use of physical and biological barriers[45] to contain exceptional risks. It should only be added that we place considerable reliance on human responsibility even when we allow the use of the most dangerous agents in a P4 facility. In this sense, the futuristic image of the P4 laboratory becomes a metaphor for our ambivalent attitude of both trust in and wariness toward all those who engage in dangerous activities that may affect us.

The persistence with which the personal responsibility of researchers confronts us as a central factor lends emphasis to the fact that the stringency of the guidelines in the higher-risk categories reflects the risks that *scientists* perceive in these agents. It should be stressed that initially it is the scientists who perceive these hazards, which become apparent only as a result of their investigations and are predictable at all only because of their training and experience. This is why the significance of individual responsibility, generally implicit in the lacunae of the guidelines, becomes explicit in the drafters' emphasis that the text "cannot substitute for the investigator's own knowledgeable and discriminating evaluation." A special section on "roles and responsibilities," making clear the inability of the drafters to anticipate every kind of experiment, elaborated on the scientific worker's personal obligations. It specifically placed a duty on investigators to increase containment beyond the guidelines when the situation called for it, while requiring institutional and NIH approval of decreases in containment levels.[46]

The guidelines placed primary responsibility on principal investigators not only to determine hazards and appropriate containment levels, but to inform staff personnel about hazards and procedures, and to supervise safety. Among other specific mandates, they required the principal investigator to report any kind of untoward incident to NIH. Moreover, the guidelines fixed on institutions in which research was done the overall responsibility for the acts of investigators, and the duty of establishing biohazards committees which were to collect information, make certifications to NIH about facilities and procedures, and advise the institution on policies. The guidelines also imposed independent responsibility on NIH study sections to evaluate biohazards and judge the appropriateness of containment facilities for each grant application. Finally, an NIH advisory committee on recombinants was charged with revision and updating of the guidelines, as well as with resolving questions put to it by the study sections and evaluating EK-2 and EK-3 biological containment systems.[47]

This is an impressive structure of scrutiny and review, but it bears repeating that in the trenches of research, operational decisions of considerable magnitude must fall on the bench scientist. This fact has both its comforts and its disquieting aspects. Presumably, the scientist's own self-interest with respect to future largesse as well as general reputation will exert a strong precautionary influence. Yet the different responses of various investigators to the draft guidelines are testimony that reasonable persons will differ in good faith about what safety measures are necessary, both on the firing line and in policy formation. Within the abstractions of the guidelines, there undoubtedly was room for corner-cutting, and there were incentives in that direction: every restriction on research costs time and drains energies that otherwise would be pointed toward discovery. The requirements for the higher levels of physical containment, and for certification of the EK-2 and EK-3 biological barriers, did seem well designed to deter the kind of conduct most likely to produce seriously injurious results. However, individual responsibility and concomitant social trust carry much weight in the mix of public regulation and professional self-discipline that is evolving around the recombinant technology.

This necessarily will continue to be so to one degree or another. One can only suggest that it is at least problematical how far we can rely on the more informal controls. Some cause for concern comes from history. One is reminded of the difficulty in stopping the use of DES in cattle feed at specified times before slaughter, and of allegations of physicians' laxity in prescribing oral contraceptives without sufficient examination or warning, especially in the early years of Pill marketing. Indeed, the early chapters of DNA research imply potential problems in relying on self-regulation. A journalistic description of Marshall Nirenberg's work in the synthesis of DNA notes that the possibility of producing a new virus might have occurred to Nirenberg, but did not deflect him from the experiment.[48] The point is that whatever that distinguished scientist's view of his subject in the early 1960s,[49] had he been tempted to take socially undesirable risks there was then no official presence peering over his laboratory bench. It is true that this research produced no monster virus, and it is a reassuring confirmation of the responsibility and foresight of scientists that there is little evidence of experiments that have loosed killer organisms beyond the confines of the laboratory.[50] It should be emphasized that whatever control was exercised in the early investigations was purely voluntary, and that the first warnings of danger about recombinant research were sounded by those who were themselves engaged in the work. Further comfort for those who believe the risk of external consequences from DNA research is minimal comes by analogy from research experience with powerful pathogens under federal control. Dr. Bernard Davis of the Harvard Medical School, who has written eloquently of the risks of limiting research as opposed to doing it, has noted that there has been only a single probable case of infection communicated outside the laboratory in 25 years of research at the government's bacteriological warfare facility at Fort Detrick, Maryland, and again only one case of infection transmitted outside of the Center for Disease Control. On the basis of this and other data, he termed the NIH guidelines "excessively conservative."[51] Without fully accepting that judgment, one is inclined to the view that the record on containment of biological research dangers is generally a heartening one. Despite this, however, the nature of the potential hazards and the remarkable spread of opportunities to use these techniques are indicative of the need for government to play a role.

An example of a possible need for checks within the laboratory appeared in the guideline making the investigator responsible for advising his staff about biohazards. The drafters of this provision rejected a suggestion that investigators must get the formal

informed consent of laboratory personnel.[52] Arguably, this was
the wrong decision. The incentives of investigators in a given
situation may be opposed enough to their employees' interests,
and the pressures for production may tend sufficiently toward
shortcuts, to make the requirement of formal informed consent
the only practical way to assure that workers are exposed to no
more than those risks they would readily assume.

Assuming the necessity for continuing review of recombinant
hazards as a threat to both laboratory workers and the general
public, some important questions involved the input by nonscientists. The NIH Director noted that the Recombinant Advisory
Committee would include scientists representing disciplines actively engaged in such research, in order to provide the "necessary
expertise to assure that the guidelines are of the highest scientific
quality." He also announced that the committee would have
members from other scientific disciplines, as well as two nonscientists: a political scientist and an "ethicist." He pointed out that it
was the existing committee which on its own initiative had recommended the appointment of a nonscientist.[53] This practice,
which tracks that followed on human experimentation committees generally, is highly desirable. Indeed, it might be advisable to
have three or four nonscientists on such committees in order to
assure diverse angles of questioning to make scientists justify their
position, and to obviate the very real possibility of a single lay
member, or even two, being overwhelmed by the appearance of
expertise.

It is well here to elaborate on a number of other matters relating to recombinant research, including the time frame it requires
to yield benefits, the familiar problem of disagreement among
scientists, and the social controversies this work is generating. In
connection with this discussion, we should make general reference to the extraordinary degree of subspecialization of modern
science. Paul Weiss has suggested the analogy of a change from a
lush, unified meadow to a "landscape of deep canyons with raging
rivers, separated by wastelands of arid mesas."[54] The metaphors
are abstract, and they imply problems to which regulation can
provide answers that are at best incomplete. But they do suggest
difficulties of communication among scientists and between scientists and laymen, as well as vast areas of ignorance about the
mysteries of biology, that lawyers and policymakers in this area
would do well to remember when confronted with problems of
uncertainty.

A particular feature of gene manipulation is that some of its perceived benefits lie much further in the future than do those associated with standard commercial products, although at this writing some recombinant research stands at the very threshold of profitable exploitation.[55] One scholar has argued that there exists a social responsibility to continue experimenting because of the possibilities for growth in "wisdom," enabling human beings to act with more "dignity and responsibility."[56] This involves a drawn-out time scale indeed. But some rather more definable goals of genetic experimentation are also fairly long-term—for example, the development of techniques to assure that newborn children are free of recessive cell genes that might otherwise have afflicted them.[57] When the uncertainties of gains as well as risks from research run over periods of years, this argues for increasing the burden on its proponents to persuade potential victims that their safety will not be compromised. It would seem especially appropriate to do that with respect to an activity in which, by contrast with the problems typically generated by industrial processes, the externalizing of dangers may precede the realization of benefits by some time.

The divisions among scientists about the guidelines, reflecting the lack of knowledge about the underlying reality, were substantial and deep. Critics not only centered on the alleged imprecision of the concept of physical containment, but expressed doubt about the concept of biological containment and its effectiveness. Besides the joining of issue on these questions, there was much disagreement about which method would be the safest and most effective.[58] This was so despite a fund of experience on the problem of keeping experimental microbiological agents isolated from the general public, embodied in classification schemes used by the Center for Disease Control for disease-causing agents and the National Cancer Institute for carcinogenic viruses.

An interesting example of the way that issues of this technicality can divide experts is provided by the disagreement in the Recombinant Advisory Committee on the use of DNA from embryonic tissue or germ-line cells from cold-blooded vertebrates. The committee voted eight to four to recommend a combination of P2 plus EK-1 for such research, with the majority taking the position that the possibility of virus transmission was "not a central problem" with cold-blooded vertebrates and that no distinction should be made on the basis of tissue origin. Other members of the committee contended that the level should be P2 plus EK-2, because of the chance that cold-blooded vertebrates could carry viruses. The director opted to support the committee recommendation for the lower level.[59] In the perspective advanced here, a four-vote minority on such a technical question presents at least a prima facie case for an administrator to require the higher level of protection. There is no definitive calculus on this point; the official must make a judgment. But when he must choose among the conflicting intuitions of experts, he should articulate the reasons for his choice. And I would argue that as the risks of given procedures become higher, his degree of risk aversion should increase markedly as significant minorities weigh in against their use.

Such disputes among scientists, as well as the rising level of public concern about matters of this kind, have tended to affect the specific form that regulation takes. Particular parts of the guidelines reflect pushes and pulls in different directions. In some cases the clear stress is on safety, even the appearance of safety. For example, when the NIH director rejected his Advisory Committee's suggestion that P1 facilities did not require an examination, he said that "we believe that all facilities should be reviewed to emphasize the importance of safety programs."[60] There coexists an insistence on precision in matching the level of containment with that of estimated risk, which manifested itself when the director turned down a proposal to merge the first two levels of physical containment. The reason for this decision lay in his belief that a merger of the levels would "tend to apply overly stringent standards for some experiments" and possibly bring about a lowering of the standards necessary for the safety of more dangerous ones.[61]

This description of the conflict in expert opinion on the recombinant question, and of the effort of the guidelines to strike a balance with an appropriate degree of risk averseness, relates to our primary focus on uncertain physical risks which will surface, if at all, only after a period of years. In a previous quotation of one commentator's paean to genetic research as a basis for getting wisdom,[62] we have hinted at an analogous problem area—the threat of long-term social risks from experimental procedures— where we might usefully apply insights derived from our study of the issue of physical hazards. A technology which can fertilize eggs in vitro, and perhaps even eventually bring them to full term in the laboratory, will likely have serious effects on the way people view themselves and society. It has been argued, for example, that the depersonalization of procreation will have dehumanizing consequences for society generally, threatening the institutions of marriage and family.[63] It is true that this is not necessarily a consequence, and personal choice, where possible, may provide a satisfactory resolution of this problem. A rationale for self-determination, where it will not cause harmful external consequences, appears in a statement by a woman who sued a scientific administrator for terminating an experiment that would have implanted an embryo in her following in vitro fertilization. Her argument for the "sacred" nature of the planned child, fully comparable in her eyes with the sanctity of a baby conceived in a normal way, emphasized the extraordinary time, skill, and emotion invested in such an artificial conception.[64] The analogy to our problem enters at the point where committed personal choice creates the possibility of unquantifiable, serious social side effects—as on family structures—over the long term. Because one is dealing in this regard with projected risks that are even harder to predict than, say, carcinogenicity, the problem is even more difficult to grasp. But it would seem that legislators could reasonably take an attitude toward such potential social dangers that is comparably risk-averse to that embodied in prescription drug legislation—or the recombinant guidelines.[65]

It also should be said with respect to the possible social risks of genetic research that it is especially difficult to calculate its counterpart advantages in light of the potential alternatives. In this connection we may consider, illustratively, the contention that if this kind of experimentation is aimed at the eventual development of programs for treatment of genetic diseases, then resources might be better spent to reduce births of children whose parents carry genes likely to produce defective progeny.[66] One conference of researchers produced a consensus that it would be better to use genetic counseling or abortion rather than gene therapy to limit birth defects. Intertwined with this problem is the question of where decision should reside. Marc Lappe opines that the choice among alternative options must be made first by the persons most immediately involved, with the remainder of the decision coming "from the scientific community in its deliberations over setting priorities." However, it must be remembered that these decisions are determined by governmental resource allocation to a significant extent. The realities of funding make this so in any event; and it probably should be the case, given the social interests at stake. Of course, with reference to the threshold problem of whether to encourage or discourage research, it is necessary to consider even rough projections of comparative risks and benefits from various strategies for reducing genetic disease. But this does not diminish the need for judgment under uncertainty, nor does it make easier the problems of social choice.

Indeed, this part of the problem strikingly illustrates the way that social controversy about the value of possible future discoveries piles upon our ignorance of scientific facts. We might note that this itself involves an uncertainty factor of sorts—namely, our lack of knowledge about the premises of policy and philosophy that will be applied to discoveries yet to be made, for which present research will lay the basis.

In concluding this chapter on an extraordinary, advanced technology of biological research which illustrates many recurring problems of law confronting science, I would like to make some general observations on the premises and problems of social regulation of this kind of hazardous activity.

I have suggested that as a general matter long-range research that is predicted to generate long-term benefits but is also apprehended to create long-term risks requires a relatively risk-averse regulatory perspective. An important corollary on the very practical question of who must produce evidence concerning both risks and benefits is that the obligation should rest principally on those who propose to act. Indeed many commentators on the NIH's proposed guidelines took the position that those proposing research designs must show that the danger is minimal and that the benefits are substantial and far outweigh the risk.[67]

The need for such a posture toward risk is clear from existing uncertainty about scientific consequences. It becomes further evident in the tentative and even imprecise quality of discourse on the subject. In illustration, referring to the question of whether genetic research should be continued or prohibited, a philosopher is characterized as saying that reason together with imagination will yield a "reasonable guess," and that this is about all that can be produced.[68] I would not deny that there is room, and necessity, for the use of intuition in our choices of regulatory strategies toward science. Indeed, we are compelled to employ a certain amount of guesswork in devising social controls for these areas of inquiry. But the very fact that it is guesswork heightens the need to be cautious in making societal choices that may bear their fruit 10, 20, or many more years later.

It is relevant in this connection that the NIH guidelines, as conservative as they seemed to many researchers, did not in fact pose insuperable hurdles to the curiosity of the extraordinary scientists who led the way onto the frontier of recombinant research. Indeed, less than a year after the issuance of the guidelines, Roy Curtiss of Alabama, a researcher originally so apprehensive of the biohazards of recombinant work that he drafted a letter in 1974 urging a thousand scientists to cease practically all these investigations voluntarily, had concluded from research done in the interim by himself and others that the dangers of many recombinant procedures were virtually nil.[69] And the physician-geneticist Stanley Cohen of Stanford, a signer of the 1974 *Science* letter who had become a leading critic of the "fictions" of the opponents of recombinant research,[70] confirmed that nature had effectively been conducting its own "recombinant experiments" to such a degree that he now believed that "our initial concerns were greatly overstated."[71] Had the guidelines halted the locomotives of research in their tracks, it would give us considerable pause. As it is, they not only produced a useful national debate on a significant scientific controversy but also generated a mountain of ingenious—and liberating—research.

It is usual for political historians to find the roots of national problems in decisions taken long before the outcropping of troubles. Yet in the case of politics, decision makers are confronted with such a multiplicity of factors that it often would be extravagantly critical to hold them to the range of knowledge that hindsight would fasten upon them. By comparison, in the activities to which this book is primarily addressed, the responsibility of decision makers is focused by the narrowness of the issue; the possible perils of a certain course of experimental action are relatively likely to be predictable as potential outcomes, at least in a general way. This tends to be so especially with reference to research aimed at culmination in particular consumer products, for example pharmaceuticals or fertilizer substitutes. In such situations the counsel of history, for example the history of oral contraceptives, is that extreme caution should be exercised when the data signal danger in a particular avenue of experimentation. The task of legislators and regulators becomes complicated in cases in which the expected end product and the risks are more diffuse, but the consequences may extend to an entire way of life. The manipulation of genes straddles these two categories of hazard. In the case of many of the safety problems raised by the recombinant technology which are discussed here, it has presented dangers that have properly stirred regulators to specific action. Many forms of genetic research pose the broader kind of problem, with risks to the public being more uncertain as to exposure in the first instance as well as to the gravity of the feared harm. When the hazards as well as the projected benefits are not as sharply in view, the task of regulation takes on a different aspect, with the satisfaction of our natural human curiosity acquiring a higher value; but we should still be guided by a general standard of risk aversion.

Whatever payoff is sought by particular lines of investigation on DNA recombinants, this research in general has had an unusually powerful effect on the public imagination, and many scientists have perceived it as presenting a unique potential for harm. As the director of NIH said in his introduction to the guidelines, the fear has been that a mishap might "initiate an irreversible process," which could create problems "many times greater" than those caused by the many recombinations that nature itself effects.[72] It may be that the caution inherent in the point of view of those who express these apprehensions stems from an implicit preference for what might be characterized as naturalness, as opposed to artificiality. A firm if inarticulate premise seems to be that in the effort to change nature, the possibility that risks will be generated artificially justifies government intervention. Thinking this way, we would be more prone to accept spontaneously occurring recombinations because they are part of nature; although we might try to prevent or modify them, we would be more disposed to philosophical resignation. This philosophical view is in turn linked to the process of mutation that has made us what we are today, creating a present condition which provides a further basis for acceptance of spontaneous natural change and for wariness of artificially induced modifications in human biology.[73] I can only suggest here that the interplay between philosophy and biology is a vital element in the development of legal rules and the choice of statutory policies, in a general way as well as specifically with respect to our degree of preference for or aversion to risk. However, whatever the relative impact of culture and nature on law and legislation, the fact seems

to be that when we try affirmatively to create new genetic processes, even if our object were to achieve reconstructions that
ameliorate suffering caused by the present state of nature, we are
risk-averse to the hazards of our own novelties. Our general view
appears to be that we should not exchange a troubled status quo
for the potential of a synthetically produced catastrophe; nor will
we countenance the shifting of injury burdens on those who have
no knowledge of the introduction of artificial elements, and no
choice in the matter.

It should be said that the very notion that the present state of
things is "troubled" is one typically born of rising expectations,
which have risen legitimately because of advances made possible
by prior opportunities for experimentation. In the modern era,
progress has been produced by our drive to rectify what we have
come to perceive as problems. Our continuing impulse to make
things better may be seen at one level as artificial, an outgrowth of
human modification of the environment; at another level, it is a
manifestation of a salutary dissatisfaction with unhappy plights,
an attitude which in a certain sense may be described as natural.
But while descriptive, this conceptual dissociation of what is artificial from what is our "nature" does not seem to capture the essence of our policy concern. Rather, the core of that concern lies
in our intuition that we should be especially wary of undertakings
that may change that nature for the worse.

9 Experimenting with the Consumer

I HAVE EXAMINED SCIENCE AND TECHNOLOGY here as creators of hazard and risk as well as social benefit. In initially describing the way scientists work in their search for knowledge, I observed how craft and judgment are indispensable tools in that enterprise. Insistently apparent was the delicate relationship between modern science and its environment, particularly its legal environment. For law—regulatory systems and liability rules—affects directions of research and influences the research choices made by individual investigators.

The quest for knowledge that has been central to human discoveries, including scientific discoveries, has brought many intrinsic benefits to the seekers. Paralleling these benefits, primarily measured as intellectual and emotional satisfactions, have been the social and economic advances won through those efforts to satisfy curiosity. Given the gains derived from scientific investigation and the necessity that it be conducted in an intellectually unhampered climate, I have proceeded on the premise that society should permit maximum freedom of inquiry and publication, and indeed of production and marketing of the fruits of that inquiry. Yet the accelerating pace of both experimentation and technological realization has been sobering. The very concept of chemical contraception illustrates the extraordinary character of these developments. In an even more fundamental way, the development of recombinant DNA technology demonstrates that we are pushing further and faster against nature than ever before. Accompanying the profound changes brought by this scientific activity has been the evolution of major exceptions to the rules of untrammeled inquiry and production. These exceptions exist because of the risks that scientific investigation and its cousin, market experimentation, pose to individual health and safety.

The book has examined scientific and technological development in areas where experimental efforts to improve human welfare have incidentally created possible hazards. An important common element in these cases has been the artificial creation of risks alleged by competent experts to be potentially grave ones. Another significant aspect of the episodes discussed here is the uncertain nature of the hazards involved. Not only is there uncertainty about the gravity of the risk to individuals who may be affected, but also about the number of persons who may be endangered. This in turn has raised questions as to what differences in treatment are merited by the risk that a product or process may cause injury to very large numbers of victims who cannot be forewarned, as compared with the hazard that may endanger only a few persons, whose identity likewise cannot be known in advance.

There is no single key to the problem. It is as complex as the life to which law responds. That complexity is evident when one undertakes to identify the factors governing legislative choice and judicial decision in cases of long-term, uncertain risk. They include:

1. The benefit anticipated from the product or process
2. The amount of scientific testimony attesting to the possible existence of the risk, and the credentials of those who offer it
3. The existence of suspicious trends in the scientific evidence
4. The type and degree of harm to individuals that is typically associated with the risk
5. The numbers of people likely to be affected by any injurious consequences
6. The possibility of synergistic effects
7. The nature of the uncertainty as to the existence of the risk, its incidence, and its physical or chemical causes
8. The time frame over which the risk may extend
9. The predictive tools available to define the risk, and their likely effectiveness early in the time period over which the risk extends
10. The time required to do the research necessary to establish whether the danger in fact exists
11. The number of people who must serve as experimental subjects to determine the existence and incidence of the hazard, either in controlled experiments or through market experimentation
12. The possibilities that consumers and other potentially af-

fected citizens may be made aware of the risk, and that they will be able to avoid harm

The strands of this web weave in and out of diverse cases that have stimulated a variety of regulatory response. These cases range from the problem of the DNA recombinants, with its historical beginnings in an effort at craft self-regulation, to the saga of oral contraceptive regulation, principally fought out in the administrative process; and they include the Reserve Mining episode, which has occupied considerable time and energy of a succession of federal judges.

I have posited that there runs through all of these efforts at private and social control a wariness of the long-term risk and a sense that uncertainties should be resolved against the creators of potential danger. The risk-averse aspect of our social response to the clusters of potential hazard presented by our modern alchemies manifests itself most clearly in the Delaney amendment with its almost uncompromising approach to carcinogenesis. It is also the stuff of many provisions of the Food, Drug and Cosmetic Act and of the NIH guidelines on gene recombinants. And it appears strikingly in the attitude of both courts in the Reserve Mining case toward conditions described as involving "uncertainty" and hazards that remained "hypothesized."

This developing consensus across a spectrum of productive activity derives from several sources, among them a strengthening of normative standards as well as an increase in expectations related to the safety of products and processes. Associated with these developments is a growing belief that given our existing stock of material benefits, many technically feasible additions to the social inventory are not so beneficial as to justify adding to the already existing personal risks in the environment. An important corollary is the idea that it is unjust to expose random persons to serious hazards about which they have no foreknowledge, and that it is even more unfair to expose them to such dangers without making provision for compensation. In a similar vein of social concern, while regulation has tended to focus on protecting against injuries on a mass scale—to cite just two, the appearance of large numbers of cancers many years after their victims have taken birth control pills or the production of uncontrollable epidemics through gene recombination—as a people we retain a parallel focus, true to our tradition, on individual tragedy. It is perhaps revealing that the literature of our law has placed labels like "disaster" upon events involving the deaths or injuries of no more than hundreds of persons.[1]

It is because of these and related reasons of economics, fairness, and social morale that we have adopted a generally risk-averse position on uncertain long-term danger. I have contended here that we have done so wisely. I have briefly suggested that the minimum requirement for those who experiment on consumers is that they must let the consumers know that they are experimental animals. In cases involving uncertain time bombs, especially where communication about the experimental nature of producing or selling is not feasible or informed choice is impossible, there should be enforcement of regulatory laws that is equal to the uncertainty and potential injustice of market experimentation.

Now I wish to summarize several considerations essential to analysis of these problems. After sketching some relevant general categories of decision-making in our society, I shall mention a number of rationales for regulation and then counterpose some factors that underlie our general commitment to freedom of scientific inquiry and technological development. I shall then outline some issues concerning valuation of human life, and attendant issues of fairness, specifically replying to the argument that the position I have advanced would place socially undesirable constraints on experimentation. Finally, taking brief note of some possibilities for analytical classification of risk, I shall re-emphasize aspects of the problem that call for the application of a broadly risk-averse point of view.

It has been an important premise of this work, both explicit and implicit, that it is the public that should make choices among risks. But to state this generalization is only to begin the discussion, because of the many faces of social choice. Using this term nontechnically to signify any decisions made by large numbers of citizens, the most common form of social choice in our political economy manifests itself through the market. By buying goods at certain prices, consumers signify acceptance of a bundle of perceived benefits and risks and indicate that they are willing to pay the external costs that these products inflict on society.

A truly public form of choice is accomplished through legislation. Often when we are dubious about the ability of individual citizens to decide about risks, or of market-pricing to reflect them, we turn to statutes and administrative regulations. Our dubiety may arise from uncertainty among experts, from the sense that ordinary persons cannot sort out the complexities of a subject, or even from a feeling that people will tend psychologically to opt for more risk than they would like if they "really" thought about it.[2] Whatever its motivation, legislation represents an extremely serious response to a perceived need for collective rather than individual decision,[3] particularly when that legislation goes beyond requirements for further provision of information and mandates product designs, or even prohibits the sale or use of certain products or processes.

The law currently governing science and technology reflects recognition of several considerations. It has implicitly affirmed the existence of market experimentation as a pervasive fact of industrial and commercial life. As manufacturers and others conducting risky activities proceed with new products and processes, it is now appreciated that the novelty and the artificiality of these creations make them experiments per se. Moreover, because of these features of market experimentation, the public's lack of knowledge about hazardous potential often negates the application of an informed choice model. Where information is not available, there is no voluntary acceptance of risk.

In controlled experimental settings, standard procedure demands at least minimal consent requirements for any contact or exposure that is not conventional therapy. And in cases of market experimentation as well as controlled procedures, when there is uncertainty about potential for physical harm, the level of regulation tends to increase when there is some expert opinion indicating that the harm may be grave and could affect relatively large numbers. Decisions for government intervention in such cases represent a belief that the dangers are great enough to require the imposition of social control, unless there is a clear showing that the apprehended detriments will be substantially outweighed by reasonably predictable material benefits. Some governmental intervention even extends to products and processes whose possible dangers are likely to affect relatively few people; the possibility that there will be such random victims may foster before-the-fact regulation on a fairness rationale, and likewise may increasingly incline legislators to require provision for after-the-fact compensation. It should be noted that when we do elect to regulate, usually the availability of less risky substitutes for the hazardous product or process is an important ingredient in the political choice of the form and stringency of intervention, which may after all range from warning requirements to mandatory safety precautions to the outright prohibition of a course of activity.

It bears emphasis that the reasons for regulating scientific activity that creates uncertain, long-term risks derive in large part from the arcane nature of those risks. The fact that the public often has no idea of their existence and no understanding of their character provides an important rationale for regulation. A related component of the problem is the inability of individuals to take precautions that will avoid personal injury. Another important factor, not often expressed, is the relative inefficacy of post injury remedies as deterrents to conduct that may cause widespread suffering only after long periods. Thus, for example, the long-range action of carcinogens makes the prospect of punishment rather unimposing as a check on officials of technology-based firms who choose to take cancer-causing risks. Even disregarding statutes of limitations for personal injury actions, many such decisionmakers will have completed their working lives before harm becomes apparent. This time problem exacerbates difficulties of proof in addition to bringing into play the tendency to forgive and forget long past conduct. Moreover, it is rather difficult both under public regulation and at common law to fix personal financial, much less criminal, liability on corporate officials for such decisions.

One facet of the general problem of consumer knowledge deserves elaboration as a basis for regulation. It concerns the multiplicity of dangers that confronts the consumer or vulnerable bystander. During the course of an average day each person meets numerous risks, some of them voluntarily, others unknowingly, and still others with only vague awareness. It is impossible for anyone to sort out and keep track of all these risks and to evaluate them in isolation. Especially when we consider products or processes which, combining with other agents, may have synergistic effects on human chemistry, the problem is beyond individual management. I do not even speak here of the increase of environmental burdens in the abstract, a separate problem of considerable magnitude, but only of the costs of acquiring and assessing information and of direct physical insult borne by individual persons. The number of risks and the magnitude of both information and uncertainty about them lend support to a risk-averse position in the fashioning of legislative responses to new product forms.

I have dealt principally thus far with the external consequences of risky innovation as they provide rationales for regulation. By contrast, it is well to mention a number of problems associated with the encroachment of regulation on untrammeled inquiry and production. Of particular concern is the tendency of increased regulation to produce disincentives to creative investigation. This is why before one advocates government intervention, it is necessary to show some reason to believe that new lines of inquiry or new production techniques or designs are hazardous. This is a principal reason that we require expert identification of risk.

Another problem arises here. Progress tends to build up establishments, scientific and otherwise. It would not be unusual that the publicizing of potential hazards should be the work of persons outside the establishment, some of whom, professionally frustrated and excluded, may have axes to grind. Others may be marginally competent or may be experts in one area but quack complainants in another. Moreover, while the flexibility of boundaries in human biochemical research promotes innovation, it also is implicated in jealousies over turf and alliances on matters of judgment that smack of scientific politics. Distinguishing expert intuition from intramural political concerns and savvy from bias may often be difficult in the assessment of allegations about risk. The truth may prevail in the long run, but often the truth hurts, and it may thus provoke responses that are not dispassionate. To listen to scientists talk informally about criticism from their brethren is an education in subtle and not-so-subtle backbiting. These problems stem from human nature as well as from human investigation of nature. They may not yield readily to analysis, but they provide a necessary perspective for society's reliance on experts to identify risks.

We also must advert to the need to differentiate among risks within fields of research and production, and the difficulty of this task. The DNA recombinant question exemplifies a case in which several kinds of potential danger, with many variations and gradations in severity of risk, tended to be lumped together by opponents into one awful menace. The basic approach of the

NIH guidelines represented a reasonable approach to this area, emphasizing as it did classification and segmentation of risks. An interesting comparison appears in the controversy over the relationship between taconite and asbestos in the Reserve case. There the judicial resolution, appropriate in that legal setting, was to equate the dangers of the two substances for regulatory purposes.

Disputes over distinctions and analogies among risks also relate to the existence of areas of inquiry and production which are cognate to those enmeshed in controversy but have been accepted parts of the social landscape. For instance, promoters of DNA research answered charges that they were "tinkering" with gene pools by pointing out that this was not a development new to the 1970s. Their citation of the original domestication of animals as well as of modern plant hybridization and livestock breeding provided historical perspective. Similarly, countless developments in modern medicine impinge, if less directly, on what otherwise would be natural selection. For example, the development of insulin has assured the survival of greater numbers of diabetics in the twentieth century, and thus the birth of more progeny whose genes carry that tendency. In the case of DNA recombination experiments, then, it is inappropriate to condemn for novelty alone a technological application that has a close analogue in previous practice.

Moreover, it is necessary in reviewing criticism of science and technology to take into account the perceived needs that fuel the demand for the fruits of these activities. The method of social accounting will differ among products. The desire for more aesthetic and reliable contraceptive techniques has stimulated invention that requires the consumer to make direct trade-offs. The existence of a market for the products of the Reserve Mining Company exemplifies the problem of indirect externalities, not bargained for by the potential victim. Both situations pose considerable difficulties related to the acquisition of information and ability to choose. Besides emphasizing the necessity to consider the needs that generate experimentation, both cases also counsel us to focus on the utility of given products as well as on their risks—and to consider the disadvantages associated with those goods to which they are preferred.

Still another consideration, which may be called the time-discount factor, further complicates analysis of hazards whose uncertain potential extends over the long term. Everyone is willing to trade a certain amount of future disadvantage for some present gains. The immediate utility of an activity may be so great that we will choose the benefit now and take our chances with the future, especially knowing that there are many other fatal events that may intervene. Culture does limit our inclination to act this way, and indeed a predominant strain of thought through most of our national history has checked this tendency, emphasizing present self-denial for future gain. Without drawing normative conclusions about this approach to life, one must note that many of the problems discussed here involve the reaping of present benefits, traded off against the risk of future harms. Because this is so, we may not concentrate solely on requiring the proponents of novelties to prove their safety; we must consider the advantages these innovations presently confer. It is interesting, however, that the case of DNA recombination presents something of a contrast to this typical profile, for its practical justification includes uncertain predictions of benefits. Though these projected advantages are paralleled by even more unpredictable risks, their very uncertainty helps to explain the especially high level of concern about the use of this technology.

This summary of conflicting policies in the background of regulation leads me to reiterate, for purposes of this general discussion of law confronting science, that differences exist not only among certain kinds of scientific judgments, but between scientific judgment and legal judgment. We have noted in connection with Reserve's discharges into Lake Superior that there is a substantial difference between assessing the probabilities that asbestos ingestion will cause illness and deciding whether to take chances over a range described by experts. The conclusion of the court's expert, Dr. Brown, exemplifies the distinctions between these different kinds of judgment. Speaking under his "medical" rather than his "scientific" hat, he declared that the public health required the cessation of fiber discharges. Interestingly, this characterization of "medical" lines up rather closely with what I have been calling "legal"—which in this case means "policy." A judicial decision to regulate the discharges represents a legal enshrinement of a normative judgment. To achieve the resulting mediation of controversy, we cannot avoid the need to distinguish between conclusions about probability and decisions of social policy. Yet we must also recognize that when cases of this sort come to courts, we cleave these concepts only initially. It should be commented incidentally that proposals for a "science court" may be founded on an overestimation of scientist-judges' ability to make these distinctions. The central point is that ultimately both scientific conclusions and social decisions must be meshed into unified judgments.

Issues of valuation and fairness, entailing the need to translate welfare into money, lend particular concreteness to abstractions of risk and benefit, and to generalizations about law's relation to science. My argument for a generally risk-averse stance on uncertain long-term risks takes into account certain realities concerning social valuations of human life and physical integrity. We do place dollar signs on lives and limbs throughout the legal system. At least in theory the most precise way this is done is the private personal injury action, although in practice these determinations are not highly calibrated.[4] Workmen's compensation and social security benefits provide rather modest valuations on an income-maintenance basis. But whatever the process of arriving at these figures, often the income transfers for deaths and injuries caused by various forms of human activity are well below the appraisals that would be made on the basis of prospective earnings or family economic contributions, not to mention money valuations of affective relationships. There is no satisfactory way to fill the personal voids caused by death or permanent disability. This is an important reason that my approach tends to emphasize regulation that limits or prohibits the exposure of citizens to potential hazards even as against after-the-fact compensation.

The position I have taken does not deny the advantages that novel product formulations and industrial processes confer on society, nor does it dispute the desirability of allowing individual consumers to decide how much they wish to pay for products whose costs are properly internalized. It does, however, give substantial weight to the difficulty that long-term uncertainty poses for social cost decisions. Moreover, I stress the significant value of an item which frequently is neglected: the suffering of victims, especially those who were initially unaware of the risks to which they were exposed, and of their families.

Related concerns appear in the problems of fairness entangled with the causation of disproportionate effects on unknowing, random victims. The abstractions of Rawls's theory of justice offer some paths to possible answers. As decision makers, we must confront issues of whether to regulate as if we did not know the circumstances that life would present for us as individuals, whether we be workers in the Reserve plant, or women wishing to prevent conception, or eaters of caponettes. The model further implies that we must make choices without knowledge of injurious outcomes to individuals, for example whether we should live free or afflicted by disease caused by asbestos or estrogens.[5] Beginning from behind this "veil of ignorance" we should act on the principle that "Social and economic inequalities are to be arranged so that they are ... to the greatest benefit of the least advantaged."[6] Attempting to reason from such broad principles to resolve the particular problems discussed here, we find diverging avenues of possible solution. For example, someone who did not know whether he would be situated like workers subjected to industrial carcinogens might decide that he would prefer that no persons should have to endure exposure to such chemicals unless very intensive attempts were made to reduce their concentrations. But it is very difficult to judge what will constitute the greatest benefit to someone who otherwise is likely to be employed in work that pays much less and whose general access to goods and services would be much lower if his work did not expose him to such hazards. Thus, one might decide that it is not "unfair" after all to expose Silver Bay families dependent on Reserve Mining's processing operation for their livelihood to the risk of cancer through air-borne asbestos; the theory would be that they should be able to appreciate that this would embody a "lesser long-run risk" to people in their position than would the prohibition of the activity.[7] This sort of dialectic could be employed with respect to a variety of risks, ranging from economic deprivation to cancer.

To pursue this form of analysis pulls us into further questions, such as how the concept of "justice as fairness" relates to the remedy. For example, might it be fair to allow a practice to continue but unfair not to compensate the eventual victims? Among still other difficulties, how can we quantify people's disinclinations to cancer, or even the risk of cancer, as compared with their preferences for effective contraception—or for hamburger instead of the pet food on which many of the unemployed subsist? If one plows still further into the territory of inarticulate premises, one would want to ask whether the lot of the working person is naturally assumed to include an unavoidably high degree of physical risk.[8] Rawls deals with the distribution of property at quite an abstract level, and he does not confront this question. Yet his premise of the personal inviolability of each human being[9] implies an especially strong commitment to defend physical integrity against harm from artificial processes. One behind the "veil of ignorance," holding to this idea of inviolability, would forgo a certain amount of gross production in order to preserve people from physical injury directly caused by it. Again, we confront the fact that at some levels of welfare, one's preference for less physical injury becomes a preference for starvation. However, I suggest that in the context of our present affluence, there is at work in the background a heightened valuation on life and limb as opposed to production, and that this bias colors the legislative choices embodied in the safety statutes I have discussed and judicial decisions like those in Reserve Mining.

Consideration of these issues of fairness forces us to confront another, vehement argument against the approach I have proposed: that it effectively makes government agencies commissars of research and development. I have stated the argument in politically emotive terms to convey the seriousness of the concern of those who advance it. But the attempt to invoke the specter of a bureaucracy practicing idea control conveys exaggerated images of future impact while ignoring a more sober representation of generally accepted present reality. Relevantly, federal review of funding proposals is already a fact of life for working scientists. And even if the position I have taken somewhat extends the potential ambit of public regulation of scientific and technological development, it does no more than elaborate on well-established roles of government. Parallel to the sizable body of statutes already reflecting a widespread concern with safety, the developing common law of public nuisance gives courts the power to restrain activities which pose prospective as well as present dangers to the community. Society only applies an established aversion to risk created by new artificial processes when it places limits on experimentation during its initial stages because of the momentum, sometimes irreversible, that it generates.

These discussions of forms of regulation and regulatory rationales, and of problems of valuation and fairness, lead us back to the major themes of uncertainty and long-term risk. The problem of long-term hazards lies at the root of many of the reasons why we may wish to prevent persons from engaging in activities which threaten their fellow citizens—and even coming generations—with future harms. Factors that support official con-

straints on such conduct include the inability of unidentifiable
potential victims to bargain, the unfairness of exposing unsuspecting persons to hazards, and the virtual impossibility of fashioning
effective deterrent penalties. The element of uncertain risk also
provides significant motivation for government action. We do indeed live with uncertainty, and in some ways we relish it. Yet our
general philosophical acceptance of it is one born of our contact
with nature through past generations. Now, when human ingenuity batters at bastion after bastion of nature, our lack of
knowledge about her possible counterattacks counsels an expanded role for legislators and judges.

Casting these factors in matrices should aid us in focusing on
the main lines of the problem. The following simplified scheme
demonstrates some possibilities as well as limitations of this approach.

Long-term uncertainty of benefit	Long-term uncertainty of risk
Short-term uncertainty of benefit	**Short-term uncertainty of risk**

This presentation of the problem makes clear that if we assume
roughly equal levels of total benefits and risks, one would generally prefer the diagonal combination of uncertain short-term benefit and long-term uncertainty of risk, and would disdain the
course of action represented by the other diagonal. If a benefit
will accrue in a relatively short period if at all, we will at least have
the opportunity to cut our potential long-range losses if it does not
come to fruition, as well as have the opportunity to try to fashion
prophylactic or curative measures in the interim. By contrast, in
the case in which the hoped-for gain would be reaped only after a
long term, we are not likely to make the wager when the chances
are that we will sustain significant losses before even knowing
whether the activity will yield measurable goods.

The answer is not so clear in either direction for one confronted with either of the two horizontal combinations. In cases in
which either of these profiles is predominant, one typically would
have to search for other elements of decision. Consider, for
example, a process whose proponents hope for quantifiable benefits only over a period of years, which also involves an uncertain

risk of substantial welfare losses over the long term. The issues in such a case would involve both the adequacy and availability of citizen information about benefits and risks, and the question of how many people are likely to be beneficiaries or victims. Complicating the problem are questions of when we should compel projections of quantifiable benefits, and what degree of precision should be required in such forecasts. On the one hand, to demand a showing of practical results may in some cases create significant disincentives to research, because the justification for scientific activity often centers more on the quest for knowledge than on commercial payoffs. On the other hand, when the possibility of widespread physical harm exists, it is proper and relevant to require rather concrete predictions of benefits.

The effort to present controlling considerations in matrix form only serves to underline the complexity of these issues. In the end, judgment is required, and it must transcend the mechanistic slotting of factors. At its best, this sort of judgment would require an extraordinary range of political inquiry and self-examination: it is critically important for decision makers to be aware of their premises, and to articulate the values on which they rely. They should declare their valuation on the search for knowledge as an abstract pursuit, the social premium they place on freedom of choice, and the negative values they assign to the kinds of death or injury that may be caused by a specific product or process. If the pressures of Congressional and agency politics make this a highly idealized catalog of decisional standards, it is worth stating them as an ideal. The closer legislators and regulators come to fulfilling that goal, the better will be the opportunity for effective political review. This would assure that eventually the profile of public law will accurately reflect society's posture toward taking the risks of given activities in light of recently accumulated knowledge about physical and chemical analogues and the general pace of scientific development.

A prime illustration of the advantages of a risk-averse perspective in cases requiring judgment appears in situations in which there has been no showing of long-term harm, but it is said that further study is needed before a clean bill of health can be issued. This syndrome, hauntingly repetitive with the acceleration of progress, forces us to subtler definition of the matrix cells. Exemplary is the report of the FDA's Committee on Obstetrics and Gynecology in 1969, which recommended a "major" research effort aimed at discovering whether oral contraceptives were human carcinogens. Such advice implies that grounds for suspicion still exist, else why should more inquiry be necessary? This is very much the kind of situation which requires government action beyond a call for further investigation. In the case of the Pill, which permitted a direct printed-word link between the producer and the consumer, it was arguably appropriate to require only the communication of uncertainty, as was done through patient labeling. Even there, it might have been desirable to make clearer the implicit suspicion of carcinogenicity on which the recommendation for further research was based. And in areas in which hazardous by-products could affect citizens who are not direct consumers of products or services, as in the Reserve case and in the conduct of gene recombinant experiments, the character of the danger may require us to go beyond cautionary statements to direct control of the potentially harmful activity itself. This, indeed, is occasionally the case with products that consumers purchase directly. When the public is ignorant, unsophisticated, or defenseless, the existence of responsibly based suspicion is enough to justify regulation of conduct.

I conclude with a further reference to a case especially symbolic of the themes I have discussed, that of the oral contraceptives. The latency period for externally caused cancer varies with the kind of chemical or physical insult, but a rough average estimate often used is two decades. When we consider the problems of uncertainty and long-term hazard posed by the various products and processes analyzed in this book, and the drama of contending forces packed into each of these episodes, we are struck by the short frame of history that has contained all of them. And both science and history enjoin us to recognize that for many of these cases, the final returns have not yet come in. Specifically, and poignantly, it is not yet twenty years since a young woman bought from her neighborhood druggist a vial of the Pill.

Notes

INTRODUCTION (pp. xi–xvi)

1. Marc Lappe, "The Human Uses of Molecular Genetics," *Federation Proceedings: Federation of American Societies for Experimental Biology* 34, no. 6 (May 1975): 1425–26.

2. Henry W. Riecken, "Social Change and Social Science," in *Science and the Evolution of Public Policy*, ed. James Shannon (New York: Rockefeller University Press, 1973), p. 136.

THE SCIENTIFIC ENTERPRISE (pp. 1–28)

1. In this regard, I accept the general proposition of Lowrance that "a thing is safe if its risks are judged to be acceptable," see William W. Lowrance, *Of Acceptable Risk: Science and the Determination of Safety* (William Kaufman, Inc.: Los Altos, Calif., 1976), p. 8, although my specific prescriptions may often diverge from his stimulating treatment of these problems.

2. John T. Edsall, *Report of the American Association for the Advancement of Science Committee on Scientific Freedom and Responsibility* (Washington, D.C., 1975), p. 4.

3. Jerome R. Ravetz, *Scientific Knowledge and Its Social Problems* (Oxford: Clarendon Press, 1971), pp. 134, 321.

4. Jacques Ellul, *The Technological Society*, trans. J. Wilkinson (New York: Alfred A. Knopf, 1970), p. 19.

5. Ibid., p. 20.

6. Ibid., p. 52.

7. Ravetz, *Scientific Knowledge*, p. 329.

8. Cf. Ravetz's comparison of "immature" and "matured" fields of inquiry with respect to the use of these techniques, *Scientific Knowledge*, pp. 156–59; chap. 14.

9. Cf. Ravetz, *Scientific Knowledge*, pp. 327–28.

10. Albert Einstein and Leopold Infeld, *The Evolution of Physics* (New York: Simon and Schuster, 1938), p. 33, quoted in Don K. Price, *The Scientific Estate* (Cambridge: Harvard University Press, Belknap Press, 1965), p. 104.

11. See Ravetz, *Scientific Knowledge*, pp. 83–86.

12. Ibid., p. 193.

264 NOTES

13. Ibid.

14. Cf. description of "change of heart" by Dr. Albert Sabin on the swine flu immunization program, in "Swine Flu: Did Uncle Sam Buy a Pig in a Poke?," *Consumer Reports* 41 (September 1976): 495–96.

15. Dr. Michael Halberstam, "The Legion Disease: So Little Still Is Known about the Body," *New York Times*, 5 September 1976, p. 7.

16. Ellul, *Technological Society*, p. 40.

17. Harold Himsworth, "Organization and the Growth of Scientific Knowledge," in *Science and the Evolution of Public Policy*, ed. James Shannon (New York: Rockefeller University Press, 1973), pp. 37–38.

18. See ibid., p. 38.

19. Cf. ibid., p. 39.

20. Ravetz, *Scientific Knowledge*, pp. 44–45.

21. *See*, e.g., H. L. Nieburg, *In the Name of Science* (Chicago: Quadrangle Books, 1966), p. 65.

22. Cf. Ravetz, *Scientific Knowledge*, p. 137.

23. See ibid., p. 138.

24. Ibid., pp. 152–57.

25. Dietrich Schroeer, *Physics and Its Fifth Dimension: Society* (Reading, Mass.: Addison-Wesley, 1972), pp. 26–28.

26. George F. Archambault, "Investigational Drugs and the Law," *Cleveland Marshall Law Review* 16 (1967): 487, 489.

27. Paul Weiss, "Living Nature and the Knowledge Gap," *Saturday Review*, 29 November 1969, p. 20.

28. Edsall, *Scientific Freedom and Responsibility*, pp. 6–7.

29. Herbert J. Muller, *The Children of Frankenstein* (Bloomington: Indiana University Press, 1970), pp. 135–37.

30. Ravetz, *Scientific Knowledge*, p. 175.

31. Ibid., p. 137.

32. Ibid., p. 138.

33. Schroeer, *Physics*, p. 117.

34. Cf., e.g., Ravetz, *Scientific Knowledge*, pp. 223–33.

35. Ibid., pp. 283–86.

36. Ibid., p. 287.

37. Ibid., p. 103.

38. Marc Lappe, "The Human Uses of Molecular Genetics," *Federation Proceedings: Federation of American Societies for Experimental Biology* 34, no. 6 (May 1975): 1425.

39. See, e.g., Barbara J. Culliton, "Legion Fever: Postmortem on an Investigation that Failed," *Science* 194 (1976): 1025, 1027.

40. Owen Chamberlain, "Government Funding," in *The Social Re-*

sponsibility of the Scientist, ed. Martin Brown (New York: Free Press, 1971), p. 98.

41. Ravetz, *Scientific Knowledge*, p. 146.

42. Schroeer, *Physics*, p. 63.

43. Indeed, the magical aura of science may have developed new staying power because of the way it serves as a replacement for traditional religious values, an insight suggested to me by Bill Austin, University of Virginia Law School Class of 1979.

44. Ravetz, *Scientific Knowledge*, pp. 122.

45. Ibid., pp. 118-20.

46. See Nieburg, *In Name of Science*, pp. 104-105.

47. Dean Schooler, Jr., *Science, Scientists, and Public Policy* (New York: Free Press, 1971), p. 50.

48. See reference to the difficulty that even experts have in keeping up with new developments in "Director's Introduction," "Department of HEW, NIH, Recombinant DNA Research, Guidelines," *Federal Register* 41, no. 131, 7 July 1976, 27,902.

49. See, e.g., "Doctors, Firms Faulted for Careless Evaluation of Drugs, Techniques," *Wall Street Journal*, 14 March 1967, p. 1.

50. Ravetz, *Scientific Knowledge*, p. 122.

51. Ibid., p. 183.

52. Ibid., p. 186.

53. Ibid., p. 95.

54. Ibid., p. 156.

55. Schooler, *Science, Scientists, Public Policy*, p. 282.

56. Ravetz, *Scientific Knowledge*, p. 311.

57. Ibid., pp. 294-311.

58. Henry Riecken, "Social Change and Social Science," in *Science and Evolution of Policy*, p. 136.

59. Emmanuel G. Mesthene, *Technological Change: Its Impact on Man and Society* (Cambridge: Harvard University Press, 1970), p. 27.

60. See, e.g., Friends of the Earth v. Potomac Electric Power Co., 419 F. Supp. 528 (D.D.C. 1976) (congressional intent under Clean Air Act).

61. Cf., e.g., General Motors v. Simmons, 545 S.W.2d 502 (Tex. Civ. App. 1976) (courts should not adopt legislative standard subsequently repealed).

62. See, e.g., Nicholas Wade, "DES: A Case Study of Regulatory Abdication," *Science* 177 (1972): 335.

63. Lee Loevinger, "Jurimetrics: Science in Law" in *Scientists in the Legal System*, ed. William Thomas (Ann Arbor: Ann Arbor Science Publishers Inc., 1974), p. 20.

64. Ibid., p. 21.

65. Price, *The Scientific Estate*, p. 271, quoted in Loevinger, *Jurimetrics*, p. 20.

66. See, e.g., Edsall, *Scientific Freedom and Responsibility*, p. 8.

67. Ibid., pp. 9–10.

68. Ravetz, *Scientific Knowledge*, p. 130.

69. Ibid., p. 349.

70. Ibid.

71. Nieburg, *In Name of Science*, p. 160.

72. Ibid., pp. 160–75.

73. Ravetz, *Scientific Knowledge*, p. 418.

74. Schroeer, *Physics*, pp. 39–40. It has been said more expansively that scientific knowledge is "something to which every reasonable person who makes the effort at understanding can subscribe." John M. Ziman, *Public Knowledge* (London: Cambridge University Press, 1968), quoted in *Physics*, p. 37. This, however, would seem to imply a reasonable person with a rather high level of specialized education, and it is a definition of knowledge which insufficiently confronts policy difficulties that grow out of the exploration of scientific discovery.

75. Ibid., p. 40.

76. This is Schroeer's characterization in *Physics*, p. 160.

77. See, e.g., "Inside Story of a Medical Tragedy," *U.S. News and World Report*, 13 August 1962, p. 54.

78. See, e.g., "FDA Chief Probing Charges of Laxity," *Washington Post*, 14 August 1975, p. A-6.

79. See Sam Peltzman, "An Evaluation of Consumer Protection Legislation: The 1962 Drug Amendments," *Journal of Political Economy* 81 (1973): 1049.

80. See Nieburg, *In Name of Science*, chap. 17.

81. Schooler, *Science, Scientists, Public Policy*, p. 280.

82. See Schroeer, *Physics*, pp. 273–74.

83. I have developed an analogous approach to governmental duties in tort in Marshall S. Shapo, *The Duty to Act: Tort Law, Power, and Public Policy*, pt. 2 (Austin and London: University of Texas Press, 1978).

84. Cf. Ravetz, *Scientific Knowledge*, p. 166.

85. Ibid., pp. 167–68.

86. Ibid., pp. 64–65.

87. Ellul, *Technological Society*, pp. 97–98.

88. Notably the Occupational Safety and Health Act, the Toxic Substances Control Act, the National Traffic and Motor Vehicle Safety Act and the Poison Prevention Packaging Act, in addition to the older Food, Drug and Cosmetic Act.

CHAPTER 2: VARIETIES OF EXPERIMENTATION (pp. 29–57)

1. Lewis Thomas, "The Benefits of Research," in *Experiments and Research with Humans: Values in Conflict* (Washington, D.C.: National Academy of Sciences, 1975), p. 35.

2. Jerome R. Ravetz, *Scientific Knowledge and Its Social Problems* (Oxford: Clarendon Press, 1971), p. 95.

3. Walsh McDermott, "The Risks of Research," in *Experiments and Research with Humans: Values in Conflict* (Washington, D.C.: National Academy of Sciences, 1975), p. 37.

4. Cf. "Ethical Principles in the Conduct of Research with Human Participants" (Washington, D.C.: *Report of the American Psychological Association ad hoc Committee on Ethical Standards in Psychological Research*, 1973), pp. 47–48 (hereafter cited as "Ethical Principles," A.P.A.).

5. See Paul A. Freund, "Introduction to the Issue: Ethical Aspects of Experimentation with Human Subjects," *Daedalus* 98 (Spring 1969): viii–ix.

6. Federal Register 40, no. 154, 8 August 1975, 33,532.

7. McDermott, "Risks of Research," p. 38.

8. Cf. Guido Calabresi, "Reflections on Medical Experimentation in Humans," *Daedalus* 98 (Spring 1969): 395.

9. Robert de Ropp, *The New Prometheans* (New York: Delacorte Press, Dial Press, 1972), p. 62.

10. Ibid., p. 63.

11. Dietrich Schroeer, *Physics and Its Fifth Dimension: Society* (Reading, Mass.: Addison-Wesley, 1972), p. 82.

12. Hans Jonas, "Philosophical Reflections on Experimenting with Human Subjects," *Daedalus* 98 (Spring 1969): 224.

13. Ibid., pp. 228–29.

14. Ibid., pp. 229–33.

15. Ibid., pp. 235–37.

16. 21 App. Div.2d 495, 251 N.Y.S.2d 818, *rev'd*, 15 N.Y.2d 317, 206 N.E.2d 338, 258 N.Y.S.2d 397 (1965).

17. "Human Experimentation: Cancer Studies at Sloan-Kettering Stir Public Debate on Medical Ethics," *Science* 143 (1964): 551, quoted in Robert D. Mulford, *Stanford Law Review* 20 (1967): 99, n. 3.

18. Letter from William A. Hyman, reprinted in *Science* 152 (1966): 865, cited in Robert D. Mulford, *Stanford Law Review* 20 (1967): 99, n. 3.

19. "Ethical Principles," A.P.A., p. 25.

20. Ibid., p. 68.

21. Ibid., pp. 43–44.

22. Quoted in Paul A. Freund, "Ethical Problems in Human Experimentation," *New England Journal of Medicine* 273 (1965): 687, 691.

23. The IND regulations appear principally in *Code of Federal Regulations* vol. 21, sec. 312 (1977), with the consent regulations at ibid., sec. 310.102 (hereafter cited as C.F.R.).

24. McDermott, "Risks of Research," p. 41.

25. *See U.S. Code Annotated* vol. 21, sec. 355(j) (1972); C.F.R. vol. 21, sec. 310.301 (1977).

26. C.F.R. vol. 21, sec. 310.102b (1977).

27. C.F.R. vol. 21, sec. 310.102(h) (1977).

28. Calabresi, "Reflections on Medical Experimentation," pp. 403–4.

29. Jonas, "Philosophical Reflections," pp. 242–43.

30. "Ethical Principles," A.P.A., p. 67.

31. Calabresi, "Reflections on Medical Experimentation," pp. 390–91.

32. Ibid., p. 394.

33. Ibid.

34. Ibid., pp. 399–400.

35. Jonas, "Philosophical Reflections," pp. 219–20.

36. Ibid., p. 222. In this passage I have borrowed heavily from Jonas's attack on the problem.

37. Calabresi, "Reflections on Medical Experimentation," pp. 388–89. Cf. Charles Fried, "The Value of Life," *Harvard Law Review* 82 (1969): 1415.

38. Calabresi, "Reflections on Medical Experimentation," pp. 388–89.

39. "Ethical Principles," A.P.A., p. 20.

40. Ibid., p. 39.

41. Calabresi, "Reflections on Medical Experimentation," pp. 404–405.

42. See generally ibid., pp. 394–403.

43. Henry W. Riecken, "Social Change and Social Science," in *Science and the Evolution of Public Policy*, ed. James Shannon (New York: Rockefeller University Press, 1972), p. 151.

44. "Ethical Principles," A.P.A., p. 71.

45. Ibid., p. 17.

46. Ibid., p. 36.

47. Ibid., p. 84.

48. Spotlighting the tension in psychological researchers' approval of the use of deceptive techniques is the condemnation by the American Psychological Association's ad hoc Committee on Ethical Standards in Psychological Research of what it calls the "particularly reprehensible practice of 'double deception' "—a second deception which is presented as part of what the participant thinks is an official postinvestigation debriefing. With almost ludicrous solemnity, the document refers to the "particular danger that the participant, when finally provided with a full and accurate clarification, will be made unconvinced and possibly resentful." The report expresses apprehension that "confidence in the trustworthiness of psychologists has realistically been shaken." "Ethical Principles," A.P.A., p. 80. Yet it is the allowance of initial trickery, particularly in situations where it can be expected to cause stress, that is at the root of the problem. This deceptive use of persons as vehicles for research creates a basis for legal intervention, as well as scarring the reputation of a discipline.

49. James L. Goddard, "Address to American Society of Clinical Oncology," 10 April 1968, as reported in *F-D-C Rep.* ("Pink Sheet") no. 16, 15 April 1968, quoted in David F. Cavers, "The Legal Control of the Clinical Investigation of Drugs: Some Political, Economic, and Social Questions," *Daedalus* 98 (Spring 1969): 427, 436.

50. Freund, "Introduction," p. xiii.

51. This view generally draws on John Rawls, *A Theory of Justice* (Cambridge: Harvard University Press, 1971).

52. See Francis D. Moore, "Therapeutic Innovation: Ethical Boundaries in the Initial Clinical Trials of New Drugs and Surgical Procedures," *Daedalus* 98 (Spring 1969): 502–3.

53. See, e.g., "HEW Proposed Rules for the Protection of Human Subjects," *Federal Register* 42, no. 10, 14 January 1977, 3076–78.

54. I am grateful to my colleague Richard Merrill for conversation which helped me to develop this point.

55. "Ethical Principles," A.P.A., p. 74.

56. Ibid., p. 59.

57. Marshall Shapo, "Swine Flu and Legal Policy: A Comment," *Pharos of Alpha Omega Alpha* 40 (January 1977): 2–6.

58. For discussion of this controversy, *see* Cavers, "Legal Control of Clinical Investigation of Drugs," *Daedalus*, pp. 441–43.

59. Cf. "Package Inserts for Prescription Drugs as Evidence in Medical Malpractice Suits" (Note), *University of Chicago Law Review* 44 (1977): 398.

60. Cavers, "Legal Control of Clinical Investigation of Drugs," *Daedalus*, pp. 436–40.

CHAPTER 3: PERSONAL CHOICE (pp. 58–87)

1. "Darvon Linked with Suicides," *American Medical News*, 29 September 1975, p. 8, citing a letter to the editor by McBay and Hudson, *Journal of the American Medical Association* 233, no. 12 (September 1975): 1257.

2. "Macrobiotic Diet Dangerous, Research Council Warns," *American Medical News*, 24 June 1974, p. 22.

3. Rodale Press, *Trade Regulation Reporter* (Chicago: Commerce Clearing House, Inc., 1976), par. 17,996 (Commissioner Elman, dissenting) (F.T.C. 1967).

4. *Medical Letter* 15 (11 May 1973): 41.

5. Kordel v. United States, 335 U.S. 345 (1948).

6. Rodale Press, par. 17,996.

7. *U.S. Code Annotated*, vol. 21, sec. 353 (1972).

8. United States v. An Article of Drug . . . "Decholin," 264 F. Supp. 473 (E.D. Mich. 1967).

9. See "Laetrile—Commissioner's Decision on Status," *Federal Register* 42, no. 151, 5 August 1977, 39,768–72.

10. *Stedman's Medical Dictionary*, 21st ed., s.v. "amygdalin."

11. "The Cancer Drug Controversy—U.S. v. Laetrile," *University of San Fernando Valley Law Review* 3 (1974): 51–52.

12. Ibid.

13. The definition of "new drug" appears in *U.S. Code Annotated*, vol. 21, sec. 321(p) (1972).

14. United States v. General Research Laboratories, 397 F. Supp. 197 (C.D. Calif. 1975).

15. 399 F. Supp. 1208 (W.D. Okla. 1975).

16. Rutherford v. United States, 542 F.2d 1137 (10th Cir. 1976).

17. "Court Ruling on Laetrile Seen as Threat to FDA," *American Medical News*, 8 November 1976, p. 3.

18. The district court's opinion on remand takes a position that lines up with this view. Tracking the court of appeals decision, it enjoined the FDA from preventing the plaintiff's importation or transportation of Laetrile until the agency could produce an administrative record on the "new drug" point. The district judge did this, he said, "in appreciation of the fact that depriving a terminally ill cancer patient of a substance he finds therapeutic, whether such benefit is physical or psychological, creates the very real risk that irreparable injury might be sustained." Rutherford v. United States, 424 F. Supp. 105, 107 (W.D. Okla. 1977).

19. I do not deal here with cases involving the peddling of remedies whose support lacks the strength of conviction which has characterized the proponents of Laetrile, including its adherents among cancer patients, and which has brought the question of that product's merits into public debate.

20. 417 F. Supp. 30 (D. Minn. 1976).

21. Within a month of the FDA's release of a full-dress review that concluded that Laetrile was not effective, see note 9 *supra*, the National Cancer Institute released a report concluding that the five-year survival rate for cancer patients had increased only 1 per cent in twenty-five years—although some experts stressed that there had been substantial progress in survival rates for a few malignant diseases. Cohn, "Cancer Statistics Show Scant Gain in Survival Rate," *Washington Post*, 26 August 1977, p. A-1.

22. "Sen. Kennedy Bids to Defuse Laetrile Publicity Campaigns," *American Medical News*, 18 July 1977, p. 1.

23. See, e.g., "Battle to Legitimize Laetrile Continues," *Science* 196 (1977): 854; "Apricot Pits, Used to Make Laetrile, Seized by U.S.," *American Medical News*, 23 May 1977, p. 3.

24. A bill passed by the Nevada senate also would have legalized a substance called gerovital, which was advertised as helpful in relieving geriatric depression. "Two More Legislatures Vote to Legalize Use of Laetrile," *American Medical News*, 16 May 1977, p. 11.

25. "Laetrile Labeled a Hazard," *Washington Post*, 10 August 1977, p. A-1.

26. E.g., one reported fatality was of a Los Angeles girl who swallowed a dose of Laetrile she had been told to inject. See ibid.

27. *U.S. Code Annotated*, vol. 15, secs. 1471–76 (1974).

28. See "Kennedy Bids to Defuse Laetrile Publicity," p. 11.

29. See summary at 2, following U.S. Department of Health, Education, and Welfare, *HEW News*, release no. B77-29, 4 August 1977.

30. F.T.C. v. Simeon Management Corp., 391 F. Supp. 697, 700–701 (N.D. Calif. 1975); 532 F.2d 708, 712–13 (9th Cir. 1976).

31. 532 F.2d at 715.

32. See Virginia State Board of Pharmacy v. Virginia Citizens Consumer Council Inc., 425 U.S. 748, 96 S. Ct. 1817 (1976).

33. *Medical Letter* 17 (October 1975): 89.

34. *Medical Letter* 18 (August 1976): 73.

35. *Medical Letter* 17 (October 1975): 89.

36. J. Martin, "Pastiche: At Last! Something to Sneeze About!," *Washington Post*, 12 September 1976, p. L-19.

37. *Medical Letter* 18 (27 August 1976): 73.

38. Auerbach, "FDA Eases Curbs on 10 Cold Remedies," *Washington Post*, 9 September 1976, p. A-1.

39. Ibid.; U.S. Department of Health, Education, and Welfare, *HEW News*, release no. 76-25, 8 September 1976.

40. National Nutritional Foods Assn. v. Weinberger, 512 F.2d 688 (2d Cir. 1975).

41. Ibid., p. 703.

42. National Nutritional Foods Assn. v. F.D.A., 504 F.2d 761 (2d Cir. 1974), *cert. denied*, 420 U.S. 946 (1975).

43. National Nutritional Foods Assn. v. Weinberger, 512 F.2d 688 (2d Cir. 1975).

44. National Nutritional Foods Assn. v. Mathews, 418 F. Supp. 394 (S.D.N.Y. 1976).

45. National Nutritional Foods Ass'n v. Mathews, 557 F.2d 325 (2d Cir. 1977).

46. *U.S. Code Annotated*, vol. 21, sec. 350(a)(1)(A), Supp. 1977.

47. U.S., Congress, "House Conference Report No. 94–1005," *U.S. Code Congressional and Administrative News*, vol. 2 (St. Paul, Minnesota: West Publishing Co., 1976): 752.

48. National Nutritional Foods Assn. v. Kennedy, 572 F.2d 377 (2d Cir. 1978).

49. *U.S. Code Annotated*, vol. 21, sec. 350 (a)(1)(B), supp. 1977.

50. Ibid., sec. 350(a)(2).

51. "House Conference Report No. 94–1005," p. 751.

52. Ibid., p. 752.

53. F.T.C. v. National Commission on Egg Nutrition, 517 F.2d 485 (7th Cir. 1975).

54. In the Matter of National Commission on Egg Nutrition, *Antitrust & Trade Regulation Reporter* (Washington, D.C.: Bureau of National Affairs, 1976) no. 776, p. E-1 (F.T.C. 1976).

55. Cf. Jerome R. Ravetz, *Scientific Knowledge and Its Social Problems* (Oxford: Clarendon Press, 1971), pp. 124–25.

CHAPTER 4: THE PILL (pp. 88–141)

1. David Sanford, "The Drug Peddlers," *New Republic*, 21 September 1968, pp. 16, 17.

2. "Drug Makers' Influence on Doctors is Criticized," *Washington Post*, 29 April 1976, p. A-1.

3. See Mintz, "Annals of Commerce: Selling the Pill," *Washington Post*, 8 February 1976, p. K-1.

4. Ibid.

5. Ibid.

6. "Man Blames Pill for 6 Children," Agence France-Press dispatch, in press story, 24 September (1974?), clipping in possession of author.

7. William D. McElroy, "The Utility of Science," in *Science and the Evolution of Public Policy*, ed. James Shannon (New York: Rockefeller University Press, 1973), pp. 22–23.

8. "The Pill—A Legal and Social Dilemma" (Note), *Temple Law Quarterly* 45 (1972): 484, 490.

9. Morton Mintz, *By Prescription Only*, rev. ed. (Boston: Beacon Press, 1967), p. 271.

10. "Pill—Legal and Social Dilemma," pp. 490–91.

11. Lawson v. G. D. Searle & Co., 29 Ill. App. 3d 670, 331 N.E.2d 75 (1975).

12. Lawson v. G. D. Searle & Co., 64 Ill. 2d 543, 356 N.E.2d 779 (1976).

13. U.S., Congress, House, Committee on Government Operations, *Drug Safety: Hearings before the Subcommittee on Intergovernmental Relations*, 89th Cong., 2d Sess., 1966, pp. 1960–61.

14. Ibid., pp. 1990–91.

15. [1963–1967 Transfer Binder] *Food Drug Cosmetic Law Reporter* [Chicago: Commerce Clearing House, Inc. (hereafter cited as C.C.H.), 1966], par. 80,155.

16. Ibid., (1967), par. 40,270.

17. Herbert B. Taylor, Nelson S. Irey, and Henry J. Norris, "Atypical Endocervical Hyperplasia in Women Taking Oral Contraceptives," *Journal of the American Medical Association* 202, no. 7, (November 1967): 637.

18. Letter from Herbert B. Taylor, M.D., to Marshall S. Shapo, 24 September 1969, quoted in Page Keeton and Marshall Shapo, *Products and the Consumer: Defective and Dangerous Products* (Mineola, New York: Foundation Press, Inc., 1970), p. 13, n.4.

19. "Oral Contraceptives Gain ACOG Favor," *American Medical Association News*, 6 November 1967, p. 5.

20. W. H. W. Inman and M. P. Vessey, "Investigation of Deaths from Pulmonary, Coronary and Cerebral Thrombosis and Embolism in Women of Child-Bearing Age," *British Medical Journal* 2 (1968): 193.

21. "FDA Watered Down Pill Warning," *Washington Post*, 5 August 1973, p. A-1.

22. Francis J. Kane, Jr. et al., "Mood and Behavioral Changes with Progestational Agents," *British Journal of Psychiatry* 113 (1967): 265.

23. Morton Mintz, "The Golden Pill," *New Republic* 2 March 1968, p. 18; James Lyons, "The Pill, A Communication," ibid., 4 May 1968, p. 37; Morton Mintz, "Perils of the Pill: A Communication," ibid. 25 May 1968, p. 38.

24. "FDA Watered Down Warning," p. A-16.

25. Ibid.

26. "Report on Oral Contraceptives," Advisory Committee on Obstetrics and Gynecology, Food and Drug Administration (1969), pp. 18–22.

27. *Trial,* December 1967/January 1968, p. 42.

28. For historical references, see Keeton and Shapo, *Products*, pp. 16–17 and nn. 11a, 11b.

29. U.S. Department of Health, Education and Welfare, "Proposed Statement of Policy Concerning Oral Contraceptive Labeling Directed to Laymen," *Federal Register* 35, no. 70, 10 April 1970, p. 5962.

30. "A Warning on the Pill," *Washington Post*, 10 September 1970, p. C-9; "AMA To Publish a Pamphlet on the Pill," *American Medical News*, 10 August 1970, p. 1.

31. "Cooperation on 'Pill' Is Cited," *American Medical News*, 17 August 1970, p. 1.

32. Turner v. Edwards [1970–1973 Transfer Binder], *Food Drug Cosmetic Law Reporter* (CCH) par. 40,422 (D.D.C. 1970).

33. Schmeck, "Hung Jury on the Pill," *New York Times*, 25 January 1970, p. 12.

34. "Birth Defects Are Found in Mice Given One Hormone Used in Pill," *Washington Post*, 27 November 1970, p. A-2.

35. "'Pill' Causes Breast Growths in Dogs," *Washington Post*, 18 October 1970, p. A-3.

36. "Firms Halt Production of Two 'Pills'," *Washington Post*, 24 October 1970, p. A-1.

37. Mintz, "High Estrogen Birth Control Pills," *Washington Post*, 3 January 1970, p. D-1.

38. U.S., Department of Health, Education, and Welfare, *HEW News*, release no. 70-13, 24 April 1970.

39. Howard G. McQuarrie et al., "Cytogenic Studies on Women Using Oral Contraceptives and Their Progeny," *American Journal of Obstetrics and Gynecology* 108 (1970): p. 659.

40. Victor A. Drill, "Oral Contraceptives and Thromboembolic Disease," *Journal of the American Medical Association* 219, no. 5 (January 1972): 583.

41. Victor A. Drill and David W. Calhoun, "Oral Contraceptives and Thromboembolic Disease: II. Estrogen Content of Oral Contraceptives," *Journal of the American Medical Association* 219, no. 5 (January 1972): 593.

42. *The Medical Letter on Drugs and Therapeutics* 14 (1972): 61.

43. Report from the Boston Collaborative Drug Surveillance Programme, "Oral Contraceptives and Venous Thromboembolic Disease, Surgically Confirmed Gall Bladder Disease, and Breast Tumours," *Lancet* 1 (1973): 1399.

44. Dwight J. Janerich, Joyce M. Piper, and Donna M. Glebatis, "Oral Contraceptives and Congenital Limb-Reduction Defects," *New England Journal of Medicine* 291 (1974): 697.

45. James J. Nora and Audrey H. Nora, "Can the Pill Cause Birth Defects?" *New England Journal of Medicine* 291 (1974): 731.

46. J. Jofen, "Long Range Effects of Medical Experiments in Concentration Camps (The Effect of Administration of Estrogens to the Mother on the Intelligence of the Offspring)," 5 August 1969, reprinted in *The Fifth World Congress of Jewish Studies* 2 (1972): 55.

47. *Ibid.* at 71.

48. "Questions Raised on Effect of Pill," *Charlottesville Daily Progress*, 23 October 1975, p. C-1.

49. Ibid.

50. George F. Archambault, "Investigational Drugs and the Law," *Cleveland Marshall Law Review* 16 (1967), 487–89.

51. *The Medical Letter on Drugs and Therapeutics* 16 (1974): 37.

52. Lawrence Fleckenstein et al., "Oral Contraceptive Patient Information: A Questionnaire Study of Attitudes, Knowledge, and Preferred Information Sources," *Journal of the American Medical Association* 235 (1974): 1331–35, citing Royal College of Physicians, "Oral Contraceptives and Health" (1974).

53. J. I. Mann et al., "Myocardial Infarction in Young Women with Special Reference to Oral Contraceptive Practice," *British Medical Journal* 2 (May 1975): 241.

54. J. I. Mann and W. H. W. Inman, "Oral Contraceptives and Death from Myocardial Infarction," *British Medical Journal* 2 (May 1975): 245.

55. Samuel Shapiro, "Oral Contraceptives and Myocardial Infarction," *New England Journal of Medicine* 293 (1975): 195.

56. Interview with Dr. George F. Cahill, "New Hope for Diabetics," *U.S. News & World Report*, 24 November 1975, p. 54.

57. "Cautions Stressed for Pill," *Washington Post*, 16 October 1975, p. A-13.

58. *Federal Register* 40, no. 207, 24 October 1975, p. 49,813.

59. See *Code of Federal Regulations* vol. 21, sec. 310.501 (1976).

60. "FDA Revises Warning on 'Pill' Labels," *Washington Post,* 29 December 1975, p. A–1.

61. Mintz, "The Pill and a Lower Rate of Fatal Heart Attacks," *Washington Post,* 8 February 1976, p. D–14.

62. Elfriede Fasal and Ralph S. Paffenbarger, "Oral Contraceptives as Related to Cancer and Benign Lesions of the Breast," *Journal of the National Cancer Institute* 55 (1975): 767.

63. Donald C. Smith et al., "Association of Exogenous Estrogen and Endometrial Carcinoma," *New England Journal of Medicine* 293 (1975): 1164.

64. Harry K. Ziel and William D. Finkle, "Increased Risk of Endemetrial Carcinoma among Users of Conjugated Estrogens," ibid., p. 1167.

65. Noel S. Weiss, "Risks and Benefits of Estrogen Use," ibid., p. 1200.

66. Kenneth J. Ryan, "Cancer Risk and Estrogen Use in the Menopause," ibid., pp. 1199–1200.

67. Weiss, "Risks and Benefits of Estrogen Use."

68. "Ban Urged on 3 Brands of the 'Pill'," *Washington Post,* 21 December 1975, p. A–1.

69. "Marketing of Sequential Birth Control Pills Is Being Discontinued," [1975–1976 Transfer Binder], *Food Drug Cosmetic Law Reporter* (CCH) (1976) par. 41,589. The decision was tempered with mercy for manufacturers who had pumped two months' supply into the stream of commerce. A stay of execution was granted for these pills, but Commissioner Schmidt suggested that women taking the sequentials finish their cycles and then seek alternative pills or other contraceptive advice from their doctors. "Sequential Contraceptives Dropped," *American Medical News,* 8 March 1976, p. 13.

70. For a summry of previous literature on hepatic tumors, see *The Medical Letter on Drugs and Therapeutics* 18 (1976): 22.

71. E. Truman Mays et al., "Hepatic Changes in Young Women Ingesting Contraceptive Steroids: Hepatic Hemorrhage and Primary Hepatic Tumors," *Journal of the American Medical Association* 235 (1976): 730.

72. Hugh A. Edmondson, Brian Henderson, and Barbara Benton, "Liver-Cell Adenomas Associated with Use of Oral Contraceptives," *New England Journal of Medicine* 294 (1976): 470.

73. Cf. Upjohn Co. v. Finch, 422 F.2d 944 (6th Cir. 1970) (neither testimonial documents nor commercial success constitute substantial evidence of drug effectiveness).

74. *The Medical Letter on Drugs and Therapeutics* 18 (1976): 21–22.

75. "FDA Panel Urges Warnings on Estrogen Instructions," *Washington Post,* 20 December 1975, p. A–2.

76. "FDA Moves to Restrict Use of Estrogen in Menopause Drugs, Oral Contraceptives," [1975–1976 Transfer Binder] *Food Drug Cosmetic Law Reporter* (CCH) (1976) par. 41,554.

77. "Estrogen Prescribing a Dilemma for Physicians," *American Medical News,* 8 March 1976, p. 13.

78. *American Medical News,* 22 March 1976, p. 3.

79. Robert Hoover et al., "Menopausal Estrogens and Breast Cancer," *New England Journal of Medicine,* 295 (1976): 401.

80. "Stronger Warnings for Estrogen Use Approved by FDA," *American Medical News,* 4 October 1976, p. 9.

81. See, e.g., *Federal Register* 41, no. 236, 7 December 1976, 53,633; corrected, ibid. no. 241, 14 December 1976, 54,544.

82. Michael P. Stern et al., "Cardiovascular Risk and Use of Estrogens or Estrogen–Progestogen Combinations: Stanford Three-Community Study," *Journal of the American Medical Association* 235 (1976): 811.

83. Royal College of General Practitioners, *Oral Contraceptives and Health: An Interim Report from the Oral Contraception Study* (New York: Pitman, 1974), pp. 37–42; S. Ramcharan, F. H. Pellegrin, and E. Hoag, "The Occurrence and Course of Hypertensive Disease in Users and Non-Users of Oral Contraceptive Drugs," in *Oral Contraceptives and High Blood Pressure,* eds. M. J. Fregley and M. S. Fregley (Gainesville, Florida: The Dolphin Press, 1974), pp. 1–16, cited in Stern et al., "Cardiovascular Risk," p. 814.

84. "Age Factor in Pill Risk, Study Says," *Washington Post,* 15 February 1976, p. A–1.

85. Fleckenstein et al., "Questionnaire Study."

86. *American Medical News,* 29 March 1976, p. 2.

87. *Federal Register* 41, no. 236, 7 December 1976, p. 53,636–40; corrected, ibid. no. 241, 54,544.

88. See *Federal Register* 43, no. 21, 31 January 1978, pp. 4230, 4233.

89. *Federal Register* 43, p. 4230.

90. It is interesting to note that this 1978 language represents a change from the statement proposed in 1976, which read, "No proof exists at present that oral contraceptives cause cancer in humans, but it remains possible they will be discovered in the future to do so." *Federal Register* 41, p. 53,640.

91. *Federal Register* 43, p. 4231.

92. *Federal Register* 41, p. 53,636. The mandate for "particular care" is repeated in the 1978 regulation, *Federal Register* 43, p. 4227.

93. "FDA Order," *Federal Register* 40, no. 203, 20 October 1975, 48,918; corrected ibid., no. 206, 23 October 1975, 49,574 (codified in *Code of Federal Regulations* vol. 21, sec. 310.501).

94. Gilmore, "Something Better Than the Pill?", *New York Times,* 20 July 1969, magazine sec., p. 6.

95. *American Medical News,* 16 February 1975, p. 2.

96. "Testing Vaccine on Pregnancy," *New York Times,* 14 March 1976, sec. 4, p. 9.

97. Rodney D. Skoglund and C. Alvin Paulsen, "Danazol-Testosterone Combination: A Potentially Effective Means for Reversible Male Contraception, a Preliminary Report," *Contraception* 7 (1973): 357.

98. C. Alvin Paulsen and John M. Leonard, "Clinical Trials in Reversible Male Contraception: I. Combination of Danazol Plus Testosterone," in *Regulatory Mechanisms of Male Reproductive Physiology,* eds. C. H. Spilman, T. J. Lobl, and K. T. Kirton (6th Brook Lodge Workshop on Problems of Reproductive Biology, Kalamazoo, Michigan, 1975), (New York: American Elsevier, 1976), p. 197.

99. Lublin, "The Man's Turn: Scientists Foresee Likely Development of Male Contraceptive," *Wall Street Journal,* 29 September 1975, p. 1.

100. Skoglund and Paulsen, "Danazol-Testosterone Combination," p. 363.

101. William J. Brenner and David M. deKretser, "The Prospects for New, Reversible Male Contraceptives," *New England Journal of Medicine* 295 (1976): 1111.

102. See text preceding and following notes 11 and 12 *supra.*

103. Walter A. Rosenblith, "Science, Technology and the University," in *Science and the Evolution of Public Policy,* ed. James Shannon (New York: Rockefeller University Press, 1973), p. 74.

CHAPTER 5: THE DELANEY AMENDMENT: ROUGH-HEWN
REGULATION (pp. 142–162)

1. U.S., Congress, House, Remarks of Representative Delaney, 85th Cong., 2d Sess., 30 April 1958, *Congressional Record* 104: 7782–83 (hereafter cited as *Cong. Rec.*).

2. *U.S. Code Annotated,* vol. 21, sec. 348(c)(4) (1972) (hereafter cited as U.S.C.A.).

3. U.S., Congress, Senate, "Senate Report 2422," 85th Cong., 2d sess., 1958; reprinted in *U.S. Code Congressional and Administrative News* (St. Paul, Minnesota: West Publishing Co., 1958): 5300–05.

4. Charles H. Blank, "The Delaney Clause," *California Law Review* 62 (1974): 1084, 1100–02.

5. Ibid., p. 1103.

6. Letter from Dr. Harold P. Blum (25 August 1959), in Remarks of Representative Leonor Sullivan, 86th Cong., 1st sess., 27 August 1959, *Cong. Rec.* 105:17,265.

7. Paper by William E. Smith, M.D. (11 July 1958), in Extension of Remarks of Representative Delaney, 85th Cong., 2d sess., 25 August 1958, *Cong. Rec.* 104:A7739.

8. Remarks of Representative Dixon, 86th Cong., 2d sess., 2 February 1960, *Cong. Rec.* 106:1827.

9. Statement of Thomas F. Carney (11 February 1960), in Extension of Remarks of Representative Barr, 86th Cong., 2d sess., 18 February 1960, *Cong. Rec.* 106:A1374.

10. Representative Dixon, *Cong. Rec.* 106:1827.

11. Editorial in *Farm Journal* (February 1960), in Remarks of Representative Horan, 86th Cong., 2d sess., 8 February 1960, *Cong. Rec.* 106:2252.

12. Remarks of Representative Delaney, 86th Cong., 2d sess., 25 June 1960, *Cong. Rec.* 106:14,350.

13. Statement of Federation of Homemakers, Arlington, Virginia, by Mrs. Ann Booras, 29 January 1960, in Extension of Remarks of Representative Wolf, 86th Cong., 2d sess., 22 March 1960, *Cong. Rec.* 106:A2563.

14. Statement of Dr. Arthur Flemming (26 January 1960), in Remarks of Representative Harris, 86th Cong., 2d sess., 25 June 1960, *Cong. Rec.* 106:14,358.

15. Ibid., p. 14,359.

16. Ibid., p. 14,357.

17. Ibid., p. 14,359.

18. Letter from Acting Secretary of Agriculture True D. Morse to Representative Oren Harris (16 May 1960), in Extension of Remarks of Representative Barr, 86 Cong., 2d sess., 25 May 1960, *Cong. Rec.* 106:A4451.

19. Guido Calabresi, *The Costs of Accidents* (New Haven: Yale University Press, 1970), pp. 56–57.

20. *U.S.C.A.*, vol. 21, secs. 376(b)(5)(C), (D) (1972).

21. Remarks of Representative Rogers, 86 Cong., 2d sess., 25 June 1960, *Cong. Rec.* 106:14,372.

22. Statement of Dr. Freddy Homburger, President of Bio-Research Institute, in Extension of Remarks of Representative Philbin, 87th Cong., 1st sess., 3 May 1961, *Cong. Rec.* 107:7259.

23. Remarks of Representative Nelsen, 87th Cong., 2d sess., 5 July 1962, *Cong. Rec.* 108:12,713.

24. *U.S.C.A.,* vol. 21, secs. 348(c)(3)(A), 376(b)(5)(B) (1972).

25. Extension of Remarks of Representative Sullivan, 87th Cong., 2d sess., 6 August 1962, *Cong. Rec.* 108:15,717.

26. *U.S.C.A.,* vol. 21, sec. 360b(d)(1)(H) (1972).

27. Blank, "Delaney Clause," pp. 1115–16.

28. Ibid., pp. 1114–15.

29. Ibid., pp. 1086–87.

30. Ibid., pp. 1093–94.

31. Paper by William E. Smith, *Cong. Rec.* 104:A7739.

32. For a discussion of "pitfalls" in scientific inquiry, see Jerome R. Ravetz, *Scientific Knowledge and Its Social Problems* (Oxford: Clarendon Press, 1971), pp. 95–100.

33. Blank, "Delaney Clause."

34. Ibid., p. 1097.

35. Ibid., p. 1098.

36. Ibid., pp. 1097–98.

37. Ibid., pp. 1110–11.

38. Ibid., p. 1107.

39. Ibid., pp. 1107–08.

40. Ibid., pp. 1103–04.

41. Ibid., p. 1103.

42. U.S., Congress, Senate, Remarks of Senator Javits, 86th Cong., 2d sess., 1 July 1960, *Cong. Rec.* 106:15,381.

43. Blank, "Delaney Clause," p. 1099.

44. Ibid., pp. 1106–07.

45. Lyons, "Saccharin Ban Faces Review," *Washington Post,* 22 March 1977, p. A-1.

46. Steven J. Kelman, "No Mad Scientists," *New Republic,* 26 March 1977, p. 11.

47. U.S., Department of Health, Education, and Welfare, Statement of F.D.A. Commissioner Kennedy, attached to *HEW News,* release no. P77-14, 14 April 1977.

48. *Saccharin Study and Labelling Act,* Pub. L. 95–203, 95th Cong., 1st sess., 1977.

49. A point made by Representative Scheuer of New York in the initial hue and cry about the F.D.A. announcement. See Lyons, "Saccharin Ban Faces Review."

50. Irving I. Kessler and J. Page Clark, "Saccharin, Cyclamate and Human Bladder Cancer," *Journal of the American Medical Association* 240, no. 4 (July 1978): 349.

51. Dr. Irving I. Kessler, quoted in Parachini, "New research defends saccharin, cyclamate," *Chicago Sun-Times,* 25 July 1978, p. 7.

52. See Blank, "Delaney Clause," pp. 1115-19.

53. Letter from Secretary of Health, Education, and Welfare Caspar W. Weinberger to Representative Harley O. Staggers, in 93d Cong., 2d sess., 21 June 1974, *Cong. Rec.* 120:20,565.

54. Marshall S. Shapo, "A Representational Theory of Consumer Protection: Doctrine, Function, and Legal Liability for Product Disappointment," *Virginia Law Review* 60 (1974): 1109.

55. U.S., Congress, House, Testimony of Representative Leonor Sullivan, 86th Cong., 2d sess., 27 January 1960, *Cong. Rec.* 106:14,370.

56. Cf. Jeffrey O'Connell and Arthur Myers, *Safety Last* (New York: Random House, 1966), p. 155, (describing "disastrous" drop in Ford sales following company's advertising campaign emphasizing safety).

57. "Report of the President's Science Advisory Committee" (May 14, 1960) in Remarks of Senator Javits, 86th Cong., 2d sess., 1 July 1960, *Cong. Rec.* 106:15,380-81.

58. Blank, "Delaney Clause," p. 1117.

59. See, *supra,* text with note 48.

60. Blank, "Delaney Clause," p. 1110.

61. Compare ibid., p. 1119.

62. *Code of Federal Regulations* vol. 40, sec. 180.107 (1976).

63. 86th Cong., 2d sess., 25 June 1960, *Cong. Rec.* 106:14,350.

64. See Blank, "Delaney Clause," p. 1089.

CHAPTER 6: DES: MAGIC WAND AND TERRIBLE SWORD (pp. 163-190)

1. 366 F.2d 177 (7th Cir. 1966).

2. Ibid., p. 182.

3. Ibid.

4. U.S., HEW, "New Animal Drugs for Use in Animal Feeds" (part 135a of chapter 1, subchapter on Drugs, FDA), *Federal Register* 35, no. 178, 12 September 1970, 14,391.

5. U.S., Congress, House, Statement of Thomas P. Carney in Extension of Remarks of Representative Barr, 86th Cong., 2d Sess., 18 February 1960, *Congressional Record* 106:A1373-74.

6. U.S., Congress, House, Committee on Government Operations, Statement of Dr. Edwards in Hearings before a Subcommittee, 92d Cong., 1st Sess., 1971, pt. 1, p. 53, quoted in Charles H. Blank, "The Delaney Clause: Technical Naivete and Scientific Advocacy in the Formulation of Public Health Policies," *California Law Review* 62 (1974): 1084, n.4.

7. U.S., Congress, Senate, Remarks of Senator Proxmire, 92d Cong., 1st Sess., 8 November 1971, *Congressional Record* 117:39,735.

8. U.S., Congress, Senate, Remarks of Senator Ribicoff, 93d Cong., 1st Sess., 28 March 1973, *Congressional Record* 119:9966.

9. Hess & Clark, Division of Rhodia, Inc. v. F.D.A., 495 F.2d 975 (D.C.Cir. 1974).

10. Ibid., p. 982.

11. 495 F.2d 975 (D.C.Cir. 1974).

12. Ibid., p. 992.

13. Ibid.

14. Ibid., p. 993.

15. Ibid., p. 994.

16. "Proposed Rule," *Federal Register* 39, no. 60, 27 March 1974, 11,299; "Notice," ibid., p. 11,323.

17. Senator Ribicoff, *Congressional Record,* pp. 9966–67.

18. Mintz, "DES May Cause Sterility in Sons, Studies Indicate," *Washington Post,* 10 December 1975, p. A–3.

19. Thomas P. Carney, *Congressional Record,* p. A1373.

20. Mintz, "DES May Cause Sterility."

21. Lawrence S. Charfoos, "DES: Bitter Aftermath of a Pill," *Trial,* May/June 1975, p. 71.

22. "Medicine's Week," *American Medical News,* 15 March 1976, p. 2.

23. Mintz, "University Finds No Cancer in Daughters of DES Patients," *Washington Post,* 27 April 1977, p. A–5.

24. Charfoos, "Bitter Aftermath," pp. 71, 76.

25. Abel v. Eli Lilly & Co., No. 74-030-070-NP (Mich. Cir. Ct. Wayne Co. May 16, 1977), summary in *Product Safety & Liability Reporter* (Washington, D.C.: Bureau of National Affairs, 1977), vol. 5, no. 22, p. 410.

26. "DES-Cancer Link Overstated, Physicians Told," *American Medical News,* 16 May 1977, p. 10.

27. It has been asserted that there is no substantial evidence of effectiveness for this purpose. Mintz, "DES May Cause Sterility," p. A–3.

28. For a representative discussion of this kind of calculus, see Charles Fried, "The Value of Life," *Harvard Law Review* 82 (1969): 1415–22.

29. "FDA Talk Paper No. T73-10," summary in *Food Drug Cosmetic Law Reporter* (Chicago, Commerce Clearing House, 1973), par. 40,833.

30. "Proposed Rule," *Federal Register* 38, no. 186, 26 September 1973, 26,809; "Preamble to FDA Order," *Federal Register* 40, no. 25, 5

February 1975, 5351; *Code of Federal Regulations* vol. 21, sec. 310:501 (1977).

31. "Notice," *Federal Register* 40, no. 39, 26 February 1975, 8242.

32. I am grateful to my colleague Richard Merrill for calling this fact to my attention.

33. "Notice," *Federal Register* 40, no. 150, 4 August 1975, 32,773.

34. Okie, "Senate Weighs Curbs on DES," *Washington Post,* 7 September 1975, p. A–11; Rich, "Senate Votes to Ban DES," *Washington Post,* 10 September 1975, p. A–6.

35. "Notice," *Federal Register* 41, no. 7, 12 January 1976, 1804.

36. *Federal Register* 41, no. 51, 15 March 1976, 10,998; *Code of Federal Regulations* vol. 21, sec. 558.225 (1978). For a later regulation permitting ear implants in lambs and cattle, respectively 70 and 120 days before marketing, see *Federal Register* 41, no. 229, 26 November 1976, 52,051; *Code of Federal Regulations* vol. 21, sec. 522.640 (1978).

37. "Agency Finds Trace of DES in Liver," *American Medical News,* 31 May 1976, p. 8.

38. "Proposed Rule," *Federal Register* 38, no. 195, 10 October 1973, 27,940.

39. Daniel Zwerdling, "Depo-Provera," *New Republic,* 9 November 1974, p. 7.

40. "Proposed Rule," *Federal Register* 38, no. 195, 10 October 1973, 27,940.

41. *Federal Register* 39, no. 178, 12 September 1974, 32,907; corrected, *Federal Register* 39, no. 198, 10 October 1974, 36,472.

42. Zwerdling, "Depo-Provera."

43. Mintz, "New Birth Control Drug May Be Linked to Cancer," *Washington Post,* 7 October 1974, p. B–14.

44. "Reanalysis of Data Related to Carcinoma in Situ," *Federal Register* 39, no. 178, 12 September 1974, 32,909.

45. Ibid., p. 32,908.

46. Mintz, "New Birth Control Drug Linked to Cancer."

47. "Stay of Order," *Federal Register* 39, no. 210, 30 October 1974, 38,226.

48. U.S., Congress, House, Remarks of Representative Price, 93d Cong., 1st Sess., 6 January 1973, *Congressional Record* 119:497.

49. See Blank, "The Delaney Clause," p. 1109.

50. Ibid., p. 1110.

51. At this writing, the product was recommended for uses varying from treatment of menopausal impact on blood vessel dilation to breast engorgement in women who have recently given birth. See *Physician's Desk Reference,* 3d ed., s.v. "diethylstilbesterol."

52. Brian Henderson et al., "Urogenital Tract Abnormalities in Sons of Women Treated with Diethylstilbesterol," *Pediatrics* 58 (1976): 505.

CHAPTER 7: ASBESTOS DISCHARGES: A SHADOW IN THE LAKE (pp. 191–217)

1. Reserve Mining Co. v. E.P.A., 514 F.2d 492, 500 (8th Cir. 1975); United States v. Reserve Mining Co., 380 F. Supp. 11, 30 (D. Minn. 1974).

2. "Judge Removed in Reserve Case Defends Actions," *Washington Post,* 8 January 1976, p. A–5.

3. 380 F. Supp. at 31.

4. Ibid.

5. Ibid. at 32, 41.

6. 514 F.2d at 501; 380 F. Supp. at 32.

7. 380 F. Supp. at 32–33.

8. Ibid. at 33.

9. 514 F.2d at 510.

10. Reserve Mining Co. v. E.P.A., 498 F.2d 1073, 1079 (8th Cir. 1974).

11. 380 F. Supp. at 48–49.

12. Ibid. at 49.

13. 498 F.2d at 1078 n.7, 1079.

14. 380 F. Supp. at 50.

15. 514 F.2d at 511.

16. Ibid. at 508 n.26.

17. Ibid. at 509 n.26.

18. Ibid. at 510 nn.29 & 30.

19. 380 F. Supp. at 43.

20. 514 F.2d at 510.

21. Ibid. at 508 n.25.

22. 380 F. Supp. at 42.

23. 514 F.2d at 510 n.32.

24. Ibid.

25. 380 F. Supp. at 43–44.

26. 514 F.2d at 510.

27. Ibid. at 512–13 n. 40.

28. Ibid.

29. Ibid. at 513.

30. Ibid. at 514–15.

31. See 514 F.2d at 515; 380 F. Supp. at 69–71.

32. 514 F.2d at 516 & n.47.

33. Ibid. at 519.

34. Ibid. at 537.

35. Ethyl Corp. v. E.P.A., 541 F.2d 1 (D.C. Cir. 1976).

36. 514 F.2d at 520.

37. 380 F. Supp. at 70–71.

38. Ibid. at 90.

39. Ibid. at 70–71.

40. Ibid. at 89.

41. 514 F.2d at 536, quoting findings of fact in 380 F. Supp. at 16.

42. 514 F.2d at 536.

43. Ibid. at 538.

44. 380 F. Supp. at 54.

45. See, e.g., 514 F.2d at 535.

46. I am assuming for the moment that the closing of the Reserve plant would have meant virtual ruination of the community, despite Judge Lord's argument that construction of facilities for abating the emissions and discharges would reasonably take up the economic slack caused by a temporary shutdown. See 380 F. Supp. at 70.

47. Minn. Stat. Ann. § 115.01(5) (1977), quoted in 514 F.2d at 528.

48. 33 U.S.C.A. §1160(g)(1) (1970).

49. 514 F.2d at 529.

50. Ibid. at 538.

51. Quoted in 514 F.2d at 523 n.57.

52. Ibid.

53. 541 F.2d 1.

54. See ibid. at 10, 28 n.58.

55. Ibid. at 28.

56. Ibid.

57. Ibid. at 28 n.58.

58. United States v. Reserve Mining Co., 417 F Supp. 789 (D. Minn. 1976).

59. United States v. Reserve Mining Co., 543 F.2d 1210 (8th Cir. 1976).

60. Reserve Mining Co. v. Herbst, — Minn. —, 256 N.W.2d 808 (1977).

61. Reserve Mining Co. v. Minnesota Pollution Control Agency, — Minn. —, 267 N.W.2d 720, 11 Env. Rep. Cas. 1568 (1978).

62. 498 F.2d at 1077.

63. See 380 F. Supp. at 56.

64. See 498 F.2d at 1077–78; 514 F.2d at 507.

65. See text *supra* with notes 55, 56.

66. See Jerome Ravetz, *Scientific Knowledge & Its Social Problems* (Oxford: Clarendon Press, 1971), pp. 76–80.

67. 514 F.2d at 516 n.46.

68. Amoco Oil Co. v. E.P.A., 501 F.2d 722, 741 (D.C. Cir. 1974), quoted in 514 F.2d 507 n.20.

69. See 514 F.2d at 507 n.20.

70. 498 F.2d at 1083 n.12.

71. See 380 F. Supp. at 46 n.29, 53–54.

72. 498 F.2d at 1084.

73. 514 F.2d at 538. It is this harmful potential which makes the case one that does in fact have "health hazard" aspects, and distinguishes it from ordinary pollution cases. Cf., e.g., 498 F.2d at 1084 *with* 514 F.2d at 527–29.

74. 380 F. Supp. at 42.

75. 498 F.2d at 1083.

76. Ibid. at 1078–79.

77. Ibid. at 1080, 1083–84.

78. Ibid. at 1082.

79. 514 F.2d at 513.

CHAPTER 8: DNA REGULATION: LAW TO TAME THE GENIE (pp. 218–247)

1. Quoted in Otto Nathan and Heinz Norden, eds., *Einstein on Peace* (New York: Simon and Schuster, 1960), pp. 294–95.

2. Paul Berg et al., "Potential Biohazards of Recombinant DNA Molecules," *Science* 185 (1974): 303.

3. See Marc Lappe, "Human Uses of Molecular Genetics," *Federation Proceedings: Federation of American Societies for Experimental Biology* 34, no. 6 (May 1975): 1425 (hereafter cited as *Federation Proceedings*).

4. David A. Jackson, Robert H. Symonds, and Paul Berg, "Biochemical Method for Inserting New Genetic Information into DNA of Simian Virus 40," *Proceedings of the National Academy of Sciences of the U.S.* 69 (1972): 2904.

5. "A Two-Edged Sword," *Nature* 240 (November 1972): 73.

6. Maxine Singer and Dieter Soll, "Guidelines for DNA Hybrid Molecules," *Science* 181 (1973): 1114.

7. See "Director's Introduction," in "Department of HEW, NIH, Recombinant DNA Research, Guidelines," *Federal Register* 41, no. 131, 7 July 1976, 27,902 (hereafter cited as "Guidelines").

8. This definition appears in "Director's Introduction," "Guidelines," p. 27,902.

9. See Richard Roblin, "Ethical and Social Aspects of Experimental Gene Manipulation," *Federation Proceedings,* p. 1421.

10. "Guidelines," pp. 27,903–04.

11. Roblin, "Aspects of Gene Manipulation," p. 1421.

12. See J. Eisinger, "The Ethics of Human Gene Manipulation," *Federation Proceedings,* p. 1412; George P. Smith, III, "Manipulating the Genetic Code: Jurisprudential Conundrums," *Georgetown Law Journal* 64 (1976): 697.

13. See Smith, "Manipulating Genetic Code," pp. 702–703.

14. See Salvador Luria, *Life, The Unfinished Experiment* (New York: Scribner, 1973), pp. 132–33, quoted in Eisinger, "Ethics of Gene Manipulation," pp. 1418–19.

15. Roblin, "Aspects of Gene Manipulation," p. 1423.

16. Berg et al., "Potential Biohazards," p. 303.

17. A summary statement of the report submitted to the Association of Life Science of the National Academy of Sciences appears in *Science* 188 (1975): 991.

18. "Guidelines," p. 27,903.

19. Ibid., p. 27,905.

20. See Lappe, "Human Uses," p. 1426.

21. "Guidelines," p. 27,902.

22. See "Department of HEW, NIH, Recombinant DNA Research, Proposed Revised Guidelines," *Federal Register* 42, no. 187, 27 September 1977, p. 49,596.

23. See, e.g., Wade, "Gene-Splicing Rules: Another Round of Debate," *Science* 199 (January 1978): 30; Fields, "Congressmen Will Try Again on Regulation of DNA Research," *Chronicle of Higher Education,* 21 February 1978, p. 6; "Senate Passes Back Gene-Splice Cup," *Science* 200 (June 1978): 1368; Simring, Letter to the Editor, "Biomedical Research: N.I.H.'s Conflicting Functions," *New York Times,* 28 June 1978, p. 30.

24. Letter from Peter Barton Hutt to Donald S. Frederickson, M.D. (3 March 1978), copy in possession of author.

25. "Guidelines," (1976) pp. 27,912–14.

26. Ibid., p. 27,915.

27. Ibid., p. 27,907.

28. Ibid., p. 27,915.

29. Ibid.

30. Ibid., p. 27,917.

31. Ibid., p. 27,907.

32. Ibid., p. 27,908.

33. Ibid.

34. Ibid., pp. 27,915–16.

35. Ibid., p. 27,915.

36. Ibid., p. 27,914.

37. Ibid., p. 27,907.

38. Ibid., p. 27,914.

39. Ibid., p. 27,907.

40. Ibid., p. 27,908.

41. Ibid., pp. 27,917–19.

42. Ibid., p. 27,909.

43. Ibid., p. 27,919.

44. Ibid., p. 27,921, n.4.

45. The allowance of vector perpetuation in only one of 10^8 host cells for EK-2 systems provides a comparison case of what might be called virtual zero tolerance. One may ask whether this should have been made a zero case, too. Yet it should be emphasized that the choice here is not so simple as one of whether to permit pipetting by mouth. The NIH director's explanation of this standard, couched in negative terms, stresses the thinness of the probability when he says that the host-vector system must have "no greater than a 10^{-8} probability of survival." Ibid., p. 27,907. From a risk-averse perspective, this has a reassuring sound, but it does leave the question of how reliable is the forecast of probability in the context of the uncertainties at issue.

46. Ibid., p. 27,920.

47. Ibid., pp. 27,920–21.

48. Robert de Ropp, *The New Prometheans* (New York: Delacorte Press, Dial Press, 1972), p. 155.

49. See the optimism about the "promise" of rapid advancement in the "molecular understanding of genetics," in the last paragraph of Marshall W. Nirenberg, "The Genetic Code: II," *Scientific American* 208 (March 1963): 80, 94.

50. However, there is at least one case in the legal literature that gives one pause. See Weller & Co. v. Foot & Mouth Disease Research Inst., [1966] 1 Q.B. 569.

51. Bernard D. Davis, "Potential Benefits Are Large, Protective Methods Make Risks Small," *Chemical and Engineering News* 55 (May 1977): 27, 30.

52. "Guidelines," p. 27,910.

53. Ibid., pp. 27,910–11.

54. Paul A. Weiss, "Living Nature and the Knowledge Gap," *Saturday Review,* 29 November 1969, p. 19.

55. See, e.g., Cohn, "'Products' of Genetic Engineering Seen Less than Five Years Away," *Washington Post,* 11 November 1977, p. A2.

56. See Smith, "Manipulating Genetic Code," p. 727.

57. Ibid., p. 726.

58. "Guidelines," p. 27,906.

59. Ibid., pp. 27,909, 27,917.

60. Ibid., p. 27,910.

61. Ibid., p. 27,906.

62. See *supra* at 241, text with note 56.

63. Ibid., pp. 708–10, 731.

64. Ibid., p. 709.

65. I do recognize, however, that constitutional distinctions may be drawn between regulation with specific health and safety features, and that designed to preserve social organization.

66. Lappe, "Human Uses," p. 1427.

67. See "Guidelines," p. 27,904.

68. Smith, "Manipulating Genetic Code," p. 730, quoting from Callahan, "A Philosopher's Response," in *The New Genetics and the Future of Man,* M. Hamilton, ed. (1972), p. 92.

69. See generally U.S., Congress, Senate, *Regulation of Recombinant DNA Research: Hearings before the Subcommittee on Science, Technology and Space,* 95th Cong., 1st Sess., 1977, pp. 50–69. Exemplary of the conclusions of Curtiss was his statement in an April 1977 letter to the NIH director "that the introduction of foreign DNA sequences into EK-1 and EK-2 host-vectors offers no danger whatsoever to any human being with the exception . . . that an extremely careless worker might under unique conditions cause harm to him- or herself." *Recombinant DNA Research: Hearings,* at p. 50.

70. See Cohen, "Recombinant DNA: Fact and Fiction," *Science* 195 (February 1977): 654.

71. Letter of Stanley Cohen, M.D., to Donald Frederickson, M.D., reprinted in *Recombinant DNA Research: Hearings,* pp. 136–37, referring to research titled *In vivo* Site-Specific Genetic Recombination Promoted by *Eco*RI Restriction Endonuclease, *Proceedings of the National Academy of Sciences* 74 (November 1974): 4811.

72. "Guidelines," p. 27,904.

73. I am grateful to my colleague Richard Merrill for conversation which helped me to develop this point.

CHAPTER 9: EXPERIMENTING WITH THE CONSUMER (pp. 248–262)

1. See, e.g., Paul D. Rheingold, "The MER/29 Story: An Instance of Successful Mass Disaster Litigation," *California Law Review* 56 (1968): 116; "The Case for a Federal Common Law of Aircraft Disaster Litigation: A Judicial Solution to a National Problem" (Note), *New York University Law Review* 51 (1976): 231; "Air Crash Litigation: Disaster in the Courts" (Note), *Southwestern University Law Review* 7 (1975): 661.

2. See Guido Calabresi, *The Costs of Accidents* (New Haven: Yale University Press, 1970), pp. 56–57.

3. See generally, ibid., chap. 6.

4. For example, it has been established in the field of automobile injuries that persons with low-value claims tend to be overcompensated and that people with very bad injuries are usually grossly undercompensated. See, e.g., Alfred F. Conard, "The Economic Treatment of Automobile Injuries," *Michigan Law Review* 63 (1964): 279, 291–92.

5. See John Rawls, *A Theory of Justice* (Cambridge: Harvard University Press, Belknap Press, 1971), pp. 17–21.

6. Ibid., p. 83.

7. Frank I. Michelman, "Property, Utility, and Fairness: Comments on the Ethical Foundations of 'Just Compensation' Law," *Harvard Law Review* 80 (1967): 1165, 1223.

8. Cf. Rawls, *Theory of Justice*, p. 78, suggesting that inequality in economic expectation between property owners and unskilled laborers is "permissible only if lowering it would make the working class even more worse off."

9. See, e.g., ibid., p. 3.

INDEX

Abortion, 243
Accidents, 42, 44
Acetaminophen, 75–77
Adenomas, 124–125
Advertising
  diet-linked, 84–87
  oral contraceptives and, 89, 97
Aflatoxin, 154
Agriculture, Department of, 169, 170
Air pollution, xi, 194, 195, 197, 202–204, 206–207, 209, 214
American Association for the Advancement of Science, 1, 10
American College of Obstetricians, 133
American Home Products Corporation, 128
American Medical Association (AMA), 103, 105
American Psychological Association (APA), 37
  Ad Hoc Committee on Ethical Standards in Psychological Research, 44, 46
  "Ethical Standards" document, 44–46, 51
Amosite, 192–193, 198, 214
Amphiboles, 192, 194
Amygdalin, 63–72
Animal feed, 149–151, 168, 179–180, 187–189
Aramite, 142, 162
Artificial conception, 242–243
Asbestos discharges, xi, xv, 52, 191–217, 255

Asilomar conference (1975), 26, 224–226, 228
Aspirin, 75
Atomic bomb, 26
Auschwitz, 114–115
Automobiles, 18, 44, 51–52

Bell v. Goddard (1966), 165–167, 177
Berg, Paul, 219, 223
Beri-beri, 5
Biological warfare, xii, 12
Birth control pills: see Oral contraceptives
Birth defects, 221
  gene therapy and, 243
  oral contraceptives and, 106, 109, 112–113, 119
Blank, Charles, 152–153
Blood clots, 92–105, 109–112, 126, 132, 178
Blood triglyceride, 130
Botulism, 155
Breast cancer, 96, 116, 121, 126, 128, 136–137, 165
Brown, Arnold, 194, 196–198, 200–203, 215, 216, 256
Burger, Warren, 210

C-Quens, 107, 108
Calabresi, Guido, 40, 41–42, 44, 46, 149
Cancer, 33; see also specific types of cancer
  asbestos issue, 192–193, 195–206, 214–217

Cancer (*continued*)
  DES issue, xi, 163–180, 187–
    189
  food additives and, 143–162,
    164
  Hyman case, 35–36
  Laetrile problem, 60, 63–72
  oral contraceptives and, 116,
    119, 120–123, 126, 128, 134,
    136–137, 262
Carney, Thomas P., 174
Cattle feed, 149–151, 168, 179–
  180, 187–189
Center for Disease Control, 228,
  239, 241
Cervical cancer, 116, 184–185
Choice: *see* Personal choice
Cholesterol, 84–87, 130
Chrysotile, 192, 196, 214
Cohen, Stanley, 245
Colds, 75–77, 87
Color additives, 147–150, 155,
  159–160, 168
Committee on the Safety of
  Drugs, 99, 118
Competition, 23
Compulsory vaccination, 34, 54
Condom, 91
Consent, 39–43, 45, 46, 47–48,
  183–184
Contraception: *see also* Oral con-
  traceptives
  Depo-Provera, 180–187
  DES and, 177–179
  male, 138–139
  types of, 91, 101, 116, 138
Corpus luteum hormone, 91
Crocidolite, 198, 214
Crout, Richard, 89
Curtis, Carl, 179
Curtiss, Roy, 245
Cryptic viral genomes, 225, 227
Cumingtonite-grunerite, 192,
  193

Cyanide ion, 63–64
Cyclamates, 157

Danazol, 138
Darvon, 59
Darwin, Erasmus, 10
Davis, Bernard, 239
DDT, 147
Deception, 47
Decholin, 61–63, 70, 78
Delaney, James, 142–145, 147,
  151, 154, 162
Delaney amendment of 1958,
  142–162, 164, 168, 188–190,
  215, 216
Depo-Provera, 180–187
DES (diethylstilbesterol), xi,
  163–180, 187–189
DES conjugate, 170–171
Depression, 97
Diaphragm, 91, 101
Diethylstilbesterol: *see* DES
Dioxyribonucleic acid: *see* DNA
  regulation
Disease, 29
Dixon, Henry, 145, 146
DNA regulation, 218–250, 254–
  256
*Dr. Atkins' Diet Revolution: The
  High Calorie Way to Stay Thin
  Forever* (Atkins), 60
Down's syndrome, 109
Drill, Victor, 109–111
Drugs
  cold remedies, 75–77, 87
  Decholin case, 61–63, 70, 78
  Depo-Provera, 180–187
  DES, xi, 163–180, 187–189
  HCG, 72–74
  investigational new drug (IND)
    process, 38–40, 65, 68, 70, 95
  Laetrile issue, 60, 63–72

oral contraceptives: *see* Oral contraceptives
vitamins, 64, 75, 78–84

E. coli (escherichia coli), 220–222, 230–232, 234
E. coli K-12, 230–231, 236
Edmondson, Hugh, 124–125
Edwards, Commissioner, 105, 107
Eggs, 84–87
Einstein, Albert, 3
Eisenhower, Dwight D., 20
EK-1, 230, 236, 238, 241
EK-2, 231–232, 236, 238, 241
EK-3, 231–232
Ellul, Jacques, 2, 26
Emergency, medical, 54–55
Endocarcinoma, 98
Endocervical hyperplasia, 98
Endocrinology, 8
Endometrial cancer, 121–123, 127–129
Enovid, 91–93, 106, 109, 110
Environmental Protection Agency (EPA), 202, 207–208
Epididymis, 139
Estalor, 108
Estrogen, 104, 108, 110–112, 114–116, 121–123, 125, 127–130, 134–136, 141, 164–166, 178
Ethinyl estradiol, 110, 125, 183
Ethyl Corporation, 202, 207–208
Ethyl Corporation v. EPA (1976), 207–208, 210
Ethynerone, 94, 95
Euglena, 221
Eukaryotes, 225, 234–235
Experimentation, xiv, xv, 25, 29–57, 248
  choice and, 38, 39, 45
  consent, 39–43, 45, 46, 47–48, 183–184

deception, 47
defined, 30
drugs, testing and marketing, 30, 38–40
emergency question, 54–55
Hyman case, 35–36
idiosyncratic subjects, 52–53
individual inviolability and, 43
inducement to, 41
investigational new drug (IND) process, 38–40, 56–57
length of, 7
market, xiv, 30, 41, 43, 128, 129, 252
nontherapeutic, 32, 34, 41
on pain, 41
pre-epidemic, 54–55
psychological research, 44–48, 51–53
rights of subjects, 37–38
selection of recipients, 48–49, 55
testing processes, 32
therapeutic, 31–32
tracing results and assigning causation, 32–33
two models of medical, 31
volume of, 48

Fad diets, 59–60
Family Planning Perspectives, 131
Farm Journal, 147
Federal Trade Commission (FTC), 61, 72–74, 84, 85
Federal Water Pollution Control Act, 206
Fermi, Enrico, 218
Fetuses, regulations on protection of, 31
Fifth Amendment, 65
Finkle, Doctor, 121–122
First Amendment, 60, 72, 73
Fleming, Alexander, 6
Flemming, Arthur, 148

Food, Drug and Cosmetic Act, 60, 64, 82, 189, 250

Food additives, xv, 8, 81, 142–162, 164, 168, 188–190, 211

Food and Drug Administration (FDA), 22, 38, 39, 56, 61, 65, 66, 71, 72, 74, 77–82

   Advisory Committee on Obstetrics and Gynecology, 99–100, 102, 119, 123, 127, 132, 177, 261

   Depo-Provera issue, 180–186

   DES issue, 163–165, 168–173, 177–180

   food additives issue, 142, 147, 155, 156, 189

   oral contraceptives issue, 91–99, 102–108, 111, 119, 123, 126–129, 133–137, 142

Fort Detrick, Maryland, 239

Fountain, L. H., 185–186

Freedom of choice: see Personal choice

Freund, Paul, 48

Friendly, Judge, 80, 82

Gall bladder disease, 112, 119

Gastrointestinal cancer, 200

Gene recombination, xv, 8, 11–12, 14–16, 25, 26, 218–250, 254–256

Genetic counseling, 243

Genetic screening, 221

Gesell, Judge, 106

Goddard, Commissioner, 48, 95, 180

Gray, Kenneth J., 94–96

Gross, Doctor, 201

Halberstam, Michael, 4

Hanson v. United States (1976), 67, 68

Harris, Oren, 148

Hart, Gary, 179

HCG (human chorionic gonadotropin), 72–74

Health, Education, and Welfare (HEW), Department of, 31, 151

Health Research Group, 174

Heart disease, 29, 33, 106, 116–119, 120, 126, 133–134

Heisenberg Uncertainty Principle, 21–22

Herbst, Albert, 175–176

Hess & Clark v. FDA (1974), 170

Hill, Senator, 154

Himsworth, Harold, 5

Hodges, Doctor, 96

Hormones: see specific names of hormones

Hyman v. Jewish Chronic Disease Hospital (1965), 35–36

Hyperplasia, 95

Hypertension, 130

Idiosyncratic research subjects, 52–53

In vitro fertilization, 242–243

Individual inviolability, 43

Infection, 33

Informed consent: see Consent

Inman, W. H., 98–99, 100, 110, 118, 126

Insulin, 222, 234

International Planned Parenthood Federation, 184

Intrauterine device (IUD), 91, 116, 138

Investigational new drug (IND) process, 38–40, 56–57, 65, 68, 70, 95

Javits, Jacob, 154

Jofen, Jean, 114–115

Joliot-Curie, Frédérick, 12

Jonas, Hans, 34, 43

Journal of the American Medical Association, 109, 111, 124
Justice, Rawls' theory of, 257–259

Kelsey, Frances, 22
Kennedy, Commissioner, 156
Kennedy, Edward M., 179
Kidney damage, 75–77

Laetrile, 60, 63–72
Lappe, Marc, 243
Laudable pus, 33
Lawson, Sarah, 92–94, 140
Lead content in gasoline, 207
Legionnaire's disease, 12
Leventhal, Judge, 170, 171
Liability rules, 55–56
Lilly, Eli, & Co., 107, 174
Liver tumors, 124–125, 126
Loevinger, Lee, 19, 20
Lord, Judge, 203, 212, 213
Lowell, Francis C., 77
Lunar Society of Birmingham, England, 10
Lung cancer, 200

Male contraception, 138–139
Manhattan Project, 26
Mann, Doctor, 116–118, 120
Mansfield, Judge, 80
Market experimentation, xiv, 30, 41, 43, 128, 129, 252
McCleery, Robert, 100, 101
McDermot, Walsh, 30, 32
Meat, DES issue, xi, 163–180, 187–189
Medical emergency, 54–55
Medical Letter, 75, 111–112, 115, 116, 126
Medroxyprogesterone acetate, 180–187
Menopause, 121–122, 127–129, 141
Merck, Sharp & Dohme, 94–95

Mesothelioma, 195–197, 200
Mestranol, 94, 109, 110, 125, 126
Microbiological research, xii
Mider, G. Burroughs, 148
Migraine headaches, 96
Military draft, 34, 54, 55
Minipill, 116, 136
Mintz, Morton, 107, 120
Miscarriages, DES and, xi, 173–176, 178, 189
MK-665, 94–95
Molecular biology, xii
Morning-after pill, 177–179
Myocardial infarction, 117–118

National Academy of Sciences, 149, 197
National Cancer Institute, 70, 184, 233, 241
National Commission on Egg Nutrition (NCEN), 84–86
National Institutes of Health (NIH), 42
  Center for Population Research, 184
  guidelines on DNA recombinant research, 227–246, 250, 255
  Recombinant DNA Advisory Committee, 223, 226, 240–242
National Research Council, 59
National security, 23
Nature, 219
Nelson, Gaylord, 103, 105
New animal drug application (NADA) statutes, 169–172
New Drug Application (NDA) stage, 38–39, 56, 65, 68
New England Journal of Medicine, 113, 118, 121, 122, 128
Nicholson, William, 194, 195, 201
Nirenberg, Marshall, 219, 239
Nitrites, 155

Nontherapeutic experimenta-
tion, 32, 34, 41
Norethynodrel, 110
Nuclear power, 218–219
Nuremberg Code, 37–38, 39, 40

Obesity treatments, 72–74
Oral contraceptives, xi, xv, 8, 51,
76, 88–141, 239, 248, 250,
262
advertising and, 89, 97
amounts of synthetic hormones
in, 108, 111–112
birth defects and, 106, 109,
112–113, 119
blood clotting and, 92–105,
109–112, 126, 132
blood triglyceride and, 130
cancer and, 116, 119, 120–123,
126, 128, 134, 136–137, 262
cholesterol levels and, 130
gall bladder disease and, 112,
119
heart disease and, 106, 116–
119, 120, 126, 133–134
intelligence in children and,
114–115
labeling of, 41, 96–97, 99–100,
119, 131
litigation over, 93–94, 140
liver tumors and, 124–125, 126
minipill, 116, 136
morning-after pill, 177–179
package insert, 104–106, 131–
134
sequential pills, 108, 123–124,
136
venereal disease and, 137
Ovulen-21, 100

Pain, experiments on, 41
Personal choice, 58–87, 251–252
cold remedies, 75–77, 87
eggs, consumption of, 84–87

experimentation and, 38, 39,
45
fad diets, 59–60
Laetrile issue, 60, 63–72
vitamins, 78–84
Pesticide, 142, 147, 162
Pfizer Laboratories, 89
Pharmaceutical Manufacturers
Association (PMA), 105
Pharmacology, 8
Phenacetin, 75, 76
Pill, the: see Oral contraceptives
Planned Parenthood, 131
Pollution Control Agency, 209
Polyoma, 235
Pooley, Doctor, 199
Population Council, 131
Poultry production, DES and,
163–167
Pre-epidemic experimentation,
54–55
Premarin, 128
Priestley, Joseph, 10
Progesterone, 91, 104, 108, 125
Progestins, 116, 136
Progestogen, 123, 108
Prokaryotes, 224, 225, 227,
234–235
Protein deprivation, 36–37
Provest, 107, 108
Psychological research, 44–48,
51–53
Publicity, 23–24
Pulmonary embolism, 92, 96, 97,
99

Rape, 178, 179
Ratner, Herbert, 131
Ravetz, Jerome, 2, 9, 11–13,
15–17, 19, 29
Rawls, John, 257–259
Reserve Mining Company, 191–
217, 250, 255, 256, 258–259,
262

Rhodanese, 63
Rhythm method of contraception, 91
Ribicoff, Abraham, 168
Richardson, Elliot, 151
Roblin, Richard, 220–222
Royal College of Practitioners, 116, 132
Rutherford v. United States (1975), 64–68

Saccharin, 156–158, 161, 189, 211
Saccharin Study and Labeling Act of 1977, 157, 190
Sadusk, Doctor, 94–96
Satellite association, 109
Schmidt, Alexander, 119, 123, 127
Science, 1–28
    collegial relationships in, 9–10
    craft characterization of, 3–4, 17, 19, 21
    dedication to, 9
    distinction between technology and, 1–2

    economics of, 6, 7
    law–science confrontation, 19
    mystique of, 13–14
    secrecy and nondisclosure, 16
    specialization and, 5
    time frame of, 6, 7
Science magazine, 218–219
Scientific journals, 7
Searle, G. D., & Co., 89, 91, 100, 101, 106, 109
Self-esteem, manipulation of, 45
Self-medication: *see* Personal choice
Self-regulation, 26
Selikoff, Irving, 196, 197, 199, 200, 215
Semmelweiss, Ignaz, 33

Sequential birth control pills, 108, 123–124, 136
Shapiro, Samuel, 118–119
Silverberg, Stephen, 123
"Simeons" method of weight reduction, 72–74
Smith, Donald, 121
Social status, experimentation and, 49
Southam, Chester, 35–36
Special Assistant to the President for Science and Technology, 20
Specialization, 5
Sternal marrow procedure, 32
Stilboserts, 164–166
Suicide, 59
Sullivan, Leonor, 150
Supersonic transport, xiii
SV40, 221, 235, 237
Swine influenza, 54
Szilard, Leo, 218

Taconite, 191, 255
Taylor, Herbert B., 98
Technology: *see* Science
Testosterone, 138
Thalidomide, 7–8, 22, 115
Thromboembolism, 92–105, 109–112, 126, 132, 178
Thrombophlebitis, 92–98
Tort law, 32
Tremolite, 198
Turner, James, 105–106

Uncertainty Principle, 21–22
University of Chicago Lying-In Hospital, 175
Upjohn Company, 107

Vaccination, 54–55
Vaginal bleeding, 96, 97
Vaginal cancer, 174–176, 178
Vaughn, Anita Lee, 100

Venereal disease, 137
Vessey, Martin, 98–99, 100, 110, 116, 126
Virology, 8
Vitamins, 64, 75, 78–84

Water pollution, xi, 191–217
Watson, James D., 223
Weight-reduction clinics, 72–74
Weinberger, Casper, 159

Weiss, Noel, 122
Weiss, Paul, 8, 240
World Health Organization (WHO), 89
Wright, George, 214
Wright, Judge, 207–208, 210

Zen macrobiotic diet, 59
Ziel, Doctor, 121